AVANT
CANADA

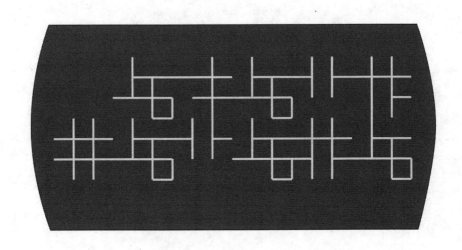

AVANT CANADA

Poets, Prophets, Revolutionaries

GREGORY BETTS
and CHRISTIAN BÖK,
editors

WILFRID LAURIER
UNIVERSITY PRESS

This book has been published with the help of a grant from the Canadian Federation for the Humanities and Social Sciences, through the Awards to Scholarly Publications Program, using funds provided by the Social Sciences and Humanities Research Council of Canada. Wilfrid Laurier University Press acknowledges the support of the Canada Council for the Arts for our publishing program. We acknowledge the financial support of the Government of Canada through the Canada Book Fund for its publishing activities. This work was supported by the Research Support Fund.

LIBRARY AND ARCHIVES CANADA CATALOGUING IN PUBLICATION

Avant Canada : poets, prophets, revolutionaries / Gregory Betts and Christian Bök, editors.

Includes bibliographical references and index.
Issued in print and electronic formats.
ISBN 978-1-77112-352-5 (softcover).—ISBN 978-1-77112-354-9 (EPUB).—
ISBN 978-1-77112-353-2 (PDF)

1. Literature, Experimental—Canada—History and criticism. I. Betts, Gregory, 1975–, editor II. Bök, Christian, [1966–], editor

PS8061.A93 2018   C810.9'11   C2018-902144-6
                                                  C2018-902145-4

Cover design by hwstudio.com. Text design by Sandra Friesen.

© 2019 Wilfrid Laurier University Press
Waterloo, Ontario, Canada
www.wlupress.wlu.ca

This book is printed on FSC® certified paper and is certified Ecologo. It contains post-consumer fibre, is processed chlorine free, and is manufactured using biogas energy.

Printed in Canada

We dedicate this book to the memory of
Dr. Barbara Godard,
a model mentor and an exemplary scholar
of the avant-garde.

Contents

List of Figures

PART I

INTRODUCTION

GREGORY BETTS
and CHRISTIAN BÖK

Time for the Avant-Garde in Canada

We can sit down, like an avant-garde, and ask who we want to be.
—*Lee Maracle*

THE AVANT-GARDE FROM BEFORE YOUR TIME

Avant Canada represents the outcome of a collaboration between two
poets, whose friendship over the course of two decades has arisen from a
shared desire to promote otherwise neglected writers from the avant-garde
community in Canada. After years of convivial dialogues about the status
of such a community, the two editors of this volume hope that their reader-
ship might enjoy what they themselves have come to love the most about
the legacy of CanLit—its embryonic, anomalous tradition of "deviant" writ-
ers who, against prudence, decide to break from the orthodox pathways to
fame in order to become not so much unseemly to their conventional peers
as untimely to their contemporary epoch. This volume constitutes a kind of
snapshot, taken at the moment when such a community, in all its diversity,
has convened at a social affair, akin to a reunion.

 Avant Canada borrows its title from a conference held at Brock Univer-
sity in St. Catharines during November 2014, at a time ripe for both writers
and critics from across the country to convene in order to map out the
current terrain of the avant-garde in English Canada. While factions of the
avant-garde at this summit might have proposed a diversity of hypotheses
about the state of the union, most attendees seem to have agreed that the

literary future involves a reconciliation with our colonial legacy. Not only must the revolutionary sensibilities of any avant-garde movement aspire to unsettle the discourses that have granted us licence to degrade both the environment and its inhabitants, but the revolutionary sensibilities of such an avant-garde must also aspire to enhance the diversity of its community by attending to the voices of both the ignored and the unheard. The editors hope that this volume contributes to such a mandate.

Avant-garde writing in English Canada has never enjoyed much more than a token degree of prestige among the literati of this country. While Canada has existed, as a nation, for as long as the tradition of the avant-garde itself, the country has perhaps yet to foster a world-class avant-garde movement of its own, although diverse writers from Canada have often contributed original insights to innovations imported from schools elsewhere in the world. When confronting the legacy of the avant-garde in Canada, writers have, at times, felt obliged to contend with a sense of either outdatedness or indebtedness, as if uptaking the newest trends after the oldest moment of their heyday. The "failure" of any avant-garde writer almost always seems to coincide with this notion of being out of step with the pace of history, arriving on the scene either too soon or too late to feel at ease in the modern milieu.

THE AVANT-GARDE FROM SOMEWHERE ELSE

Renato Poggioli has described the avant-garde as a class of bohemians whose specific agendas may differ, but whose artistic stances have much in common, adopting attitudes that remain agonistic, alienated, neophilic, technical, objective, and difficult, with respect to the conventions of the status quo—each movement aspiring to consummate an alliance between artistry and politics. According to Poggioli, the avant-garde consists of "lost generations,"[1] either "decadent" or "futurist" in their fashions: the first, seeing itself as tragic, having arrived at the apocalypse of an old history, now exhausted, awaiting the next ages with anxiety; the second, seeing itself as heroic, having arrived at the beginning of a new history, now restarted, inviting the next ages with fervour.[2] The avant-garde, for him, must transit these fashions, inventing itself anew, after each novel agenda becomes a tired cliché.

Peter Bürger goes on to suggest that the avant-garde aspires to make a kind of art that criticizes the institution of art itself, using shock to call into question all precedents for the relationship between our artistic labour and the artistic market.[3] The modern milieu of art thus becomes a series of reflexive, political critiques, in which art questions the prevailing definition of art, after which institutions strive to absorb this redefinition. The avant-garde tries to marry artistry to politics, so as to reintegrate the otherwise dissociated relationship between living and making, but, according to Bürger, the avant-garde fails at this venture, with its critiques becoming yet another specialization of work, selling aesthetic novelties for our conspicuous consumption.[4] The rejection of every prior style of art for the sake of a social agenda becomes a newer style of art to be copied in the available repertoire of history.

Matei Călinescu even goes so far as to argue that the avant-garde exaggerates these conditions of exhausted decadence to foment what he calls a "culture of crisis,"[5] in which time itself expresses its victory over traditions that might have, otherwise, seemed both ageless and eternal, including perhaps the very idea of the avant-garde itself. Each vanguard movement in art constitutes an elite group that aspires to abolish the elitism of the arts, rendering them demotic for all—but by doing so, the avant-garde embarks upon a suicidal campaign, in which the avant-garde, if successful, eliminates the necessity for its own existence.[6] The avant-garde aspires to achieve a time beyond itself—a time to which the prefix "post-" might become attached as a signifier for both the obsolescence of itself and the supersedence of itself. The avant-garde thus becomes the herald of its own demise.

Reginald Shepherd has even suggested that, for poetry, the avant-garde has perhaps entered what he calls a "post-avant" phase in which the lessons of the avant-garde have become so institutionalized that each poet has become a magpie, who can enjoy the "eclecticism"[7] of all schools of writing, neutralizing them or synthesizing them (making them either equalized in value or interbred in style), doing so without any sense of either utopian anticipation or elitist renunciation. The avant-garde is thus, for him, no longer untimely in its modern moment (even though his use of the prefix "post-" might not indicate the foreclosure of every avant-garde, so much as the prefix might indicate an impatience that, despite all efforts to the contrary, we have yet to surpass this moment—and thus we must pretend to have done so, long before we have actually produced a more advanced paradigm to replace it).

Temporality, for every avant-garde, might hinge, in fact, upon the doubled meaning of the word *avant* itself—both the French adverbial form for "earlier" or "in advance of" (as in "before") and the French adjective form for "forward" or "in advance of" (as in "beyond"). If the avant-garde includes the visionaries ahead of us (the legendary soldiers of a better hereafter, daily promised), the avant-garde also includes the visionaries aback of us (the forgotten pioneers of a bygone yesterday, never attained). If the avant-garde can issue a prognosis about the near future, whose advent always seems postponed too late, the avant-garde can also nurse its nostalgia about a lost future, whose advent always seems abandoned too soon. The avant-garde in Canada confronts these tensions of interrupted temporality—tensions caused by waves of vanguards (soldiers and pioneers, all with their utopian agendas).

THE AVANT-GARDE FROM SOMEWHERE HERE

Louis-Armand, Baron de Lahontan, in his *Memoires de l'Amerique Septentrionale*, from 1703, documents the story of his service as an officer in New France between 1683 and 1694. Lahontan recounts that, after arriving as the young scion of a French aristocrat, he quickly becomes fluent in Wyandot, then leads a troop of Canadien *habitants* and Wyandot warriors into battle against the Haudenosaunee—but the superior, military prowess of this nation causes his retreat, whereupon Lahontan joins forces with the Outaouas, becoming a deserter, breaking ranks entirely from the French colony. His memoir constitutes the first usage of the term "avant-garde" to refer to the people of Canada,[8] and he uses the term to describe the elite bands of Haudenosaunee, praising them for their ability to protect their hunters from skirmishes with the colonizers. The avant-garde in Canada originates with these Indigenous warriors.

Bertram Brooker (the Canadian painter) later evokes the idea of the avant-garde in 1929 to refer to the radical artists of his era in Canada (twenty years after the debut of Futurism in *Le Figaro*). When Brooker defines the avant-garde as "the first men of a new civilization whose implications are incalculable,"[9] he argues that the avant-garde is "never narrowly contemporary";[10] instead, the avant-garde breaks the relics of the past, to bypass the limits of the present, so as to foster the growth of the future. The avant-garde thus aspires to, what the editors of this volume might call, a kind of "untimeliness," either by being *before its time,* addressing an as yet unforeseen future audience (doing so from a modern viewpoint in a tone of historic anticipation), or by being *beyond its time,* addressing an as yet unawakened modern audience (doing so from a future viewpoint in a tone of historic renunciation).

Northrop Frye has noted, for example, that the Canadian experience of time remains different from the experiences of time for British writers of our colonial heritage. Whereas such authors might imagine themselves contributing to a linear series of heroic models, all of which remain cumulative and modifiable, with a grand story of progress, literati in Canada encounter a "kaleidoscopic whirl with no definitive shape"[11]—a whirligig of anachronistic, international traditions, whose patterns and meanings conflict with each other, excluding the Canadian from any sequential, historical trajectory through such a kaleidoscope. How have avant-garde writers in Canada navigated this refracted condition of feeling either outdated or indebted, unable to pass through the fray, while striving to make themselves anew? How do such writers relate to their moment in history when they have arrived on stage, off cue?

Barbara Godard has noted, for example, that "writing a history of the present is always a fraught project when the only clock is variation."[12] Without a stable "clock" that might underpin the centre of our culture, writers in Canada cannot easily situate themselves within their own time; and consequently, they cannot map a line of descent, whose pedigree might legitimate their own progressive development within a grandiose, unilinear history. Godard coins the term "ex-centrique" to describe this experience of the avant-garde in Canada, equating this experience of "de-centering" with the exclusion of the feminist agent (if not the colonial other) from the historical centrality of any grand story about the past: "ex-centriques, thus avant-garde."[13] The history of the avant-garde might therefore seem to inhabit an array of anomalous timelines, all of which depart from the mainstream, diffracting into a welter of stories about an, otherwise eccentric, tradition.

Daniel Coleman has described such a kaleidoscope of timelines, when he defines four "chronotopes"[14] in Canadian literature: first, an *isochronous, Imperialist time;*[15] second, a *nationalist, Postcolonial time;*[16] third, a *dispersive, Emigratory time;*[17] and fourth, a *concentric, Indigenous time.*[18] The first chronotope measures time according to the standards of the global market, with everyone racing against others through linear history at a metered pace, toward progress. The second chronotope interrupts the first, restarting the clock at the moment of national independence from an imperial forebear, while the third chronotope interrupts the first two, restarting the clock at the moment of diasporic displacement from an original homeland. The fourth chronotope measures time according to the standards of an innate ritual, with everyone moving through cyclic history at an organic pace, without finality.

Paul Huebener has, likewise, argued for a "multitemporality"[19] in Canadian literary criticism in order to accommodate the timing of these interruptions by such vanguards of either combatative deployment (soldiers) or exploratory settlement (pioneers). Such interruptions might fracture history, if not stratify history, into parallel stories, each with its own imagined, possible future for the country itself. Such a reading of history makes room for the anachronism of voices out of sync with the pace of their time (perhaps because they goad us from a lost past or perhaps because they call us from the next ages). The history of the avant-garde (much like the history of Canada itself) might consist of no singular heritage, conforming to one timeline, marching toward progressive improvement; instead, the history of the avant-garde might consist of multiple legacies vying with each other across time.

The editors of this volume might even go so far as to add a fifth chronotype to such studies of "multitemporality"—arguing on behalf of an "avant-garde time" that remains both *anachronous* and *speculative*, either by appearing *before its time* or by appearing *beyond its time* (in keeping with the doubled meaning of the word *avant* in French). The avant-garde writer almost always opposes the present, interrogating its exposés of "nowness" and "newness" in order to offer experimental alternatives (some derived from unused options, aback of us in a neglected time; some derived from unborn options, ahead of us in a predicted time)—but options that might, in both cases, transect the flow of these other four chronotypes. The fifth chronotope might intervene in the other four, perhaps to impede them, to sunder them, to mingle them, to divert them, agitating to diversify each potential that they might afford us.

THE DISPOSITIONS OF THE AVANT-GARDE

With these four conflicting chronotypes in mind (their histories, juxtaposed and stratified), the editors hope to highlight the diversity of attitudes about the trajectories of the avant-garde over the course of the last five decades, since the 1960s. The editors have taken inspiration from the table of contents for *Canadian Literature* (the most esteemed academic journal in the field), structuring the anthology into two modes of writing: critical articles (including twelve *essaies* by scholars) and literary examples (including twelve oeuvres by literati). The editors want the audience for this book to encompass both critics and writers alike, in part because the avant-garde often explores the porousness of boundaries between genres (intermixing personal, creative artistry with detached, academic analysis so as to imagine hybrid models for expression).

The editors have also organized these materials to reflect four dispositions of avant-garde practice in English Canada over the last five decades: first, *concrete poetics*, which explores limit-cases of inscrutability (accenting the materialist conditions of a mark); second, *language writing*, which explores limit-cases of referentiality (accenting the signifiable conditions of a text); third, *identity writing*, which explores limit-cases of expressibility (accenting the intractable conditions of a self); and fourth, *copyleft poetics*, which explores limit-cases of conceivability (accenting the speculative conditions of a rule). All these practices might take inspiration from each other, but each one emphasizes its own limit-cases, arguing that, for the avant-garde, the literary extremes of an inscrutable mark, of a referential text, of an expressible self, of a conceivable rule—all have a political, not just an aesthetic, dimension to their practice.

Each of these four dispositions receives scholarly attention from two academic literati (for a total of eight essays about work from the 1970s onward). The editors have added, as a preamble, two more essays about the counterculture of the 1960s during the Centennial, using both Leonard Cohen and bpNichol as touchstones. The editors have then framed these ten essays with four less scholarly, more anecdotal, texts: first, a reminiscence by Lisa Robertson about the avant-garde in the 1980s (followed by an account from Liz Howard about issues of cultural reimagination); later, an account by André Alexis about crises of cultural appropriation (followed by a conversation with Jordan Abel about the avant-garde in the 2010s).

GREGORY BETTS AND CHRISTIAN BÖK

Each of the four dispositions (concrete poetics, language writing, identity writing, and copyleft poetics) also features exemplary ephemerae by three creative writers.

Avant Canada begins with a reminiscence by Lisa Robertson, who writes a "lyric essay," recounting her experiences at the Kootenay School of Writing (KSW) in the 1980s, doing so in a style characteristic of her poetry from the period. Robertson discusses the degree to which avant-garde writers plagued with disaffection might nevertheless find solace in their engagement with a community of peers, all working together upon a collective enterprise of resistance. *Avant Canada* also begins with an account by Liz Howard, who describes how her practice, as an Anishinaabe writer, testifies to the *survivance* of her cultural heritage in the face of colonial pressure to assimilate. Howard suggests that, for a marginal identity, all such acts of *survivance* constitute an expression of the avant-garde, no less radical and no less extreme than the insurgency of a quixotic literary movement that promotes an innovative aesthetics.

Avant Canada closes with an account by André Alexis, who writes a "newsy essay," recounting his impressions of the controversy surrounding the scandals of Amanda PL and Hal Niedzviecki, both of whom have encountered social rebuke for their unfaddish attitudes about entitled, artistic licence. Alexis plays the role of a thoughtful questioner, wondering about the adverse impacts of such rebuke upon the literary dialogue across cultures in CanLit. *Avant Canada* also closes with a conversation by Jordan Abel, who comments upon the development of the avant-garde since the Kootenay School of Writing in the 1980s, doing so at a time when his work has received endorsement from the Griffin Poetry Trust. Abel describes how his practice, as a Nisga'a writer, touches upon concrete poetics, language writing, identity writing, and copyleft poetics, in an era of Truth and Reconciliation.

While the contributors to this anthology might pursue eclectic literary interests, addressing a diverse variety of radical writing, the editors might suggest that, after 1965, during the cultural outburst of the Centennial, the avant-garde in Canada has taken much of its inspiration from the counterculture of the period. Kristine Smitka, for example, discusses how the reception of *Beautiful Losers* by Leonard Cohen owes much of its success to the marketers at McClelland & Stewart in the 1960s; likewise, Stephen

Cain, in turn, discusses how the inception of Ganglia Press by bpNichol owes much of its impetus to the community at Sigmund Samuel Library in the 1960s. Such achievements by Cohen and Nichol have, perhaps, become hallmarks for later poets, who have, at times, taken heart from the success of such writers (both of whom have won the Governor General's Award and have received international commendations for their work).

The Canadian exponents of "concrete poetics" have since then politicized the values of the inscrutable mark, disrupting the norms of functional literacy so as to interrogate the normative protocols of reading. Julia Polyck-O'Neill argues that the art show *Concrete Poetry*, curated by Michael Morris (et al.) at the University of British Columbia Fine Arts Gallery in the late 1960s, establishes a confluence of literacies between the visual poetry of Canadian writers and the conceptual aesthetics of Canadian artists. Mike Borkent, in turn, argues that *Grease Ball Comics*, by bpNichol in the early 1970s, breaks the unilinear, narrative sequence of reading in comics so as to foreground the networked relations among an array of self-reflexive, self-addressed pictures. The editors have solicited creative work from Kaie Kellough, Kelly Mark, and Eric Schmaltz to illustrate some of these aesthetic attitudes.

The Canadian exponents of "language writing" have, likewise, politicized the values of the referential text, disrupting the norms of neoliberal exchange so as to interrogate the normative protocols of meaning. Michael Roberson, for example, argues that, when members of the Kootenay School of Writing resort to both disjunctive syntax and disruptive themes in a manifesto entitled "Coasting," these poets of the West Coast challenge the equivalence of meaningful expression with profitable transaction. Kit Dobson goes on to deploy the theories of Michel de Certeau to examine how critiques of referentiality in both *The Vestiges* by Jeff Derksen and *Kern* by Derek Beaulieu challenge the fiscal values of poetic labour under capitalism. The editors have solicited creative work from Dorothy Trujillo Lusk, Erín Moure, and Donato Mancini, to illustrate some of these aesthetic attitudes.

The Canadian exponents of "identity writing" often politicize the values of the expressible self, disrupting the norms of subjective lyricism so as to interrogate the normative protocols of telling. Myra Bloom, for example, argues that *How Should a Person Be?*, by Sheila Heti, challenges the biographic conventions of confessional, performative writing, often extolled in literature written by men, but impugned in literature written by women. Sonnet L'Abbé, in turn, discusses how diverse writers such as Garry Thomas Morse, Shane Rhodes, Jordan Abel, and M. NourbeSe Philip use tropes of textual erasure to highlight the degree to which the expression of marginal identity often occurs under erasure in the interstices of an official document. The editors have solicited creative work from Lee Maracle, Leanne Betasamosake Simpson, and Anneharte to illustrate some of these aesthetic attitudes.

The Canadian exponents of "copyleft poetics" often politicize the values of the conceivable rule, disrupting the norms of individual aptitude so as to interrogate the normative protocols of writing. Katie L. Price, for example, argues that Dan Farrell practises a kind of pataphysical speculation about the psychology of the Rorschach test when he lists the responses of patients, portraying these answers as a poetic series of imaginary solutions to a textual problem of interpretation. Darren Wershler has, in turn, argued that many of the impersonal techniques of avant-garde writing have begun to infuse the ordinary, everyday practices of people who do not identify as literati, but who nevertheless use a procedural constraint to generate offhand, amateur works of interest to avant-garde poets. The editors have solicited work from Derek Beaulieu, Moez Surani, and Dani Spinosa to illustrate some of these aesthetic attitudes.

While these four dispositions in the Canadian avant-garde might often exhibit overlapping interaction with each other (blurring the boundaries between them), and while their practitioners might respond to more than one of these aesthetic attitudes at the same time, these four dispositions do represent well the variety of literary factions, attending the "reunion" in great force. While the editors have not addressed work by every manifestation of the avant-garde in Canada (especially among writers in Quebec, for example), the editors have, nevertheless, assembled the most extensive (if not most inclusive) selection of people in attendance for the conversations at this historically significant conference. This selection of writing spans fifty years of activity by the Canadian avant-garde in English, from the 1960s to the 2010s, providing a sample of material about otherwise unorthodox writing in the country.

THE AVANT-GARDE FROM AFTER YOUR TIME

Stephen Collis asks: "[D]oes the term 'avant-garde' do any productive, liberatory work anymore?"[20] The editors suggest that, while tensions often exist among factions of the avant-garde, with groups disputing the merits of either their aesthetic aims or their political ends, the revolutionary sensibilities of the avant-garde still continue to argue for the expansion of both liberty and licence throughout our everyday, creative lives. The avant-garde still persists in the imagination of writers, despite many reasons to quit (including decades of critical reproach, demands of economic exigency, rewards of ordinary practice, or changes in literary interest). The editors continue to find inspiration, not in the dogmatisms of the avant-garde, but in the doggedness of writers willing to take a risk, testing the limit-cases of their art form, despite the likelihood of hateful censure (if not wilfull neglect) by their culture.

Pauline Butling has suggested that, after the last half of the twentieth century, the avant-garde now constitutes a "historiographic project"[21] that strives to reclaim the story of radical writing from the shortcomings of its own retelling, wresting this narrative from the dominant timeline of a dominant identity in the past. Butling suspects that any story of progressive improvement aligns itself with the discourses of neoliberal capitalism itself. Ergo, she does not privilege the prefix "post-" (with its neoteric, temporal visions of both obsolescence and supersedence); instead, she privileges the prefix "re-" (with its visions of both lateral movement and reverse movement, all spiralling backward in time to return to what they then must revise—"a re poetics"[22] of both re-reading and re-writing). For her, the avant-garde must re-articulate the chain of events in the chronotopes of its own history.

Lee Maracle has noted that, for Aboriginal expression, "[w]e cast the picture in the direction of the future before we speak, so that when we speak we are speaking the same sense … as our remembered ancestries."[23] The Canadian avant-garde has perhaps, likewise, begun to address the future in such a way, aspiring to speak to an anticipated, emancipatory outcome ahead of us in response to an unfulfilled, conciliatory promise aback of us. The Canadian avant-garde often questions the cultural themes, if not the humanist values, of both the nation and its people, and in an era of globalization, when these two signifiers have become fractured and displaced, the avant-garde may find itself better poised to assess the millennial anxieties about our heritage, interrupting history at such a moment of crisis to remind us of our capacity for resistance, if not revolution. Now is the time for the avant-garde.

NOTES

The epigraph is taken from "Memory and the Avant-Garde in Canada", a keynote address given by Lee Maracle for the conference Avant Canada: Artists, Prophets, and Revolutionaries at Brock University in November 2014.

1 Renato Poggioli, *The Theory of the Avant-Garde* (Cambridge: Harvard University Press, 1968), 76.
2 Poggioli notes: "There is no great difference between the decadent's dream of a new infancy ... and the futurist's dream of a new maturity." *The Theory of the Avant-Garde*, 76.
3 Peter Bürger, *Theory of the Avant-Garde* (Manchester: Manchester University Press, 1984), 80.
4 Bürger notes: "The culture industry has brought about the false elimination of the distance between art and life, and this also allows one to recognize the contradictoriness of the avant-gardiste undertaking." *Theory of the Avant-Garde*, 50.
5 Matei Călinescu, *Five Faces of Modernity: Modernism, Avant-Garde, Decadence, Kitsch, Postmodernism* (Durham: Duke University Press, 1987), 124.
6 Călinescu notes: "The avant-garde is compelled by its own sense of consistency to commit suicide." *Five Faces of Modernity*, 124.
7 Reginald Shepherd, "Who You Callin' 'Post-Avant?'," *Harriet*. https://www.poetryfoundation.org/harriet/2008/02/who-you-callin-post-avant/.
8 Louis Armand (Baron de Lahontan), *Mémoires de l'Amérique Septentrionale* (Amsterdam: Chez François L'Honoré and Co., 1703), 165.
9 Bertram Brooker, "When We Awake!," in *Yearbook of the Arts in Canada 1928–1929* (Toronto: Macmillan, 1929), 12.
10 Brooker, "When We Awake!," 15.
11 Northrop Frye, "Canada and Its Poetry," *Northrop Frye on Canada* (Toronto: University of Toronto Press, 2003), 32.
12 Barbara Godard, "Notes from the Cultural Field: Canadian Literature from Identity to Hybridity," *Essays on Canadian Writing* 72 (Winter 2000): 209–247. 221.

13 Barbara Godard, "Ex-centriques, Eccentric, Avant-Garde: Women and Modernism in the Literatures of Canada," *Room of One's Own* 8.4 (1984): 57–75. 58.

14 Daniel Coleman, "From Contented Civility to Contending Civilities: Alternatives to Canadian White Civility," *International Journal of Canadian Studies* 38 (2008): 234–237.

15 Coleman, "From Contented Civility," 231.

16 Coleman, "From Contented Civility," 232.

17 Coleman, "From Contented Civility," 233.

18 Coleman, "From Contented Civility," 234.

19 Paul Huebener, *Timing Canada: The Shifting Politics of Time in Canadian Literary Culture* (Montreal: McGill-Queen's University Press, 2015), 22.

20 Stephen Collis, "The Call to Be Disobedient," *Jacket 2.* http://jacket2.org/article/call-be-disobedient.

21 Pauline Butling, "(Re)Defining Radical Poetics," *Writing in Our Time: Canada's Radical Poetries in English (1957–2003)* by Pauline Butling and Susan Rudy (Waterloo: Wilfrid Laurier University Press, 2005), 19.

22 Butling, "(Re)Defining," 21.

23 Lee Maracle, "Memory and the Avant-Garde in Canada," Keynote speech, Brock University (November 2014).

PART II

PROLOGUE

LISA ROBERTSON

The Collective

A school alit on a moment. It felt electric, erotic, uncomfortable, necessary. Because they noticed, the moment expanded, scaffolded by a low-rent materiality. They entered this temporal suspension by climbing narrow and steep stairways to the upper floors of neglected Edwardian storefronts in a decrepit downtown neighbourhood. They trundled book boxes, or helped the older ones. But beyond the scaffolding and the dusty scent of the hallways the school itself was immaterial, and infinitely mobile, like many of its precedents: single Black Mountain lectures sprawling magnificently across days; beer-fuelled livingroom readings attended by loggers, architects, camp cooks, lefty lawyers, and students; the communal meeting halls of 1871 Paris in the month of March, where radical shoemakers, seamstresses, and preschool teachers lectured on citizenship; the experimental chemistry clubs of seventeenth-century, revolutionary London; the romantic meteorologists of Cambridgeshire; Fourier's passionate associations and phalanstries; the peripatetic conversants of the Epicurean garden, where women and men shared the lively and living pursuit of philosophy, in contradiction to the discourses of the state.

A resurgent energy pulses into shimmering expression in a city, a room, a street, beneath certain trees, when necessity sends acute though necessarily covert signals. Clearly there must be more than one person or the frequency can't alight. The reception isn't willed. The receivers emanate a superb, almost obscene, attractive force having to do with their absolute disrespect for the ordinary sinecures. Only in retrospect does it appear that fate plays a role in the swerve-like transmission. The receivers of this synchronic worthiness transmit the communal moment of an insurrection across their sentences. The resultant vibrations alter the shape of cognition. This has to do with people's speech, its self-authorization, its communal autonomy. In retrospect, I see their protest as collective ceremony, although they themselves would have definitively scorned the notion. Their values were narrowly secular. But terms they violently rejected as insufficiently materialist can now become useful, because the collective can't be described with precision from within the field of their own vocabulary. An outer vantage is needed. So I'll return to them now the odours and the ceremonies and the ritual protocols their radical self-identity occluded. I'll indulge in the praise of their utter vulgarity.

I was never a founder. For certain periods I was absent. My interpretation of events corresponds to my own heightened, even hackneyed, desire for a story, my own attraction to a vulgate. I never felt really equal to the magnetism of my companions. This account is quite wrong factually.

As for the forms of protest—often they were unrecognizable, except belatedly. The most stringent protest evades spectacle, nonchalantly preserving its transformative force for the propitious moment, the most apt and unsuspecting initiates, the casually secretive gathering. Some of them believed the resurgence pertained to syntax, and adored repeating that word. Some believed in the complicated and conflictual duration of group consensus as a model for change. Yet whom they kissed or didn't, how long the empties sat, the fruit flies hovering above them, the way the notebooks splayed across the stained blue carpet for days at a time, the books never returned to the library and the books found lying on sidewalks, the borrowing and filching and thrifting, the use of Letraset, glue stick, and carbon paper in their quotidian rituals, the Smith Corona Selectric that came after the loud manual, the placement of the folded bath towel under the manual late at night to protect the shared wooden house from staccato retort, the use of roach chalk on thresholds … these exigencies necessarily infiltrated their grammar. And grammar pertained not only to linguistic coherence and distribution and its reinvention, but to community and domestic form. They practised the evasion of enforced subordination in favour of horizontal structures of intensification, composition and multidirectional exchange. Their task was very large, like a decades-long emotional science project. They believed they would be endlessly robust; they believed the same for their texts.

In a sense, time was their medium. They wanted glamorous seminars to fling open and demolish all expectations regarding the regularization of time. They wanted the spontaneous eruption of intense intellectual newness. Time spontaneously translated to new time. Some of them wanted to experience historicity as radically simultaneous: the medieval wandering poets would be among their most urgent contemporaries, or the epistolary writers of the long eighteenth century, or the gentlemen naturalists of early Romantic England meandering up Adanac Street, or the baroque philosophers tracing their ellipses in the forests of UBC. To help the collapse of time as metrics, and encourage its transformation into a luxuriously shared lubricant, an enticingly shimmering and moving fabric, a shared yet contested décor, the collective welcomed end-narratives: the end of femininity, the end of nature, the end of work. They believed that each ending was necessarily the site of a transformation. This was their cosmology. They were good at surviving.

Actions create language in the present at the same time that their historical traces paradoxically remain latent within language across long durations. I think language is a mobile, immaterial archive of a very long history of human gesture. The collective linguistically seized the paradoxical status of the universal commune; now, because in their shabby neighbourhoods they moved into then unknown social futures, because they made poems from these movements, intense collective potentials hover as forms in the present. These forms animate the visceral knowledge that the poem is the opposite of capital.

They said that the task of each minute was to differentiate between the mind's thought and the state's thought. They had a queer agreement that the mind is a wandering organ. They said the state's thought is an inert placebo for an actual relationship with form. Capital gives everything its emptied double—form can't live there so relationships won't change. Thus there are two thoughts. One pulsed in low-budget shadow. This is a theory I wish to open. In the current era of capital, it could be that the mind's thought must live in hiding, in inconspicuous parallel to the official institutionalizations. Their shabby, difficultly accessible rooms were spiritual havens, as in the

Epicurian mandate: live in hiding. Because they could recognize, originate and exchange the mind's thought, time in the collective's spaces and texts was the highly diversified energy of combined innovation and contemplation. Time was not the metrics of the reproduction of capital. They weren't strivers. They scorned tenure. They had arrived at this obscure place by exercising their shared piety for horizontal discursive extremes in others. Lovingly they addressed the bodies of the future.

From the present point of view, it might seem that what the collective produced, and what remains of both its covert and its gregariously public activities is a catalogue of linguistic and intellectual artifacts: the poems, essays, journals, chapbooks, and various paper ephemera that will show up in personal and institutional archives, or slip from the pages of casually retrieved volumes of American Language poets, or Frankfurt School theorists, or Montreal feminists, as well as the concepts associated with these movements and texts. All this will remain in circulation for at least the near future. But now I believe that what the collective produced most importantly was a mode of autonomous, plural existence. Deeply, almost like animals, they understood how to live together. They made for a moment a precariously inhabitable social sculpture. Since a way of living is the more evasive and inconspicuous artifact, more evanescent than the texts and material detritus, it is what I wish to describe. This living shall be traced through bodily memories of gestures, of caresses, of mythic spills, the charged air in certain rooms, the movement of thoughts and objects and texts across neighbourhoods, transformations in relationships and self-perception and recognition. How do people find each other, recognize afresh the secretive necessity, proliferate and associate with almost painfully new ideas? How do they make situations for one another's most exigent and elegant strangeness? How do these spaces exist in contradictory relation to the dominant histories and economies, evading, for dizzying spans, the oppressive propaganda of institutional assimilation? What is transmission? Must transmission be unbroken or regular in order to be actual? I think not. It will fountain, unannounced, unanticipated, by means of desire.

If there was conflict, it was because of the complex nature of the desire that indeed manifested itself in an irregular continuousness. Part of their work was to learn how to recognize new desire, and carefully to separate it from hegemonic compulsion. That was an ongoing task. It was sometimes tiring. They drank and they puked and they judged and often they were not kind. They enjoyed it. They often didn't like things. There was conflict because there were many desires, erotic imaginations of new forms of intellection, interlocution, composition, and political movement in the city. To bring these multiple desires into temporary resonance was the repeating collective task. Fights could erupt. In this way, an undulant social harmonics was composed, a vibration that provided a buzzing ground for the individual compositions. The collective made a space where the extremities of a multifocal yearning were sheltered by the shared belief in its political necessity. This was a value. Tent-like, its space needed to be repeatedly reinstated, re-erected, since the materials, structure and dimensions underwent permanent improvisation, as thought veered, as the city transformed, as the economy mushroomed. They dissociated the political from the economic without abandoning the critique of materiality and its relation to power. But their living together opened the certainty that a part of political practice is immaterial.

I'm insisting on the word desire because of the feeling that was in the air in those shabby rooms, both in the collective spaces—the meeting rooms, bookshops, galleries, and bars—and in the apartments the poets moved among. Those rooms were livid with sparks. They rendered defunct the boundaries between the intellectual, the political, the aesthetic, and the erotic. Who kissed whom, who proofed whose texts, who collaborated in what studios, who moved in together, which bands made their ears ring for days after the concerts, who fought at kitchen and bar tables over the vocabulary of political analysis—I can't separate these queries from my imagination of those spaces. They enjoyed the sensation of being impassioned by an idea; they throve in the defensive ambiance. Ambiguity, cathexis, and dispute were expressions of collective love and hate, where love and hate changed places with always unanticipated thoroughness. Any evening, any meeting, any table could achieve the character of an eruption. I heard that somebody punched someone as they smoked on the street between readings. One made Scotch-tape sonnets. The other invented virtual coalitions. One is still working; the other has disappeared.

As well as disappearance, shared boredom was a content. They passed much time each month hunched over long brown formica tables, hung over, folding 8½-×-11 sheets of paper twice, to fit into business-sized envelopes, as the scent of stale beer drifted from corners. They licked stamps. Those were the press releases, typed on Selectric, scarred by white-out, their authors decided by consensus at the long, frequent, meandering meetings, as were the rosters of readers, lecturers, workshop leaders, panel conveners, and so forth.

The collective expression was contingent on leisure as a rescued value. Beyond financial and demotic metrics, they made time to spend together, and time to think. This time had a particular stretchiness, an opacity, an intensely deregulated quality. It was synthesized among thinking bodies. Late starts, overlong readings, closing down bars, thence to crowded kitchen tables and 2 a.m. call-in beer delivery, the long sleep-ins, the sleep-overs on hard futons and sprung couches, the afternoon reading groups or editorial meetings extending again to the small hours of the following morning, spontaneous road trips to Seattle or Portland to ferry visiting poets, lying at border crossings, deferred or abandoned degrees, unconventional domestic structures, suspension of reproduction, underemployment, non-profit work, chosen self-employment and freelancing, low rent, welfare, sharing: they made themselves time-rich through the avoidance or lack of conventionally defined work. And here I should mention that their unstymied reproductive self-determination, via free and open access to birth control and abortion, played an important part in the advancement of poetical agendas. This access was enabled by still other collectives—the Vancouver Women's Health Collective, and the Pine Free Clinic occupied cluttered upstairs spaces and drab storefronts that didn't feel dissimilar to the ones the poets frequented. If the work of thinking together was gloriously careening onwards, it's because the reproductive labour of capital was ignored, in as many ways as possible. The collective produced leisure, wilfully. Leisure had specific textures—worn-out, silk-thin band T-shirts under mended overalls, plaid on damp plaid, Styrofoam cups of Kelowna wine, sentences without subordination. Leisure anticipated new composition. It opened the possibility that language belongs to those who divert its energies towards the multiplication of collective joy.

As resurgent as it surely was, as synchronic in its expression of a recursive communal necessity, there is something particular about the historical time of the collective—it catapulted into being in 1984 in its province as the government was systematically replacing responsibility towards citizens with the overarching, non-responsive rationality of capital. They did not then know the term neoliberalism. They called it Capital. A rural university in the interior of the province was closed down, said the governors, because it failed to produce profit. I recall how weird and irrational this politically constructed reason then seemed. The students quickly understood the danger, without yet realizing that such edicts would accumulate into the single banal and smothering fabric now termed global. Protests, letter-writing, and fundraising readings followed. The government wouldn't budge; the arts program in the mountains folded. The disbanded students regrouped independently from the recognizable institutions. They moved to the city, associated themselves with the artists, found a cheap downtown space, installed a telephone, a desk, and a meeting table. They researched new funding structures, found a pro-bono left-wing lawyer, and succeeded in acquiring a non-profit legal status. They bought a few dozen black wooden folding chairs. They formed a mailing list and sent out press releases. They taught each other how to write grants. They taught each other how to read and how to argue. And they did argue, in baroque duration. They documented everything in bulging spiral-bound ledgers, in poems, and on cassette tape. When the office was frequently burgled, for safekeeping they stored the tape archive in the trunk of somebody's Valiant.

Henceforth the collective traced an irregular path, in shifting nodes of six or ten members, and audiences of one to several dozen, depending. The site drifted among several upstairs spaces, most within a three-block radius, in a poor neighbourhood that in those days didn't have a name since it wasn't for sale. They shared crappy storefronts with galleries or bookshops. Lulls and disquietudes and uncertainties were interspersed with unparalleled intensity and rushes of rigorous excitement and consequent activity, continuing in this way for around thirty years, collective members holding on, disappearing, announcing, and renouncing one another until, grants tapering off, no longer able to afford to rent a meeting space, its library in storage, its archive shunted off to the university special collections, it dwindled and fizzled. I recently heard in an email from a longtime member that the collective is now defunct. Defunct was his word.

Here I want to consider that the apparent failure of the collective is actually a condition of potent latency. In the way that the Paris Commune of 1871 expressed afresh an altered form of eighteenth-century revolutionary citizenship, which itself responded to the brief English Revolution of the seventeenth century, future communes will announce themselves in manifestations as yet unrecognizable. Resurgent collectivity will burst afresh when an intensity stumbles on a snag in the machinations of the political economy, and people decide on a dime to coax open that potent flaw to create a site. Continuity must be irregular in order to effectively cluster the potencies of linguistic subjectivity and political life apart from capital's metrics. Continuity must be vulgar.

The duration of the collective, from 1984 until 2016, is the period that saw the deepening and zenith of the political and administrative expression of neoliberalism, globally, and also particularly in the real estate markets of their city, a place historically determined by impolitical and socially violent real estate practices since its colonial "founding" on Indigenous territories in 1886. For a long time the financial colonization was incomplete, and border zones flourished, but I could say that now the price of everything has made leisure itself an overpriced product. In the current city any residual underemployed working class is displaced by the rents. Bookshops close and discourse narrows. It's a way of outlawing non-financialized leisure. It isn't unusual that the collective should have dwindled as the economic rationalization of political life usurped the active practice of the public. It began with such an incipient financialization, in the cauterization of the role of higher education; it ended at what appears to be the new liberal economy's full realization. The fabrication of a description of this thirty-year moment will yield information about the relationship of subjectivity and its formations and movements to neoliberal determinations of political personhood. I use the word *subjectivity* in a resolutely collective, un-private, and non-possessive sense, considering that it is the historical energy that travels between voices. For three decades the collective exponentially expressed and opened the incompletion and inefficiency of the liberal state, by producing new forms of linguistic subjectivity. No takeover is ever entire.

Now I think that the collective's most important trait was its vehement resistance, coupled with its gregarious linguistic inventiveness. Distribution was not an issue. They rejected the ideology of accessibility, in favour of the realism of difficulty. They were resisting the totalizing movement of capital and its usurpation of both individual and collective time, but they were resisting by widely varying means: Marxist class critique, avant-garde experiment, conceptual rigor, feminist rejections of gendered hierarchy, woman-centred editing practices, queer identity explosions, post-colonial and anti-racist actions. Some used images, or alcohol, or archives, or housing, or sex as the resistant material, experiencing these inseparably from language. Myriad groupings of identifications and practices ripped through and animated the collective fabric. Part of what this new subjectivity showed them was the absolute profanity of happiness, and the existence of that happiness outside of duration. Resistance became a form of life, a form of lived coexistence. This form of life included the structure of group conversations, the improvised ways decisions were made and tasks were allotted, the chaotic fidelity with which records were kept and events and meetings were documented, how a generous unspoken agreement to take each person's intellect completely seriously underwrote vicious arguments, conflicts and opaque inventions, as well as the ways ideas moved or were blocked between smaller friendship dyads or triads and the larger group. It would include the ways they cared for one another's health and appetites, the ways they helped each other's animals and plants and households, the kitchen haircuts they excelled in, the thrifted garments they exchanged, the various textures of relationship with other collectives and groups. Most of them survived. Many of them later scattered. Some returned. The collective translated communal time to the radically leisured time of the poem.

A question remains open. What is the relation between the poem and a form of life? What are the terms and means of this vital translation? I believe that this is the query that the collective elaborated. That immaterial phalanstery still guides the trajectory of my own activities in poetry.

LIZ HOWARD

Against Assimilation I Rose into Poetry

Here I am in the land called Canada. Canada is a problem and I am a problem, too. I am both settler and First Nations, an anglophone with Franco roots, a thoroughly rural person who, due to the fact of my strangeness and need for education, has left her homeland for the Big Smoke. And I am a poet, perhaps a poet first in this indulgence. An avant-garde poet, a feminist poet, a decolonial poet, a poet. The problem of Canada, and ultimately of myself, I could argue, has been the driving force behind my work.

   In the process of arriving at this essay, I've tried to locate in myself the site from which to write in/against Canada. The waters of my thought have rushed through the myriad approaches I could take, the theoretical frameworks, the modes of address. My mind is simultaneously a Steinian room in which I "act so that there is no use in a centre"[1] and the carafe of blind glass that is an "arrangement in a system of pointing,"[2] the lip pointing of my mother and Annharte, needle of some internal compass pointing north which is home, the divining rod of my cognitive waters and what it means to call down the sky. To enter the tent of one's consciousness bound by colonial ligatures/strictures and to be released into a charged divinatory field of manidoog[3] language of which poetry can act as translator on the portage to self-determination and self-knowledge, against assimilation toward a radical form of transgressive excess, a potlatch, a talk show in which everybody gets a poem, towards what Lisa Robertson has called an "illustriously useless poeisis."[4]

The site of my arrival assumes the form of an anecdote wherein I first met James Douglas Wesley, then an elder of the Oji-Cree Brunswick House First Nation in my hometown of Chapleau, Ontario, a small, isolated logging community, formerly a Hudson's Bay fur-trading post, tucked just inside the arctic watershed. It was the fall of 2001. I was sixteen and had attended the birthday party of my friend Lyndsay, herself a member of the Fox Lake Cree Nation. She and we party guests decided to parade into the heart of downtown in our conical, cartoon party hats trailing streamers and helium balloons to go hang out where the youth often gathered, outside the convenience store at the main intersection where one of the town's few traffic lights blinked orange in all four directions, perpetually. When we arrived there were also three adult First Nations men outside the store. One man approached me, and I saw that he had only one arm, his face grew closer in the intermittent light. He introduced himself as *James Douglas Wesley, from the old folks home at Duck Lake* (Duck Lake being the local name for Brunswick House First Nation), and then he placed his only hand on my head, his lower palm cupping my brow, and what he said I can only paraphrase: he said he was calling down the sky to save me, asked the Great Spirit to help me, to heal me, to aid me in "getting out of this town." I was sixteen years old, and I looked into the face of James Douglas Wesley, his eyes half shut, I looked into the blink of the orange traffic light and knew for certain then that I had to leave. That I could leave. That against the Canada that I knew, the Canada that prefers me impoverished or better yet dead, that I would continue and in that continuance I rose into poetry.

Years later I would learn that James Douglas Wesley was a residential school survivor, and it is not my role or right to speak of what I learned about his time in Rez School, but I will offer that it was horrific.

I want to take a screen shot of my recollection that is the scene of our meeting and use it to explain who I was in that moment and then fast-forward from there to who I am today, having written my book *Infinite Citizen of the Shaking Tent,* and being one who has been invited to write here as a citizen of the current body politic, and these sores on my mind, on the body of my work—who are they for when I have both a name and a country that try to erase me? There is both the moon and the fall of my day clothes on the cheap flooring of this apartment that equivocates on the former floor of Lake Iroquois. The resurrection of the ancient oppressed is radical, is an avant-garde, as I tell the police there is nothing amiss here, nothing amiss other than the fact of my crying because over the phone my mother has threatened suicide. Please do not kill me. It is within the realm of possibility that I am not even actually real.

In that screen shot I am a young woman who only knew the half-truth about her origins. At that time I knew I was of both settler and First Nations ancestry. My mother told me my absent father was Ojibway, Anishinaabe in the language, and that he was a very kind and intelligent man who fell into addiction and took himself away before I was a toddler. He fell into addiction in part because he was taught to hate who he was, "a half-breed Indian." We lived on welfare as my father, in some other town, worked on killing his own liver, either too embarrassed or too ambivalent to speak to me, even as he knew he was dying. When he was dying I was summoned to him at the age of twenty-nine. Alone flying to Halifax to witness the state of a father I never knew, not fully realizing that he would die after I kissed his cheek, holding his hand as his body went cold, blood coming up though the tubes connected to the body of my father, this body this face this skin, that is mine, that I see as myself, that is now dying, that is now dead, my yellow-white hand grasping the dead brown and jaundiced hand of my father. I so wish this could've been different. I want to come back and see you on your best day of collecting garbage, before you cash it in for beer. I want to see the truth of your eyes in the light of March where you might have been humorous. Deadbeat dad, you no longer have to worry about a thing. I watched as my father passed from my unknowing into eternity.

Today I am a person who has done the hard work of reconciling conflicting/problematic origins, traditions, and the trauma of my family, the multigenerational trauma sewn into our DNA,[5] the survivance that is my word, my account, my fractured story along both the waters of this page and of my book. Gerald Vizenor wrote that

> Survivance is an active presence, the continuance of native stories, not a mere reaction, or a survivable name. Native survivance stories are renunciations of dominance, tragedy and victimry. Survivance means the right of succession or reversion of an estate, and in that sense, the estate of native survivancy.[6]

The estate of my survivancy is poetry. In poetry I am never a victim. I am most alive. During the composition of my book I held in my mind, simultaneously, a First Nation's approach to poetics, whereby I engaged with "the action of weaving the old stories with new contemporary realities,"[7] and that of innovative feminist poetics in which the consideration of "interrogating or undermining the subject's relation to writing … [is tied up with] working out problems *in* rather than simply *with* language."[8] In my book I have written both of Western philosophy and science and also of Anishinaabe creation and migration stories, of both the city and the Boreal forest I was raised in. I have tried to write in conviviality with what Leanne Betasamosake Simpson has written: "Ethically it is my belief that the land, reflected in Nishnaabeg thought and philosophy, compels us towards resurgence in virtually every respect."[9]

When I stand on stage or at the entrance of every poem I've written, the fact of my body, its myriad histories, deep histories are inscribed their too. My body is of the land and my mother who bore me upon that land. The land of northern Ontario where my great-grandfather trapped beaver, where, in front of her shack, my great-grandmother smiles out from a picture taken on Atikameksheng Anishnawbek[10] land, where I fascinated over lichen as a child, where I wrote my first poem. Against the land now called Canada I endeavour to write another future wherein I have not only survived but reclaim the land in my work and to acknowledge also how this reclamation/resurgence is problematic. I continue to stand at the entrance of my every thought. Everything is a question, a poem, a father, a mother, a procedure, an account. I do not always know if I have done right by what has been given me. I do not know if I could call down the sky.

How does exercising/exorcising one's particular unknowing in verse make it avant-garde? I recall how David Antin wrote that if you can't respond to (or perhaps write towards or out of) the reality of relation, empathy, and ambiguity then "youre [sic] not in the avant-garde."[11] An interesting notion, one that has stuck with me. And I think of James Douglas Wesley, what would he think of my writing? That in my book I have written:

lux   *below the sole blinking traffic*
sucrose   *light in the centre of town*
norepinephrine   *an elder diabetic amputee from*
                         the farthest reserve placed

whether our engine of the possible?
asked this atomic history of silt
in the watershed

his last hand on my brow
called upon Gitchi Manitou
to call down my exit
from the sky[12]

I think also of Rosanna Deerchild who has written about her mother's experience of residential school:

us kids eh
conspire in Cree
pass notes

sneak past
praying nuns
in chapel
tonight

hide in treeline between
school and [am]bush ...

one lone whistle
slow and long ...

sound snags shawl
we sing her to earth ...

at least that night
us kids eh

we called down the sky
to save us[13]

My own practice of resurgence has been to celebrate my disparate origins, to not deny an Indigenous presence in my work, the remnant and still dancing Indigenous figure of my voice, within the problem that is Canada, the problem that is both mine and yours. I invoke the transgressive excess of the West; science, *écriture féminine*, the sonnet and also Nanabush stories,

stories from the land and the idea that the master's tools will never dismantle the master's house.[14] The sky was called down to save me. I made my work into a Shaking Tent. I have not been murdered. I have not been erased. Some have said I have created an exceptional thing, it was everything that was in me to give. I still endeavour to inscribe along the other side of this day the birthright of my name-place: I rose into poetry. And if this fact is not perceived as radical, then perhaps we must reconsider what it means to be avant-garde.

LIFE CYCLE OF THE ANIMAL CALLED SHE

I made a line without continuation. My name in red
Wife   Letters along the belly of this curve. How to cure him
Mother   Of the colic, the bed wet, the conquest, or the lack
Mistress of consent? I haven't got it in my purse, in my nerve,
Or in a hospice of milk. Everything we see could also

Be otherwise. I had another beginning. I took love down
Waitress From its shelf and inserted it into my orifice. The century
Nurse   That flattered me begged also in roses and spring, I am
Whore   But a sinner yet retreating. The limits of my language
Are the limits of my world. I took love out of my orifice
And buried it by the river.

The picture is a model of reality. I have no sense because
I am between genders in the west end of this dying city.
Maid   Give me a balm of women's kisses. The flame of my dessert.
Maiden I woke up and texted you: It's over. I woke up to get myself
Crone   Some meat. I made a mask of all the features that are receding.
The light a bawdry infant disclosed amid a lawn of cosmos.

There is an amber coloured skull in the painting called *Vanitas*
Birth   That is my son. My son cannot speak because I have no son.
Marriage I have a brother on the spectrum. He drives a rig hauling metals.
Grave   He is my brother but we do not share a father. It is impolite

To speak of such things. My headstone could read that I was
An animal unafraid to breathe these title's their speaking.

Subpoena my belief. Love doesn't work here anymore.
I lifted my face into distraction. I lifted my hair at its roots,
My breasts with wires. When I dreamt the Indian Agent
He was the accountant of persuasion. I let down my limbs
Address And replicated. I do not know any other door through
Occupation Which to enter. Castigate my own body in service to
Age The tyranny of will which is no altar. There is no take
Away in the forest. Who will be invited to eat and devise
A plot of land? Make this mantle disappear: the world
Is independent of my will. I've said this. Nothing in me
Can ever truly pay the lease.

NOTES

1 Gertrude Stein, *Tender Buttons* (Mineola: Dover, 1997), 43.

2 Stein, *Tender Buttons*, 3.

3 Anishinaabe Spirits who communicate the future (or matters distant in place) during the conjuring ceremony known as the Shaking Tent.

4 Lisa Robertson, "Untitled," *Nilling: Prose* (Toronto: BookThug, 2012), 87.

5 See http://indiancountrytodaymedianetwork.com/2015/05/28/trauma-may-be -woven-dna-native-americans-160508.

6 Gerald Robert Vizenor, *Manifest Manners: Narratives on Postindian Survivance* (Lincoln: University of Nebraska Press, 1999), vii.

7 Neal McLeod, "Introduction," *Indigenous Poetics in Canada* (Waterloo: Wilfrid Laurier University Press, 2014), 3.

8 Kate Eichhorn and Heather Milne, "Introduction," *Prismatic Publics: Innovative Canadian Women's Poetry and Poetics* (Toronto: Coach House Books, 2009), 13–14.

9 Leanne Betasamosake Simpson, *Dancing on Our Turtle's Back: Stories of Nishnaabeg Re-creation, Resurgence and a New Emergence* (Winnipeg: Arbeiter Ring, 2011), 18.

10 My family's former reservation located just outside of Sudbury, ON.

11 David Antin, *What It Means to Be Avant-garde* (Toronto: Emergency Response Unit, 2010).

12 This was the original line in my chapbook: *Skullambient* (Toronto: Ferno House Press, 2011), 8.

13 Rosanna Deerchild, *Calling Down the Sky* (Markham: BookLand Press, 2015), 48–50. Reprinted with permission of BookLand Press, www.Booklandpress.com, and of Rosanna Deerchild.

14 See Audre Lorde, "The Master's Tools Will Never Dismantle the Master's House," *Sister Outsider: Essays and Speeches* (Berkeley: Cross Press, 2007), 110–114.

PART III

THE CENTENNIAL

KRISTINE SMITKA

The Sublation of Obduracy: Nationalism and the Avant-Garde Marketing of Beautiful Losers

Upon publication, *Beautiful Losers* (1966) sparked public debate: Was it excessively pornographic and worthy of condemnation, or was it, as Stan Dragland has argued, daringly Canada's first postmodern novel, worthy of national praise? Cohen's mixture of the sacred and the profane, his experimentation with the formal elements of the novel, and his incorporation of popular cultural products firmly root the text in the sixties and result in comparisons between Cohen and the likes of William S. Burroughs and Thomas Pynchon.[1] Despite these virtues, the novel posed a challenge for its publisher, McClelland & Stewart, who feared it would be banned due to its pornographic content.

Regardless of this concern, Jack McClelland, McClelland & Stewart's general manager, could not bear the thought that an American firm might publish a new novel by one of Canada's great authors before a Canadian publisher released it.[2] Thus, he planned a pre-emptive strike against public dissent, which consisted of a seven-part promotional scheme: first, a carefully planned launch party for 400 of Toronto's most prominent artists and critics; second, a promotional card including artwork by Canadian abstract expressionist artist Harold Town, which was mailed to bookstores, reviewers, and libraries; third, another promotional card displaying additional work by Town, which was released the following week; fourth, a double poster, mailed to bookstores a few days after the second promotional flyer; fifth, another mailing, consisting of background on the novel's composition, accompanied by quotations from Cohen's work; sixth, the release of more advanced opinions by experts; and seventh, the purchase of ad space, with little more than the title, author, and price of the book.[3] Throughout the advertising campaign, Harold Town's illustrations, as well as his review of the novel, positioned Cohen's work as part of the emergence of a Canadian avant-garde.

Considering McClelland's fear of an obscenity charge, the choice of Town at first appears counter-intuitive. However, this careful pairing helped McClelland situate *Beautiful Losers* within an ongoing debate about freedom of expression in Canada. This essay investigates McClelland's marketing scheme's strange mixture of avant-garde imagery and nationalist rhetoric through the lens of what Jochen Schulte-Sasse calls "the social impotence" of the avant-garde, particularly when it comes to destabilizing the economic power structures that enable a bourgeois celebration of art as detached from social praxis.[4] I argue that McClelland sought to stabilize two forms of institutional power: nationalism and democracy. On the one hand, McClelland's tactics interpolate Town's and Cohen's critique of the institutions of bourgeois culture within McClelland & Stewart's own nation-building practice. However, this accusation may be anachronistic, given that at the time nation-building was also an expression of a radical politics of decolonization. In this sense, the growth of Canadian publishing in the 1950s and 1960s, of which McClelland is often lauded as its symbol, can be seen as its own radical social formation. The economies of scale of Canadian publishing ensure that national publishing endeavours run counter to market forces. Herein lies the challenge of applying canonical theories of the avant-garde to a Canadian context, for surely the anxieties of the Futurists, Dadaists, and Surrealists in Europe and the United States were inflected differently from artists reacting against the institution of art within a Canadian context.

This essay's definition of the avant-garde builds from Peter Bürger's *Theory of the Avant-Garde*, which argues that art decoupled from life in the eighteenth century, when art ceased to be a conduit for religious ritual or monarchical power, and instead became a site of worship in its own right. *L'art pour l'art* movement, and bourgeois society more broadly, severed art from "the praxis of life."[5] The avant-garde did not so much react against the styles and techniques of its artistic predecessor's investment in aestheticism (as did the modernists), but rather attacked the very institution of art that enabled the artist to stand at a distance from the social sphere. Bürger gives the example of Duchamp's *objets trouvés*, which disavow the relationship between individuality and artistic creation. However, Duchamp's ready-mades lose "their character as antiart" at the moment when they are installed in the gallery.[6] While Duchamp's experiments fail to integrate art into social praxis, they nevertheless succeed in highlighting the art galleries' power to sanctify what constitutes art. The avant-garde's revolutionary ambitions may have failed, but they remain important for exposing the institutions that govern cultural formations.

In 2010, Bürger responded to common critiques of *Theory of the Avant-Garde*, clarifying that the "paradox of the failure of the avant-gardists ... [manifests when t]he provocation that was supposed to expose the institution of art is recognized by the institution as art."[7] However, "[o]ne could almost say: in their very failure, the avant-gardes conquer the institution."[8] The interpolation of avant-garde art into the gallery does not mean that the gallery remains unchanged. Rather, Bürger invokes Hegelian sublation to explain the dialectical transformation of the institution that results from the recognition of the everyday object as worthy of artistic scrutiny. Thus, Bürger redefines failure: the avant-gardists succeeded in provoking attitudinal changes, yet failed to incite revolution.

The comfort with which McClelland absorbs Cohen and Town into McClelland & Stewart's nation-building practice highlights a similarly paradoxical failure by demonstrating how neither artist occupies the vanguard positions from which they claim to speak. Instead, the marketing scheme for *Beautiful Losers* reframes the agonistic logic that typifies avant-garde discourse:[9] the "we" of Canadians against the cultural imperialism of a villainous American "them." However, we may ask what this failure can teach us about the ideological seams of nation-building, especially given that McClelland did not see the avant-garde in Canada as at odds with his own nationalist endeavours.

CONFESSIONS OF A LITERARY NIBBLER

In 1965, the year before the publication of *Beautiful Losers*, McClelland began soliciting advice on how best to position the novel in the Canadian marketplace. In a letter to Northrop Frye, dated 29 December 1965, he explained that

> Because we consider Cohen an extremely important Canadian author, and because it is going to be published outside this country regardless of what we do, I have concluded that we must publish here despite the fact that we are almost certain to run into an obscenity charge either in Ontario or in the province of Quebec. The recent action in connection with Dorothy Cameron has convinced me that we are probably going to have trouble.[10]

In 1965, The Toronto Police Morality Squad raided Dorothy Cameron's Yonge Street art gallery and confiscated Robert Markle's nudes, forcing her to close the exhibition space while she awaited trial on obscenity charges.[11] McClelland feared his publishing house would meet a similar level of censorship. In the name of national pride, and Canadian publishing more specifically, he planned a pre-emptive strike against public dissent.

At the centre of the seven-part marketing scheme was new artwork by Canadian abstract expressionist artist Harold Town, who was to feature prominently on all advertisements, as well as the book's jacket. As McClelland explained to Corlies M. Smith at Viking Press, which was Cohen's American publisher, Town was not only a contemporary and a friend of Cohen, but also "Canada's best known and most highly regarded contemporary artist. At least to the younger group."[12] For McClelland, both attracted a similar audience, comprised of modern youth who epitomized the next generation of contemporary art.

In pairing Town and Cohen, McClelland made a comparison between abstract expressionism and the scope of Cohen's work. As Serge Guilbaut notes, the artistic abandon of abstract expressionism came to be associated with the idea of freedom during the Cold War.[13] A backlash to the realist propaganda employed in wartime, combined with both a resistance to Marxist thought in New York in the 1940s and the stifling effects of McCarthyism in the 1950s, produced a "self-proclaimed neutrality" among abstract expressionist artists.[14] As a result, avant-garde artists "were soon enlisted by governmental agencies and private organizations in the fight against Soviet cultural expansion."[15] The dynamic colours and sweeping brushstrokes of this anti-representational style were "for many the expression of freedom: the freedom to create controversial works of art, the freedom symbolized by action painting, by the unbridled expressionism of artists completely without fetters."[16]

Thus, McClelland's choice to employ Town's abstract expressionist imagery in the marketing of *Beautiful Losers* can be read in two complementary ways: first, it is another instance of McClelland looking to the United States for a product that he could rebrand with a maple leaf. McClelland & Stewart's New Canadian Library serves as another example of this logic, because it draws not only its format, but also its name, from The New American Library.[17] American practices heavily influenced McClelland's understanding of national publishing. If abstract expressionism stood for American freedom, then Harold Town represented Canada's ability to produce similar symbols of nationalist liberation. Second, it suggests a tempering of McClelland's (and perhaps Town's) commitment to the idea of an avant-garde revolution, a tempering also exhibited in Cohen's novel, which sees American culture as the environment in which the characters swim. However, this failure to break out of these systems could also be read not as a wavering of their commitments, but rather as what Bürger calls an awareness of the impossibility of success. Quoting Pierre Naville's *La Révolution et les Intellectuels* (1927), Bürger describes the avant-garde motto: "Notre victoire n'est pas venue et ne viendra jamais. Nous subissons d'avance cette peine."[18]

In addition to providing visual interpretations of the text, Town penned a review for *The Globe and Mail* entitled "Confessions of a Literary Nibbler," on 25 December 1965, arguing that *Beautiful Losers*

> is the sort of work that inquisitional censors pray they will find under the Christmas tree; it makes *Tropic of Capricorn* seem like Winnie the Pooh, but is, I think, the first real proof that Cohen has authentic genius and that rarest of abilities, the power to create tenderness in a horrifying context.[19]

Town, as a figure in Cohen's milieu, vouches for the writer's "authentic genius" three months before the majority of the public could purchase the work. He also positions "inquisitional censors" against exceptional artists, encouraging readers to invest in a definition of the artist as a remarkable individual, who must be afforded freedom of expression in order to ensure that his insights reach the general public. In 1964, Marshall McLuhan published *Understanding Media*, in which he made a similar argument: The "serious artist is the only person able to encounter technology with impunity, just because he is an expert aware of the changes in sense perception."[20] Both McLuhan and Town position artistic vision against the general public's blindness, thereby rendering censors unqualified to judge art, because censors operate from the disadvantaged position of the sightless. Town's review then underwrites Cohen's authority, by claiming clarity of vision, a privilege afforded only to genius artists.

Here, Town exhibits the paradoxical position of an avant-gardist who both erects the category of genius to justify his review and yet ostensibly deconstructs such categories, and the institutions that make these categories visible to the general public, in his artistic practice. The very notion of a "serious artist" presupposes a hierarchy of artistic practice that elevates certain artists to a canonical vantage. This oxymoronic impulse—to both fight against institutional power that severs art from everyday life and base this argument on the idea of genius, which is a concept at the heart of institutional power—drives avant-garde discourse. While the interpolation of avant-garde art into the art gallery often denotes failure in the counterculture, the inability of the avant-garde to find a way out of the use of the category of genius, represents another important failure, as exemplified by Town's justification of reputational power as a necessary evil in the fight against systemic power.

Town's review was part of McClelland's strategy to sway public opinion with as many positive advanced critical reviews as possible. In an outline for the promotional program, dated 28 January 1966, McClelland informs his staff that the novel will "confound most of the critics, and certainly most of the public unless they are told in advance what they should believe."[21] This tactic sought to leverage the reputations of esteemed professionals, such as Town, in the service of Cohen's novel. Simultaneously, it dispersed responsibility over a larger body of critics, relying on the cultural capital of others employed in the creative industries not only to buttress Cohen's reputation, but also to protect McClelland & Stewart against public scrutiny.

FIGURE 1 Pre-publication advertisement for Leonard Cohen's *Beautiful Losers*, featuring original artwork by Harold Town (1966).

FIGURE 2 Post-publication advertisement for Leonard Cohen's *Beautiful Losers*, featuring original artwork by Harold Town (1966).

The first advertisements for the novel consisted of a two-part series of black-and-white cards that were distributed to libraries, book reviewers, and employees of the book trade in advance of the launch. These cards paired Town's abstract expressionist illustrations with justifications for the publication of the controversial novel. The illustrations for both cards depict human forms, but the black-and-white images abstract the body to the point of confusion. The first (Figure 1) shows a long-haired figure bending forward so that a cascade of tresses blocks his or her face from view. The second illustration (Figure 2) shows a bird-like body with legs that end in large claws and arms that fold into wing-like shoulders. Both androgynous bodies lack facial details and have a grotesque beauty. Situated on a flap that folds over the accompanying text, these illustrations occupy one-third of the card and can be turned, like opening the cover of a book, to reveal the full text of the advertisement.

The first card asserts, "[o]urs is a serious publishing house. This is a serious and carefully written work by an important Canadian writer. We believe that it is not only our privilege but our obligation to publish it."[22] This justification shifts attention away from the novel and towards the publisher, leveraging the "serious[ness]" of McClelland & Stewart's brand to vouch for the quality of the book.[23] McClelland fails to name the cause for which he feels an "obligation."[24] Be it an obligation to the nation, or an obligation to the publishing profession and literature more broadly, McClelland invokes nationalist sentiments to explain his support for a controversial work of art. The use of Town reiterates Cohen's position as a prominent Canadian artist. Thus, McClelland frames dissent against the novel as an attack on both artistic freedom and nationalism.

The second version of the card, mailed to the same recipients the following week, addresses Cohen's novel more directly. Although it begins with a reference to the work as a "controversial new novel," it concludes that it is a "disagreeable religious epic of incomparable beauty."[25] While conceding that the novel "will mean different things to many people," the inclusion of an anonymous interpretation provides a positive reading of the novel that could be adopted by the general public.[26] McClelland often employed this tactic, most notably in the introductions that accompanied each edition in the New Canadian Library, where Canadian scholars leveraged their reputations to attest to the value of Canadian literature. These paratextual elements manage the reputations of the texts that they envelop; as acts of canon-formation, they highlight McClelland & Stewart's role in cultivating the authority of its writers.

Both advertisements for *Beautiful Losers* conclude with an aside to direct the reader back to the illustration by Town: "Yes! The drawing is by Harold Town. It will be the basis for our jacket motif," and "P.S. You're right! That is another Harold Town illustration. It will be part of our jacket design."[27] The emphasis on Town positions Cohen's novel at the forefront of the Canadian avant-garde. Fiercely critical of the Canadian art world's lack of support for local artists, Town worked as an activist for Canada's creative community. The hopeful impetus behind activist endeavours demonstrates what Gregory Betts describes as the key assumption of avant-gardism: that current tastes are inadequate and that "society can be remade."[28] While Town's prominent role in the public sphere may at first resemble a public intellectual—"in 1966 alone, [Town] appeared in seventy-two articles in the three Toronto daily newspapers"[29] (more than any avant-garde artist)—these two concepts are not immediately at odds within Canada's postcolonial context.

In *Avant-Garde Canadian Literature: The Early Manifestations*, Betts delineates Canadian avant-gardists' complicity in both commercialism and nationalism in the face of the dominant "colonial imagination."[30] The Canadian iteration of this future-oriented movement did not subscribe to total revolutionary change, so much as it advocated for Canadian artistic production, and thus "postcolonial agency" from both Britain and the United States.[31] By borrowing European aesthetic models to advocate for Canadian artistic institutions, the Canadian avant-garde did not seek "to recondition the general category of reality and restart history," but rather "sought to recondition the experience of reality in Canada and to envision the start of a truly Canadian" artistic history.[32] While Betts grounds his book in literary history, his argument readily applies to Town's advocacy work.

Town refused to relocate to the United States, despite the affordances of the art market to the south. Instead, he positioned himself in Toronto's artistic milieu, receiving the Order of Canada in 1966 and the Canada Centennial Medal the year after.[33] Town remains most famous for his role in Painters Eleven (1953–1960), a movement without a manifesto, which nevertheless stood in opposition to the landscape paintings of the Group of Seven (1920–1931).[34] In the catalogue for the Art Gallery of Ontario's 1986 exhibition of Town's work, David Burnett argues that the unifying concept of Town's career was a consistent attack against "the armies of the bland."[35] However, Town used his prominence in the public eye to attack not only boring art, but also institutions of power and domination that obfuscate social injustice.

In 1964, Town represented Canada at the prestigious Venice Biennale with his exhibition *Enigma*. During the Biennale, a cardinal ordered two of the *Enigma* drawings removed.[36] The compositions depict professional men and woman (doctors, priests, judges) in positions of submission and domination to investigate, what Town claimed were, the "social wrongs and follies, of the hypocrisies, complacency, and self-seeking of those who hide behind the mystique of professionalism or the cosseted power of institutions."[37] While Town referred to these drawings as his "political cartoons," others called them pornographic, misogynistic, obscene, bestial, savage, and satiric.[38] Town's explicit politics, combined with his artistic technique, express the avant-garde belief that "art has a socially consequential role only when it is somehow related to a socially relevant discussion of norms and values and thus to the cognition of society as a whole."[39] In fact, it is this investment in rescuing art from its isolation in artistic institutions and resituating it within social praxis that distinguishes avant-garde from modernist art. Both avant-garde and modernist artists react to growing industrialization, globalization, urbanism, and mass culture precipitated by capitalism; however, the avant-garde remains distinguishable from modernism in its will to political power, "tempted by the opportunity to see their revolutionary projections realized in a world in need of revitalizing."[40]

THE MOST REVOLTING BOOK EVER WRITTEN IN CANADA

When the CBC called Town to ask him to comment on *Enigma*, he revelled in the criticism: "[i]t's such an honour being banned in Italy, the mother of sensuality [he explained.] It's like being asked to straighten your tie in a bordello."[41] The litany of criticism Town received for *Enigma* parallels the media frenzy that erupted concerning Cohen's work *Beautiful Losers*. Although the book was never banned, as McClelland feared it would be, its reception was polarized. Upon release, *The Globe and Mail* described it as "verbal masturbation," and *Toronto Daily Star* critic Robert Fulford called it

> The most revolting book ever written in Canada.... I believe everything he writes is entirely within the proper range of literature, but it seems to me his book is an important failure. At the same time it is probably the most interesting Canadian book of the year.[42]

Many bookstores, most notably W.H. Smith and Simpson's, decided they did not want the risk of carrying it, a decision that considerably decreased sales.[43] In contrast, avant-garde poet and publisher bill bissett raved, "i give th book of cohens a good review, a great review, easily million stars [*sic*]."[44] When asked to defend the book in an interview with Adrienne Clarkson on her show *Take 30*, on 23 May 1966, Cohen responded,

> I'd feel pretty lousy if I were praised by a lot of the people who had come down pretty heavy on me. I think in a way there's a war on. It's an old, old war....

[I]f I had to choose sides ... I'd just as well be defined as I have been by the establishment press.[45]

The old war Cohen identifies pitted those who hold institutional power against a new wave of creative energy.

Cohen's dichotomy between the "establishment press," which censors artists, and the "new vanguard," which battles for freedom, falls apart when read in the context of Donald Brittain's and Don Owen's National Film Board (NFB) documentary, *Ladies and Gentleman ... Mr. Leonard Cohen*, which proved "crucial in launching his performance career," advertising the poet to John Hammond of Columbia Records.[46] At the end of filming the directors invite Cohen to a private screening so as to catch his reactions on camera. These remarks close the documentary. The footage reveals Cohen in the intimate acts of domestic life: sleeping, bathing. Confessing the staged nature of these private moments, Cohen admits, "the fraud is that I am not really sleeping."[47] While bathing, he writes in black marker on the wall behind the tub "*caveat emptor.*"[48] When asked to translate the phrase, Cohen explains it means "buyer beware ... I had to warn the public that [my performance] ... is not entirely devoid of the con."[49] Cohen's work as a self-proclaimed "double-agent" productively effaces the truth-claims of documentary film, proving him trustworthy.

This "ironic accommodation" of the documentary form constitutes a fairly common modernist response to the institutions that promote literary celebrity.[50] Joe Moran, however, ascribes this quality to all literary celebrities, who must present themselves as both extraordinary and familiar, as their lives and work are "ransacked for their human interest at the same time as they are lauded for their difference and aloofness."[51] This celebration of paradox marks the reader's "nostalgia for some kind of transcendent, anti-economic, creative element in a secular, debased, commercialized culture."[52] By unmasking the apparatus—the conscious techniques that support documentary's truth claims—Cohen appears to rise above them. As such, he presents himself to the viewer as authentic, diffident even. Essentially, Cohen distances himself from the blatant act of self-promotion—starring in a film that only furthers his presence in the public sphere—by drawing the viewer's attention to the constructed nature of such projects. In so doing, he becomes the biographical subject and the biographer at the same time. This distancing from the media apparatus is echoed in his term "establishment press," but the binary between established and marginal falls apart in the Canadian context. While the NFB certainly employs film as a "citizen building technology," and had the expressed purpose of naturalizing new immigrants, this nationalist initiative is firmly located in the nation's transition from a British to an American sphere of influence.[53] As Canada moves from being a literal colony to a colony by virtue of both capital and cultural interpolation, the NFB operates from an anti-colonial position.

The NFB's documentary on Cohen was screened at the very expensive launch party for *Beautiful Losers,* which was held almost a month before the novel's publication, on 29 March 1966, at the Centennial Ballroom, located at the Inn on the Park in Toronto. The 400-person all-star guest list for the carefully orchestrated, open-bar affair included Pierre Berton, Marshall McLuhan, Harold Town, and almost every prominent writer in the Toronto region.[54] However, Cohen failed to attend the party. Disappointed with sales figures, Cohen implored McClelland to mount a more extensive advertising campaign. On 9 May 1966, McClelland composed a six-page response to defend the publisher's efforts, which outlined the 300 copies of the novel sent to reviewers; the numerous press releases, specialty coasters and posters; and the expensive launch party that Cohen had failed to attend. In fact, McClelland claimed it had received "more direct promotional effort than any other book [had] received."[55] McClelland then berated Cohen for his failure to participate in this promotional process. In an attempt to distance himself from the marketing of his work, Cohen instead lobbied McClelland to invest in more advertising. In this way, Cohen asked McClelland to claim responsibility for the commoditization of his art, so that he could maintain a critical distance from the tarnishing effects of the market. When read in this context, we can see how Cohen's agonistic statement about the "establishment press" attempts to erect what Stephen Voyce calls "the moral superiority of the 'we' against the banality of the 'they,'"[56] but Cohen is colluding with the "they" behind the scenes.

BEAUTIFUL LOSERS

Linda Hutcheon reads *Beautiful Losers,* a novel sprawling in its scope, as an allegory for Canada's political history. The novel's four prominent nationalities—the First Nations (represented by Edith and Catherine Tekakwitha), the French (represented by the Québécois separatist F.), the English (represented by the anglophone professor I.), and the American (represented by the invasion of American mass culture in the form of comic books, advertisements, and cinema)—create a hierarchy of domination and pose the ethical question of the novel: How do we "become 'beautiful losers' able to deal with our loss without taking it out on someone else?"[57]

Robert David Stacey's recent work on the novel delineates the tension between I.'s banal "repression and violent introjection, symbolized by his dedication to the past and his chronic and painful constipation" and F.'s doctrine of "futurity."[58] F.'s aesthetic vision, which seeks to "connect nothing,"[59] nevertheless reveals an obsession with systems in general. As the spokesperson for newness as a disciplined regime, F. reveals the megalomaniacal-ego at the heart of creation:

> If Hitler had been born in Nazi Germany, he wouldn't have been content to enjoy the atmosphere. If an unpublished poet discovers his own image in the work of another writer it gives him no comfort, for his allegiance is not to the image or its process in the public domain, his allegiance is to the notion that he is not bound to the world as given, that he can escape from the painful arrangement of things as they are.[60]

As a separatist, F. asserts that Canada represents one such "painful arrangement." However, F.'s admission that Hitler displays a similar mania to poets paints history's most villainous politician and avant-garde artists with the same wary brushstroke. Both strive towards radical social formations, but their legacy-oriented motivations call their projects into question.

Here Cohen demonstrates his awareness of the close relationship between fascism and the avant-garde, both of which assert "violence as an ethical and regenerative force."[61] In his work on the close relationship between Georges Sorel and the French avant-garde, Mark Antliff argues that "[t]o be truly beautiful, Sorelian violence had to express the creative and moral transformation of each individual, otherwise it would resemble the brutal, immoral violence of the tyrant."[62] The justification of literal violence as a necessary force to destabilize systemic tyranny not only parallels the representational violence foregrounded by avant-garde artists, but also surfaced in the political allegiances of anglophone writers like Wyndham

Lewis, who praised Hitler, and Ezra Pound, who supported Mussolini. These Vorticist writers "realized that controlling language, and by extension the media, meant controlling the culture and all those in it. This realization (and the revolutionary impulse to correct the denigrating course of Western culture that it inspired) led both Pound and Lewis to fascism."[63]

When McClelland marked *Beautiful Losers* as Canadian literature by stamping it with the McClelland & Stewart brand, he interpolated F.'s separatist imagination within the publishing house's nation-building practice. With the book's transformative exploration of extreme violence, as exemplified by many of the masochistic characters, McClelland's ability to locate this text within the canon of Canadian literature perhaps represents one of the book's important failures: its aggressive sexuality and violent politics are assimilable into a national discourse. McClelland sublated the novel's pulpy sexuality, positioning the book as literature by publishing it in a hardcover format with an "expensive jacket and a good binding."[64] In fact, the four thousand copies of its first print run sold for $6.50 a book, making it slightly more expensive than other books on the market.[65] While Malcolm Ross, the editor of McClelland & Stewart's New Canadian Library, refused to include Cohen's novel in the series on the grounds that it was "obscenity for obscenity's sake,"[66] it was the first book added to the series upon Ross's retirement in 1978. From the initial marketing scheme to its position in the New Canadian Library, McClelland absorbed the more agonistic aspects of the text into his national publishing framework.

Although McClelland worked in publishing from 1946 to 1987, he did not become general manager of McClelland & Stewart until 1952, essentially taking over the firm from his father.[67] Throughout his tenure, McClelland tried to balance the heterodoxical objectives of running a profitable business, a service company, and a philanthropic enterprise; as McClelland said, McClelland & Stewart's objective was "not profit, but profit from a particular field of endeavour," specifically the service of Canadian authors.[68] McClelland's dedication to Canadian publishing was founded on an awareness of postwar trends. When McClelland took over the company he felt "that upswings in population numbers, education opportunities, leisure time and improved communications boded well for books."[69] This was a time of unprecedented growth in secondary and post-secondary education as a result of the baby boom. The ballooning of higher education translated into additional textbook acquisitions, the growth of libraries, and higher literacy rates. Nevertheless, a small population, a large geography, and competition from the south made Canada a difficult country in which to grow a national publishing culture. In opposition to the cultural invasion from the south, McClelland worked as Co-Chairman for the Committee for an Independent Canada (CIC), an organization that lobbied government for limits to foreign investment and ownership.[70]

Internationally, the postwar period saw rapid decolonization, and Canada, along with other post-colonial nations, sought to find independence on the world stage. As Canada became politically and economically tied to the United States, culture came to be viewed as one of the last fields of independence. Although nation-building is often understood to be a top-down project, McClelland used the firm, which he inherited from his father, to serve a nationalist agenda. The field of cultural production looks different from a Canadian perspective because of the country's colonial heritage, proximity to the United States, small population, and relatively short history as a nation. In a Canadian context, the world of symbolic capital aligns not so much with avant-garde artistic endeavours as with domestic production, because the economically successful side of the field is occupied, almost entirely, by foreign production. Thus, domestic production becomes symbolically valuable as the antithesis to a British or American mass-media invasion.

McClelland's dedication to domestic production resulted in the Guadalajara International Book Fair proclaiming him, in 1996, "the outstanding Canadian publisher of his generation."[71] In a letter of support for the award, fellow publisher Anna Porter named Jack McClelland the "prince of publishing,"[72] a nickname that stuck. After the prince had abdicated his throne and retired, Leonard Cohen wrote him, proclaiming, "[y]ou were the real Prime Minister of Canada. You still are. And even though it has all gone down the tubes, the country that you govern will never fall apart."[73] Cohen's elegy asserts Canadian publishing's integral contribution to nation-building, but it also betrays his nostalgia for a kind of postwar optimism predicated on a desire for Canadian cultural independence.

Beautiful Losers, both the novel and the epitextual material, highlights how the Canadian avant-gardists were seeking to harness the burgeoning power of the nation state to create a home for their revolutionary projections. However, this case study also exposes how this failure has a particular inflection when located in a postcolonial context. If abstract expressionism came to stand for freedom during the Cold War, as Guilbaut has argued, we might ask what this same technique tells us about freedom in a Canadian context. In the Canadian milieu, with its particular tensions of cultural imperialism and decolonization, freedom also meant freedom from American cultural invasion, and thus the erection of protectionist policy in the service of national artists. Ironically, this freedom to create art necessitated institutional structures and systems to support it.

NOTES

1 See Dennis Duffy, "Beautiful Beginners," in *The Tamarack Review* 40 (Summer 1966); and John Wain, "Making It New," in *Leonard Cohen: The Artist and His Critics* (Toronto: McGraw-Hill Ryerson, 1976).

2 In the end, McClelland & Stewart published simultaneously with Viking Press in the United States.

3 McClelland Box 20, File 1.

4 Jochen Schulte-Sasse, "Foreword: Theory and Modernism versus Theory of the Avant-Garde," *Theory of the Avant-Garde*, by Peter Bürger, trans. Michael Shaw (Minneapolis: University of Minnesota Press, 1984), xlii.

5 Bürger, *Theory*, 49.

6 Bürger, *Theory*, 57.

7 Peter Bürger, "Avant-Garde and Neo-Avant-Garde: An Attempt to Answer Certain Critics of *Theory of the Avant-Garde*," *New Literary History* 41.4 (2010): 705.

8 Bürger, "Avant-Garde," 705.

9 Stephen Voyce, *Poetic Community: Avant-Garde Activism and Cold War Culture* (Toronto: University of Toronto Press, 2013), 13.

10 Jack McClelland, Letter to Northrop Frye, 29 December 1965 (McClelland Box 20, File 8).

11 "Cops Ban 'Lewd' Drawings," *This Hour Has Seven Days*, 6 February 1966 (CBC Digital Archives).

12 Jack McClelland, Letter to Corlies M. Smith (McClelland Box 20, File 8).

13 Serge Guilbaut, *How New York Stole the Idea of Modern Art: Abstract Expressionism, Freedom, and the Cold War*, trans. Arthur Goldhammer (Chicago: University of Chicago Press, 1983), 201.

14 Guilbaut, *How New York Stole*, 11.

15 Guilbaut, 11.

16 Guilbaut, 201.

17 The New American Library was an autonomous publishing company that broke out of Penguin Books (Janet Friskney, *New Canadian Library: The Ross-McClelland Years, 1952–1978*, 36).

18 Bürger, "Avant," 700.

19 Harold Town, "Confessions of a Literary Nibbler," *Globe and Mail*, 25 December, 1965, A14.

20 Marshall McLuhan, *Understanding Media: The Extensions of Man* (Toronto: McGraw-Hill, 1964), 18.

21 McClelland Box 20, File 1.

22 McClelland Box 20, File 1.

23 McClelland Box 20, File 1.

24 McClelland Box 20, File 1.

25 McClelland Box 20, File 1.

26 McClelland Box 20, File 1.

27 McClelland Box 20, File 1.

28 Gregory Betts, *Avant-Garde Canadian Literature: The Early Manifestations* (Toronto: University of Toronto Press, 2013), 17.

29 Iris Nowell, *P11 Painters Eleven: The Wild Ones of Canadian Art* (Toronto: Douglas & McIntyre, 2010), 171.

30 Betts, *Avant-Garde*, 65.

31 Betts, 62.

32 Betts, 63.

33 Nowell, *P11*, 162–167.

34 See Lynda Shearer, *Painters Eleven*, and Brandi Leigh, "An Introduction to the Group of Seven."

35 David Burnett, *Town* (Toronto: McClelland & Stewart, 1991), 98.

36 Nowell, *P11*, 165–166.

37 Town quoted in Nowell, *P11*, 166.

38 Nowell, *P11*, 166.

39 Schulte-Sasse, "Foreword," xiii.

40 Betts, *Avant-Garde*, 203.

41 Town quoted in Nowell, *P11*, 166.

42 Robert Fulford, "Leonard Cohen's Nightmare Novel," *Toronto Daily Star* (26 April 1966).

43 McClelland Box 20, File 1.

44 bill bissett, "!!!!!" Rev. of *Beautiful Losers*, *Alphabet* 13 (June 1967), 94.

45 "*Beautiful Losers* Praised and Condemned," *Take 30*, hosts Adrienne Clarkson and Paul Soles, CBC Digital Archives.

46 Keith Harrison, "*Ladies and Gentlemen … Mr. Leonard Cohen*: The Performance of Self, Forty Years On," *Image Technologies in Canadian Literature: Narrative, Film, and Photography* (Brussels: PIE Peter Lang, 2009), 69.

47 Donald Brittain, dir., *Ladies and Gentlemen, Mr. Leonard Cohen*, perf. Leonard Cohen (National Film Board of Canada, 1965).

48 Brittain, *Ladies and Gentlemen*.

49 Brittain, *Ladies and Gentlemen*.

50 Aaron Jaffe, *Modernism and the Culture of Celebrity* (New York: Cambridge University Press, 2005), 177.

51 Joe Moran, *Star Authors: Literary Celebrity in America* (Sterling: Pluto Press, 2000), 8.

52 Moran, *Star Authors*, 9.

53 Zoë Druick, *Projecting Canada: Government Policy and Documentary Film at the National Film Board* (Kingston: McGill-Queen's University Press, 2007), 4.

54 Ira Bruce Nadel, *Various Positions: A Life of Leonard Cohen* (Toronto: Random House of Canada, 1996), 138.

55 McClelland Box 20, File 1.

56 Voyce, *Poetic Community*, 14.

57 Peter Wilkins, "'Nightmares of Identity': Nationalism and Loss in *Beautiful Losers*," *Essays on Canadian Writing* 69 (1999), 25.

58 Robert David Stacey, "Mad Translation in Leonard Cohen's *Beautiful Losers* and Douglas Glover's *Elle*," *English Studies in Canada* 40.2–3 (June/September 2014), 179.

59 Cohen, *Beautiful*, 17.

60 Cohen, 59.

61 Mark Antliff, *Avant-Garde Fascism: The Mobilization of Myth, Art, and Culture in France, 1909–1939* (Durham: Duke University Press, 2007), 5.

62 Antliff, *Avant-Garde Fascism*, 6.

63 Betts, *Avant-Garde*, 201.

64 Nadel, *Various Positions*, 439.

65 Nadel, 439.

66 Ross quoted in Janet Friskney, *New Canadian Library: The Ross-McClelland Years, 1952–1978* (Toronto: University of Toronto Press, 2007), 113.

67 James King, *Jack: A Life with Writers: The Story of Jack McClelland* (Toronto: Alfred A. Knopf, 1999), 308.

68 King, 108.

69 King, 43.

70 The desire to block out American investment was complicated later in his career by McClelland's initiative to "create a larger market for Canadian books by forming an association with … Bantam Canada" (King 308). This new option, which had been forbidden by Canada's Foreign Investment Review Agency until 1977, allowed McClelland to benefit from the improvement to the economies of scale, arising from combined markets.

71 Roy MacSkimming, *The Perilous Trade: Book Publishing in Canada, 1946–2006* (Toronto: McClelland & Stewart, 2007), 118.

72 MacSkimming, *The Perilous Trade*, 118

73 Cohen quoted in King, *Jack*.

STEPHEN CAIN

"A Vision in the UofT Stacks": bpNichol in the Library

In discussing the unusual format of Book Six of *The Martyrology*, Stephen Scobie once remarked: "What is it that bpNichol has against bibliographers, some Oedipal resentment from the days he worked in a library? How is a poor librarian supposed to catalogue a book that gives a different title on its title page from the title it gives on the cover?"[1] Although this is clearly a humorous rhetorical question, it is nonetheless something I want to consider here: What is the influence of the library on the poetry and poetics of Nichol? Not just the physical building, although that does play a part, but how does the very idea of the library—as an institution, as an image, as a metaphor—function in the work of Nichol? I wish to suggest that rather than seeing the library as an antagonistic force, one which Nichol might have looked at with resentment as a young writer, the library was an enabling and productive element in Nichol's poetics: one which fostered a poetic community, one which provided the material conditions that inspired some of his poems, and one which continued to influence his ideas about writing and research as a place of contestation and play.

In many of Nichol's earliest interviews, he often commented upon the effect of working at the University of Toronto library when he first moved to Toronto in the spring of 1964. For example, responding to Jack David's query about the library's influence on him in 1978, Nichol replied:

It impressed me with the narcissism of much literature. It took away from me the illusion that I was simply, by writing books, going to change the world;

59

there were probably much better vehicles for it. When you spend day after day under the dusty stacks of the well-meant words of millions of people, it changes your view of literature and what the point of it is. I ceased, at that point, to have a view of myself as reaching out and 'changing the masses'.[2]

Indeed, one can certainly sympathize with the 22-year-old Nichol, fresh from a failed career as a primary school teacher in British Columbia,[3] hauling countless books in the formidable UofT library known colloquially as "Fort Book," examining its vertiginous shelving, and despairing of ever writing again. Robarts Library, in fact, with its hexagonal atrium, and imposing, brutalist architecture, might be seen as an attempt to manifest Jorge Luis Borges's infamous Library of Babel which, in his short story of the same name, describes a library "composed of an indefinite and perhaps infinite number of hexagonal galleries"[4] containing books of identical appearance, all with 410 pages, and using twenty-two characters which contain every possible permutation of those characters so that the books express, in all languages

> Everything: the minutely detailed history of the future, the archangels' auto-biographies, the faithful catalogue of the Library, thousands and thousands of false catalogues, the demonstration of the fallacy of those catalogues, the demonstration of the fallacy of the true catalogue ... the true story of your death, the translation of every book in all languages, the interpolations of every book in all books.[5]

Faced with this near infinite total, or universal, library, many of the librarians of Babel respond by committing suicide or dwelling in "excessive depression."[6]

Rather than reacting in such a nihilistic manner, however, Nichol, at this point in his life, appears to have first been humbled by the library, relinquishing some aspects of the authorial ego that he had previously held and, rather than seeing the library as overwhelming, responded to the library's vastness by producing books that were somehow "different"—books that by their format and design questioned what constituted a book, and moreover the type of content that a book could contain, including visual poetry, sound performance scores, comics, paper sculptures, and much more.

That Nichol's response to the library was enabling rather than despairing might also partly be explained by the fact that when he refers to working at the UofT library he is not referring to "Fort Book" (Robarts Library had not yet been built when Nichol was employed as a stack boy) but the more idyllic Sigmund Samuel Library, featuring an impressive reading room, but not as overwhelming as the former's Fisher Room. While still a formidable collection, "Sig Sam" housed just over a million titles in 1964; in contrast, Robarts Library would hold more than double that, with two and a half million titles, when it opened in 1972.[7] But it is not just the scale of the library that differs; I would also suggest that Sigmund Samuel Library, being primarily a humanities-based collection, also attracted a different type of patron and worker, allowing for the growth of a particular poetic community.

For example, in the introduction to my recently edited collection of Nichol's early long poems, *bp: beginnings* (2014), I describe the importance of the friendship of the senior Modernist poet Margaret Avison (1918–2007) to Nichol's poetic development, and in particular her commentary on, and encouragement of, his lyric poetry (and eventual publication of those early lyrics in the anthology *New Wave Canada* in 1966) when they first met at the UofT library.[8] Jason Wiens has also written of Nichol's relationship with Avison in "Avison and the Postmodern 1960s," and Frank Davey's biography of Nichol lists the fellow poets whom Nichol met while working at Sig Sam.[9] Yet, in the commentary of these critics, and in Nichol's own interviews, we do not learn how Nichol and Avison actually came to meet, and whether Nichol and Avison were both employed at the library, or whether Avison merely studied at the library while Nichol was working there. In a 2002 interview with Sally Ito, Avison contextualized their first meeting, recounting a story worth quoting in full:

We met in the University of Toronto Library stacks in the early 1960s. He was then employed putting away books on a lower level where I had a carrel, a desk where my work materials could be left, during M.A. studies. As I walked towards that desk one morning, bp, an unknown stack boy, was waving a fist with a rolled up manuscript in it, saying softly but intensely to a co-worker 'It's good. It's really good. They send it back after a half-glance, if that. Won't anybody READ my poetry?' Without breaking pace as I approached, I said 'I will', and without a beat missed, bp slammed it into my hand. Instead of doing dutiful work at my desk, I read it with growing delight, and, when time came to go, I left a small note, promising the precious manuscript back the next morning—although I made it clear that my enjoyment did not mean I could move bp any closer to publishers.... Of course I enthusiastically offered any words he wanted to use as a blurb. Over the months our correspondence flourished, on scraps of paper, just fun to light the lower level where we were immured.[10]

While Nichol and Avison might conceivably have eventually met under other circumstances, it is hard to envision a more appropriate encounter for a first meeting and textual exchange. And it is the site of the library that enables this encounter—I can't imagine Nichol waving a manuscript around the Hart House common room, for example, or in the dining room at Victoria College, attracting Avison's attention. The textual and collegial atmosphere of Sig Sam made this connection possible. As Avison claims that Nichol was unknown to her, this encounter was indeed fortuitous—although it is also certainly possible that Nichol had been well aware of who Avison was all along, and purposely set up that scene with his co-worker for Avison to overhear, and for just that intended result.[11]

Nevertheless, the friendship between Nichol and Avison resulted in much correspondence, some of which can be found in *bpNichol Comics*,[12] and this encounter led to Nichol producing some of Avison's more experimental work, such as the poem *Sliverick*, through his Ganglia Press in 1969. *Sliverick* approaches sound poetry insofar as it consists of many nonce words, and it appears inspired by hearing crowds cheering at a sports event while the poet is at some distance from the action, possibly listening from a window while at the library. Indeed, this impression is consolidated by Nichol's comments on the poem when it was republished in his anthology of concrete poetry, *Cosmic Chef*, in 1970: "[this] delightful poem ... was written a few years back in a study space in the UofT library."[13] The writing of poetry by Nichol and Avison on small scraps of library notepads and call cards might be compared with William Carlos Williams composing poems on prescription pads. The small-scale composition space might explain the focus of all three poets on the individual word and their attraction to similarly minimalist poetry.

Nichol published Avison not only in his mimeo pamphlet series from Ganglia Press, but also in *Ganglia* magazine proper, the periodical that he began while working at the library with fellow poet David Aylward. Again, we see the importance of the social space of the library for the development of this journal, with Nichol and Aylward first meeting at the library, and then editing and discussing the magazine while they worked in the stacks:

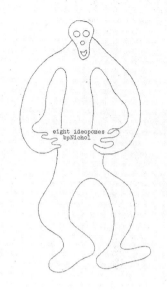

> David Aylward & i began GAN-
> GLIA when we were both working
> at the UofT library. the idea was
> to have a mag that published the
> poetry & prose one or the other of us

FIGURE 3 Cover image of *Ganglia* 1.1 (1964).

> saw as not getting the exposure it should. in my case this meant a number
> of west coast writers ... as time passed the amount of work to be published
> began to surpass the amount of work published & David and i decided to
> bring the magazine to an end.[14]

Avison appears, as the first poet in the very first issue of *Ganglia*, but Nichol also features his own work in the issue which represents, in fact, some of his earliest published poems. At this point in 1965, he had published only one translation and four concrete poems in bill bissett's *blewointment*, and he had a short series of visual poems published by d.a. levy's 7 flowers press in Cleveland (*Cycles Etc.*). As can be discerned from the title page preceding Nichol's poems in *Ganglia* (Figure 3), this was so early in Nichol's poetic career that he was still calling his visual poems "ideopomes," not yet having discovered the international concrete poetry scene.

When the editor of a first issue of a new magazine publishes his or her own poetry in that same issue, readers are often encouraged to read these poems as examples of work that the editor is seeking for future issues, or even as a personal poetic manifesto. At the very least, it is through these poems that Nichol, a relatively new poet at this time, is presenting himself to a national audience. And what is the first of these eight ideopomes? "THIS IS A POME ABOUT WHERE I WORK."

A Marxist critic would argue that one's working conditions always shape one's poetic output, but this seems even more blatant than the most pedantic historical materialist could possibly expect. Nichol's workplace is clearly the central focus of his poetics at this time. Looking at this poem, we can see it is similar to some of his "Cycle" poems, in which Nichol permutates a word looking for words within that word or puns that can be derived from association.[15] It begins by meditating on the types of books that can be found in the library ("drama books" and "cook books") then moves to draw out the word "ram" from "drama," which then suggests another animal—a horse or "steed"—before suggesting emotive responses to being surrounded by books. Books are frightening ("BOO"), can bring a "stack boy" to tears ("boo hoo"), and can also be pests to be warded off ("BOO(shoo!)"), until the poet finally reaches a sense of resignation: books are "O.K." From this point of acceptance the poem then moves to a drama, drawing attention to the idea that the work of librarians is a form of performance ("poses"), where some comic librarians "ad-lib," where other revolutionary librarians might commit "heresies," and where some librarians might best be avoided altogether ("not her ... no other librarian"). This brief theatre performance is, however, speculative ("suppose ...") and the poem then returns to acceptance of the role of working in a library: "books" are "O.K." Thus, rather than being an assault on the working conditions of the library, or a critique of institutional practices, it appears that Nichol sees the library as a site of play, performance, and acceptance of the material conditions (and materials) found in the library.

Returning to Scobie's comment regarding Nichol's possible Oedipal resentment toward the library, the publication schedule of *Ganglia* does appear to disrupt the normal ordering and chronology of periodicals and may be working to frustrate conventional librarians. That is, issues 1, 2, and 3 of the magazine came out in order during 1965, but then *Ganglia* skipped three issues and the next issue that appeared was issue 7 (confusingly subtitled FOUR) also carrying the announcement that issue 8 would be

```
                  THIS IS A POME ABOUT WHERE I WORK
        ABOUT WHERE THIS IS A POME              I WORK


                        books  (drama
                        books    drama
                        (cooks and a
                        looks)   ram)
                        books    drama

                          steed
                        o       a
                          steed

                          (tee  anyone  ?)

                                  one
                          steed
                      BOO

                      boo hoo boo hoo boo hoo
                              books
                                BOO(shoo!)
                              books
                              books

                              O.
                              K.

                          books
                          books
                          books
                          books
                          books

                          suppose.......

        35                        O!
        34                      (poses
        33                            everyone)
        32
   ACT 3: SCENE 2:
        30              librarian
        29          ad-lib(arians
        28          a librarian  - such
        27  another librarian        heresies
        26  other librarians'        heresies
        25
        24                        HERE!
        23

        22  another librarian
        21
        20    o
        19  not
        18      her
        17  another
        16  ano
        15
        14  no
        13  no
        12
        11  no
        10   other librarian
        9
        8                        :EXIT
        7
        6          books
        5           books
        4          books
        3          books
        2         books
        1         O.
        O.K.O.K.O.K.
```

FIGURE 4 bpNichol's "THIS IS A POME ABOUT WHERE I WORK," *Ganglia* 1.1 (1964).

65

Ganglia's last. Then issue 5 appeared, then issue 4, which was a full collection of bill bissett's poetry (*We Sleep Inside Each Other All*) in 1966, followed by an announcement that the first series of *Ganglia* was over and that a new series, *Ganglia* 2, was beginning with a new editorial board. Issue 6 and 8 of the first series did not appear at this time.[16] In the first issue of the second series of *Ganglia* we encounter this editorial:

> dave aylward and i launched ganglia out of a feeling of mutual desperation engendered by working at the u of t library. pretty well all the editorial assistants mentioned worked at the u of t too – sukhamol khasnabish john riddell marv ross et cetera. ganglia arose out of that community and out of a desire to present in a linked format trends we saw developing on the west coast & in the east that nobody else seemed to be picking up on ... then it ended. i quit the library & the need for ganglia disappeared ... anyway a bunch of old friends (among them john riddell—that all important library link) with that same old feeling of community said let's launch a second series & here it is. the second series of GANGLIA. in contrast to the first series this one is published by GREEN PLANT PRESS (which will probably confuse libraries for at least a while). david & i both hope it flowers.[17]

Here we see the importance of the library as a site for literary community ("that all important library link"), since all the editors were also employed at the UofT library, but also we see that when Nichol quits the library, he loses interest in the magazine. The second series, in fact, lasted only two issues without the presence of Nichol. There is some mention that the magazine's sequencing and change of publisher might prove confusing, but only for a limited time. I think this reveals that, rather than being a Dadaistic gesture to disrupt the library system, Nichol views his sequencing as merely "alternative"—logical in its own way, and not intended to be explicitly destructive. Even though issue 6 and 8 of *Ganglia* did not appear in the 1960s, Nichol has indicated that *The Ganglia Press Index*, issued in the 1980s, represents the eighth issue of *Ganglia*, and that the entire run of grOnk can be said to represent issue 6 of *Ganglia*.[18]

Nichol quit the library due to his increasing involvement with Therafields, but also due to a desire to concentrate more on his own writing practice, which included hands-on press work at Coach House Press.[19]

One series of publications that Nichol produced concurrently with that of *Ganglia* reflects this move from the library as a source of inspiration and material to that of Coach House and its experiments in letterpress printing. The "TONTO or" series of publications may very well be the least discussed significant series of Nichol's publishing enterprises, and Nichol rarely mentions them in his interviews and biographical sketches. Part of the reason for this might be the limited nature of these publications: only nine were issued in the series, and the print run for each pamphlet was less than thirty (the smallest run being nine copies). Nonetheless, I believe this series to be significant since they all consisted, with one exception, of Nichol's own work, and they were site-specific to Nichol's move to Toronto and employment at both the library and Coach House.[20] That is, from the title of the series alone, we have the emphasis on Toronto, with the name derived from Nichol's paragrammatic play on the city, becoming "TONTO or." Whereas *Ganglia* was conceived as a site where West Coast poets could intermingle with eastern Canadian poets, "TONTO" or focused exclusively on Toronto and Nichol's own work. That the series is a supplement to *Ganglia* is also suggested by the emphasis on Tonto, the companion to the Lone Ranger— but the "or" also suggests a possibility that he (and the series) can stand independently.

The series begins by reflecting upon the material conditions of Nichol at the UofT library, what with the hand-drawn poetic portraits of fellow employees (*Portrait of David*), or else the series draws inspiration from the site of the library itself (*A Vision in the UofT Stacks*), before shifting to letterpress printing for the last three issues (*Alaphbit*, *Stan's Ikon* and *Birth of O*). The series ended, appropriately, when Nichol definitively quit the library.

The most evocative piece in the series is also the most ephemeral: *A Vision in the UofT Stacks* circulated in an edition of nine. Looking at it, we can see that its cover has been taken from a printout of some sort of index at the library, listing the beginning of entries with the prefix "Art." What follows is a series of rubber-stamped designs in the form of mandalas, with the impression being taken from rubber stamps available to university librarians: LIBRARY MAIL, UNIVERSITY OF TORONTO PHOTOCOPY SERVICE, MICROFORM AVAILABLE FROM THE NATIONAL LIBRARY, LIBRARY, DELIVERY TO PROFESSORS, CIRCULATE AS MONOGRAPH, DATE DUE, and finally, BEING REPLACED.

FIGURE 5 Cover of bpNichol's *A Vision in the UofT Stacks* (TONTO or, 1966).

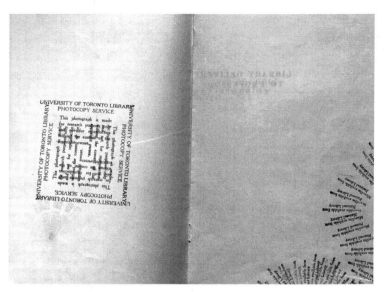

FIGURE 6 bpNichol's "University of Toronto Photocopy Service" from *A Vision in the UofT Stacks* (TONTO or, 1966).

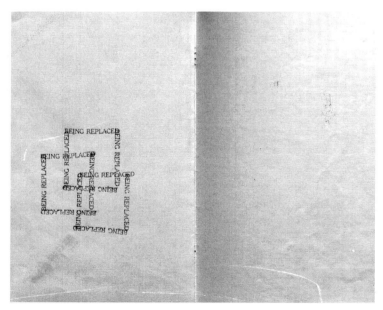

FIGURE 7 bpNichol's "Being Replaced" from *A Vision in the UofT Stacks* (TONTO or, 1966).

Obviously, this sequence could have been produced only by someone working in a library, and the sequence uses the material at hand in an almost *bricoleur* fashion. Moreover, it seems to anticipate the views of later small-press publishers, like Jason Le Heup, many of whom suggest that the micro-press is produced in a parasitic fashion, where materially limited young poets and publishers siphon off the resources from their day jobs (stealing paper, using the company photocopier to print their 'zine, and so on).[21] But the choice of rubber stamps in conjunction with the poem's title is quite telling.

Visionary poetics have a long history in English literature, but considering Nichol's influences at this time, "A Vision" suggests a connection to such figures as William Blake and Allen Ginsberg.[22] In the case of these poets, a vision suggests revelation,[23] and so what the poet of Nichol's poem saw in the stacks was transformative, perhaps relating to his own poetic practice: that through this vision his own poetics changed, and that he became a different poet. Here the mandalas suggest a religious experience, but in their visual manifestation, they suggest that Nichol has been granted a vision, in which he should pursue concrete or visual poetry rather than the lyric. And indeed, Nichol's next major publication following this pamphlet would be the collection consisting solely of typewriter-concrete poems, *Konfessions of an Elizabethan Fan Dancer* (1967).

Yet a vision can also suggest an insight into future events, and we might read this sequence as a prophecy regarding both book culture and labour. In the latter reading, thinking of Nichol's employment at the library, and of the possible Marxist implications of his early *Ganglia* poem discussed above, the sequence might relate to precarious labour in the institution and academy, with professors and librarians "being replaced" by new technologies of circulation and pedagogy. Looking further at Nichol's choice of the words found on the rubber stamps, a common theme is the replication and displacement of the book object: photocopies, microfilms, but also circulation, delivery, and mail, all of which end with the repeated phrase "being replaced." Considering Nichol's interest in the book as object, even at this early stage of his career, we can read "being replaced" as Nichol's lament at the destruction, or at least displacement, of the traditional book object. Conversely, and thinking about Nichol's desire to expand the possibilities of what the book can convey, "being replaced" might be an imperative: that the standard codex needs to be replaced by other forms of inscription. In the latter case, Nichol's own rubber-stamped pamphlet suggests an alternative: a return to handcrafted circulation of textuality.

As a rubber-stamp publication, each is unique, and bears the trace of the author's own body in the act of pressing the stamp to the paper: it is a type of holograph. This piece is, I believe, also the first sustained use of a rubber stamp in the creation of concrete poetry in Canada, appearing nearly a decade before Steve McCaffery's more radical use of the rubber stamp in *Carnival: The Second Panel* (1973). Considering McCaffery, and the concept of carnivalization, leads to the Toronto Research Group (TRG), the collective enterprise of Nichol and McCaffery from 1973 to 1982. Nichol's continued interest in the library is demonstrated through this project, since the library functions prominently in "The Toronto Research Game," a game with dice and board, created by Nichol and McCaffery in the 1980s. The presence of this game and its rules suggest that the library was not a passing subject of interest to Nichol and continued well beyond the period when he was employed at UofT. More importantly, that the library provides the scenario for a game not only alerts us to the interest of both Nichol and McCaffery in game theory, but also anticipates the idea of research and writing as a form of contestation. One might compare this gesture of the TRG to that of Guy Debord, who designs the *Game of War* as a way of teaching modes of resistance for potential revolutionaries.[24] The TRG may be alerting future students and scholars about the potential pitfalls and dangers (if not excitements) of conducting research:

Reading and Writing: The Toronto Research Game

"Reading and Writing" is a simulation of what the Toronto Research Group goes through writing *their* essays. Now you can experience the excitement of the competitive search for knowledge as you vie with other players to find and read the books that will help you garner that groundbreaking might into the process of READING and WRITING. In the campaign version of the game you'll have the chance to build a REPUTATION as the *real* thinker in the TORONTO RESEARCH GROUP.[25]

Although this introduction to the game emphasizes the (potentially) glorious nature of research, the library designed by Nichol and McCaffery seems to be a rather dangerous place: one where a dice roll determines daily events, so that there is a 1-in-16 chance of a disaster in the library—a fire, a bomb threat, or a flood. The library is an absurdist or parodic space where another die roll determines the librarian's mood and, consequently, whether or not the player-researcher will receive any archival material for the day.

The development of the TRG library game indicates that Nichol's interest in the poetics of the library continued long beyond the period when he was working at the UofT library. In fact, he continued to explore the library right until the end of his career. In the final section of "A Book of Hours" collected in *The Martryology Book 6*, the last volume that Nichol published before his death, he addresses the library directly:

> because there are words & more words
> uncounted books deploring our inhumanity
> prizes for those who merely spoke from conscience
> a competition & a judging
> because there is now the tyranny of quantity
> the sheer mass of literature
> that concept becoming clear
> the old notion of immortality seen for what it is
> a preening in the brief light history reflects
> – READ ME – READ ME –
>
> the weight of words shifts

> (in the library stacks the shelves grow fuller, the buildings forced to expand, the budgets cut, nonexistent, of course the voices become more muted, even tho they are screaming, even tho they have things to say, things that you might want to hear, the words disappear into the dust, the darkness, the books closed and noone here to read them, noone here to take them from the shelves, anything anyone of us might say becoming simply what it is, ink on yellowing pages, disappearing into this wait of words, the unvoiced endless hours)[26]

Here, twenty years after his employment at the UofT library, with Nichol in his early 40s, we can see that his impression of the library might now be closer to Borgesian despair. We now have a "tyranny of quantity" in the "sheer mass of literature." Yet there is also the sense that the books them-selves are victims, sentient entities (similar to some of Nichol's concepts of the book in *Craft Dinner*):[27] "they are screaming," "they have things to say," and they are chanting "READ ME." Moreover, unlike the tomes in the Library of Babel, the majority of which contain nonsense, the books in Nichol's imagined library "have things to say," particularly in "deploring our inhumanity." Even at this late stage of Nichol's career and life, the library still demanded to be scrutinized; it was a site of activity and common humanity, and it continued to speak to his own vision of himself as a writer.

NOTES

1 Stephen Scobie, *Signature Event Cantext* (Edmonton: NeWest Press, 1989), 91.

2 Jack David and Caroline Bayard, *Out-Posts/Avant-Posts* (Erin: Press Porcépic, 1978), 18–19.

3 See Frank Davey, *aka bpNichol: A Preliminary Biography* (Toronto: ECW Press, 2012), 48–49.

4 Jorge Luis Borges, "The Library of Babel," *Labyrinths: Selected Stories and Other Writings* (New York: New Editions, 1964), 51.

5 Borges, "The Library," 54.

6 Borges, 55.

7 See Robert H. Blackburn, *Evolution of the Heart: A History of the University of Toronto Library up to 1981* (Toronto: University of Toronto Press, 1989), 326.

8 Avison, at her first meeting with Nichol in 1964, had already published her first collection of poetry, *The Winter Sun*, which had won the Governor General's Award for Poetry in 1960, and she was at work on her second collection, *The Dumbfounding*, as well researching her M.A. thesis on Lord Byron at the University of Toronto (Avison, *I Am Here and Not Not-There*, 348).

9 See "Introduction" (Cain 9–10), *aka bpNichol* (Davey 52, 76); and Jason Wiens, "Avison and the Postmodern 1960s," *Canadian Poetry* 59 (2006), 33–34.

10 Margaret Avison, "Interview with Sally Ito: The Quiet Centre Inside," *I Am Here and Not There: An Autobiography* (Erin: Porcupine's Quill, 2009), 312.

11 Nichol would have been aware of Avison through *The Winter Sun* (published in London by Routledge) and her prestigious Canadian literary award, but she might also have been attractive to him due to her participation in the Vancouver Poetry Conference during the previous summer in 1963. Nichol had not attended the conference, but had instead travelled to Toronto to visit his

brother for the summer (Davey 43). For details about Avison's involvement at the Vancouver conference, see Wiens, "Avison."

12 See Carl Peters (ed.), *bpNichol Comics* (Vancouver: Talonbooks, 2002), 49–62.

13 bpNichol, *The Cosmic Chef: An Evening of Concrete* (Ottawa: Oberon Press, 1970), 79.

14 bpNichol, *Ganglia Press Index 1964 to 1983* (Toronto: Ganglia Press, 1983).

15 Some of Nichol's "Cycle" pomes can be found in *Konfessions of an Elizabethan Fan Dancer* and in *bp: beginnings*.

16 The dates of publication and sequencing of *Ganglia* are based on my reading through Scott Library's bound copies of *Ganglia*, with pencilled notes by librarians on each issue. Advertisements found in each issue, and the eventual *Ganglia Press Index*, also support this chronology.

17 bpNichol, "Another Disgustingly Sentimental Editorial," *Ganglia* 2.1 (1969).

18 "Ganglia #8: INDEX to all GANGLIA PRESS publications (see grOnk s 8 #7)" and "GANGLIA 6 became grOnk. thus consists of all 64 issues of grOnk" (Nichol, "Index").

19 See Davey, *aka bpNichol*, 89 and 80.

20 Nichol's own description of the series, from the *Ganglia Press Index* reads: "Limited edition xeroxed & typeset poem pamphlets—xeroxes done at the UofT Library, letterpress handset by the author at the Coach House Press—all titles from 1966 & all by bpNichol except as noted."

21 "The parasitic relationship to larger institutions is central to the activity of most small publishing. Paper, photocopies, stamps, and envelopes are quietly siphoned from English departments and day jobs to sustain a teeming world of marginal magazines. Page layout is done between assignments and copy editing accomplished while the boss is at lunch" (Le Heup vi). Frank Davey's biography of Nichol also characterizes Nichol's publishing at this time as "parasitic" and based on the material conditions of working both at Sig Sam and Coach House: "The shop [Coach House] was also a source for Barrie of random pieces of paper left over from commercial printing work, and suitable for irregular pamphlets. Much of Ganglia was printed on a hand-cranked mimeograph machine, but some of Barrie's first self-published ephemera, and some of the grOnk releases, would be hand-set by Barrie on [Stan] Bevington's proof press and then xeroxed at the Sigmund Samuel Library" (80).

22 Gregory Betts has also suggested that Nichol might be referring to W. B. Yeats's *A Vision* (1925), which in turn was an influence on Jack Spicer, an author who

would publish a poetic sequence on Billy the Kid, just as Nichol would in 1970 (private correspondence to author).

23 See, for example, Ginsberg's "Sunflower Sutra" of 1956.

24 See Alexander R. Galloway, "The Game of War: An Overview," *Cabinet* 29 (2008), 68. Galloway claims that Debord thought that his game "had future potential in training and cultivating a new generation of militants." See also McKenzie Wark, "The Game of War: Debord as Strategist," *Cabinet* 29 (2008), 75. Wark argues that Debord's Game of War suggests revolutionary action through its emphasis on fluid, improvisational strategies: "Key to playing the Game of War is a talent for judging the moment to move from the tactical advantage to the strategic. Plans have to be changed or abandoned in the light of events."

25 Steve McCaffery and bpNichol, "Part 5—READING & WRITING: THE TORONTO RESEARCH GAME," *Rational Geomancy: The Kids of the Book Machine* (Vancouver: Talonbooks, 1992), 199.

26 bpNichol, *The Martryology Book 6* (Toronto: Coach House Press, 1987).

27 The opening text of *Craft Dinner* constructs a narrative in which the book itself appears to speak directly to the reader: "you turn the page & i am here that in itself is interesting to me at least it is interesting since my existence begins as you turn the pages & begin to read me."

PART IV

CONCRETE POETICS

JULIA POLYCK-O'NEILL

Words With(out) Syntax:
Reconsidering Concrete Poetry:
An Exhibition in Four Parts

In this chapter, I undertake a close reading of a cultural artifact: the catalogue from the art show *Concrete Poetry* (exhibited at the University of British Columbia Fine Arts Gallery in 1969)—a show co-organized by Alvin Balkind (the curator of the UBC Fine Arts Gallery), Michael Morris, and other significant cultural figures from Vancouver and beyond. I elect to do a material reading of the catalogue, meaning that I read the work as both a physical entity and a conceptual entity, pointing to the two levels of signification implied by the term "material." On the one hand, I examine the tangible components of the text, both as an object of study and as evidence of an event; on the other hand, I explore and discuss the context of this art show as central to a greater politico-cultural movement, taking place at a specific moment in history. These readings are intertwined, and, as such, I present a faceted reading of a heterogeneous text. I also discuss how this event remains paradigmatic in the shaping of Vancouver's cultural identity, showing how this exhibition partakes of an avant-garde discourse still tangible in the life of the city. By examining debates surrounding renewed attention to the exhibition, I draw attention to how Vancouver's position within the context of both regional and international art historical movements led to a geographically specific interpretation of text-based art. In this context, according to the avant-garde theories of Peter Bürger and Matei Călinescu, curatorial intention is revealed to be a matter of the institutional politics of art in Vancouver, rather than one of art historical or literary taxonomies. These concerns are the reason this exhibition can be understood as a pivot point for the inter-rogation of the generative, but oftentimes ambivalent, relationship between Conceptual Art and concrete poetry.

The catalogue's title, *Concrete Poetry: An Exhibition in Four Parts*, alludes to the four parts of the exhibition itself as well as the four parts of the accompanying publication (plus one, if we include the portfolio itself in this enumeration). The catalogue comprises three booklets, variously contain-ing textual works and visual essays, a selection of prints of concrete poetry,[1] as well as a box-like portfolio upon which is printed a number of lists. The four sections of the exhibition, according to the catalogue, are as follows: nineteen collages by Ray Johnson, twenty-four letter drawings by Michael Morris, a selection of recent concrete poems by international artists, and what the catalogue describes simply as "film, sound poets on tape, and a selection of slides."

The catalogue correlates to the exhibition insofar as the included book-lets provide reproductions of Morris's twenty-four letter drawings, while the portfolio lists the slides shown during the show, presumably to contex-tualize concrete poetry in the broader cultural history of art and literature; moreover, the booklet titled "Ray Johnson" includes only three reprints of his collages, while opting to list the titles of the remaining sixteen. Addi-tionally, the catalogue's format, with its extensive tripartite bibliography and numerous essayistic components, suggests that the catalogue serves as a supplement to, rather than simply a documentation of, the exhibition. The impressive selection of images and their unbound, loose format con-tributes to this idea, suggesting that this grouping of literary elements and visual components speaks to the philosophy underlying concrete poetry itself: such poetry is not necessarily restrained by the conventions of the book; indeed, it confounds convention in many ways, and, at the very least, it speaks to alternative, emergent traditions of art and writing in the post-industrial, if not postwar, era.[2]

Understanding that the curator invariably occupies the apex of power inherent to any exhibition remains key to approaching this catalogue. Bal-kind's "Acknowledgements" is a seemingly banal document, but in fact, it disseminates a number of significant, contextual cues. In it, Balkind lists the exhibition's contributors, starting with the members of the exhibition committee: Edwin Varney, Stephen Scobie, Werner Aellen, Ian Wallace,

Douglas Eliuk, Michael Rhodes, Illayas Pagonis, and Jeff Wall. Balkind next thanks Michael Findlay (the vice-president of the Feigen Gallery) and Dick Higgins (owner of Something Else Press), both out of New York. Balkind also thanks the following publishers: Very Stone Press, Vancouver, and Coach House Press, in Toronto; the Wild Hawthorn Press in Edinburgh, Scotland; Hansjörg Mayer in Frankfurt, Germany; and the Letter Edged in Black from New York. Last on this list are Blew Ointment Press and Radio Free Rain Forest Press, both in Vancouver. Balkind then acknowledges, without naming, the contributing poets, while naming an individual officer from the Canada Council of the Arts (Mr. Naïm Kattan), along with a variety of specific figures from the University of British Columbia, all of whom have provided support in varying capacities.

Balkind's list of acknowledgements is not particularly unusual, but, like all such lists, it points to an underlying structure of power and architecture of influence within the framework of the exhibition, while underlining a series of classist, colonial, and gendered dynamics, typical of such a historical, institutional context. These dynamics are particularly relevant to my reading of the catalogue, since the notion of an inherent hierarchy is implicit to much of the political spirit shaping the discourse of the media celebrated in the exhibition: that of a simultaneously anti-institutional (if not non-institutional) politicized art form (occurring mainly at the exhibition's surface), and the innate recognition that institutional discourse shapes avant-garde rhetoric in the post-industrial age. The overarching, institutional nature of the exhibition creates a generative tension within the context of the catalogue—since the event receives support from a variety of Canadian establishments, but the event also plays host, not only to the counter-institutional gestures of concrete poetry and mail art, but also to the contra-institutional gestures of conceptual movements in the visual arts.

The tension between radical politics and institutional realities features prominently not only in the catalogue, but also in the exhibition itself. Such tension speaks to contradictions generally inherent to the avant-garde (as defined by Peter Bürger in *The Theory of the Avant-Garde*, in which the theorist argues for a dialectical relationship between radicalism in art and the political, historical conditions of the institution of art). Musing on historical, avant-garde movements, with special consideration of what he identifies as the limitations of Renato Poggioli's reductive, modernist theory,[3] Bürger notes how, previously, the presence of an institutional discourse in art has disrupted or neutralized "the political content of the individual work,"[4] whereas more contemporary, late-capitalist emanations enter into a "new relationship to reality"—one that necessarily recognizes how the initial intentions of the avant-garde, constructed according to the false dichotomy of "pure" art, on the one hand, and political art, on the other, are doomed to collapse.[5] Bürger deduces that, finally, "it is art as an institution that determines the measure of political effect avant-garde works can have," and he concludes that "art in bourgeois society continues to be a realm that is distinct from the praxis of life."[6]

Such dynamics are representative of the specific historical moment from which the exhibition emerges. According to Stephen Voyce in *Poetic Community: Avant-Garde Activism and Cold War Culture*, participants in the post-industrial avant-garde have productively joined forces with institutions, reaping the benefits of doing so during the politicized 1960s.[7] Indeed, avant-garde artists at this time have frequently co-opted the language of the institution, as evidenced perhaps by Ray Johnson's deliberate misspelling in his collective mail-art enterprise, the *New York Correspondence School*,[8] suggesting an overarching, reflexive awareness of the institutional roles played by academies within such practice. Building on Bürger's conceptualization of the avant-garde (and its critical tension with post-industrialism), Matei Călinescu in *Five Faces of Modernity: Modernism, Avant-Garde, Decadence, Kitsch, Postmodernism* (1987), discusses how, "[c]ompared to the old avant-garde, the new, postmodernist avant-garde seems ... more systematically involved in theoretical thinking."[9] Furthermore, he underlines how "the enjoyment offered by postmodern art ... comes in the form of a broadly defined, parodic practice, in which some commentators have discerned a more general characteristic of our cultural times."[10] Broadly, he points to the general self-consciousness of position prevalent within the avant-gardes of this period, highlighting how creative praxis is both critical of, and complicit with, institutional dynamics. While the avant-garde often finds itself adopted by the discourse of modernity, the undeniable influence of a figure like John Cage, from the Black Mountain School, within concrete poetry does imply, or at least anticipate, the presence of postmodern ideation within the genre, and certainly within the 1969 show.

In his list, Balkind first names several important figures circulating within the institutional culture of not only Vancouver in particular, but also British Columbia and Canada in general, including the following two artists and scholars: first, Ian Wallace (a professor of art history at the University of British Columbia, and a central figure in the development of Vancouver photoconceptualism); second, Douglas Eliuk of the National Film Board. Balkind then lists the various contributing art galleries and small presses, identifying the nodes of a network for concrete poetry and mail art, both domestic and international. These names, however, do not belie the aforementioned tension in the remainder of the list, and although there is nothing conspicuously aberrant in the conventional format of Balkind's letter (since the contributing artists are listed elsewhere), the prioritization evident in the explicit naming of institutional figures before all others does speak to the contradictory impulses outlined by Bürger.

The selection of slides identified on the list in the catalogue seems especially relevant to this observation, since the curator has included them to provide an accessible conceptual context for the ideas advanced in the exhibition; the inclusion of these slides speaks to self-reflexivity and a sense of discursive encoding, including that of parody. Among the slides listed are an Egyptian papyrus, a Mongolian manuscript from the eighteenth century, George Herbert's visual poem "Easter Wings" from the late seventeenth century, and a number of Dadaist, Futurist, and Russian Constructivist typographic works, including selections by Marcel Duchamp (*Machine Optique*, 1920) and F. T. Marinetti (*Les Paroles en Liberté*, n.d.). The images, when grouped together, suggest a number of different themes: the visuality of language; the evolution of communication; and the instability of language systems. Moreover, the images collectively suggest concrete poetry's trajectory of influence, showing slides of such artworks in chronological order so as to demonstrate how written language does, in fact, lend itself to visual interpretation. Again, these references gesture ironically to institutional discourse, while also highlighting the conceptual foundations of the medium: concrete poetry is a hybrid form, borrowing from both the visual realms and the linguistic realms.

In his unconventional review of the exhibition, "Incoherent Thoughts on Concrete Poetry," John Noel Chandler assembles a variety of textual sources in order to flesh out the definition of the composite medium, citing quotes, for example, by the following two artists: first, John Cage, who defines such poetry as "words without syntax, each word polymorphic"—and second, Ian Hamilton Finlay, who says: "It may be a case of separating the letters of a word in order to disclose new *decorative* and semantic possibilities."[11] Certainly, the optical aesthetics of language are brought to the forefront in the visual work represented by the catalogue, while the sonic, performative elements are merely listed, and as a result, become secondary.

Jeff Wall's review of the exhibition offers a more resolute response to the event. Notably, Wall is mentioned in Balkind's acknowledgements—and for this reason, Wall's review, although at times polemical, speaks to a specific, nuanced experience of the show. He asserts: "The presence of an extremely intellectualized method of art-making was evident," explaining that

> [t]here is an awareness of the critical or theoretical position of the artist, his public position in regard to the interpretation and historical significance of his work. As well, a general conviction seems to exist among these artists that the poems defy specific interpretation or commentary, and that what can be talked about can include the artists' intentions, the relation of his activity to the major literary or esthetic traditions, his relation to the system or lack of system he employs in his work, his role as a distinct "presence" in his work—in other words, there is a good deal of discussion "around" the objects themselves.[12]

Indeed, such reviews, when combined with the essays included in the catalogue by Michael Morris, Ian Wallace, and Michael Rhodes (as well as the reproduction of letters by Ray Johnson) give weight to the broader context of the exhibition.

The essay "Literature—Transparent and Opaque" by Ian Wallace, which concludes the orange, unpaginated booklet, expands upon this discourse of intellectualism, with its theoretical familiarity. He alludes to the apparent constraints of language being challenged by the exhibition and the creative strategies therein, noting how "situated within a literary format and literature as a creative activity, concrete poetry plays a special role in the modernization of literature, a role that becomes more important as the power of rhetoric becomes exhausted." He advances ideas such as the "material integrity" of the icon and the psychoanalytic potential of the purely visual renderings of concrete poetry. Calling critical attention to the different ways that literature and concrete poetry treat language: "what is said" versus "something to say," respectively, he revisits the historical context of these distinguishing linguistic features. He points to, what he calls, "the vacuum of experience" resulting from the advent of modernism, and he identifies how the effects intrinsic to developments in electronic media influence the "act of reading" in such a way as to transform the role of the poet. He argues that the poet's role becomes one of "locating consciousness in space and time" rather than one of mere expression. His erudite, if abstract, response to the exhibition echoes Morris's more playful contextualizing statements about the show.[13]

Additional support for these texts is found in the selection of images provided in the catalogue, all of which serve to document works that form the central core of the exhibition, if not the textual documentation in the catalogue itself. The black-and-white photographic reproductions afforded by contemporary technologies work well with the graphic nature of the concrete poems, as well as the documentary photographs of Stephen Scobie's installation, *Computer Poem* (n.d.). The concrete poetry included in the catalogue varies in style and form: some works are more recognizably language-based, such as bpNichol's typewriter poem, *dear deanna* (n.d.), whereas bill bissett's *Vancouver Mainland Ice and Cold Storage* (n.d.) is collage-based and constructed of found materials. Indeed, the diversity of the works included in the show speaks to, and builds upon, early debates that continue to surround the position of concrete poetry within the Canadian avant-garde.[14]

The works frustrate literary analysis. The semblance of literary form confounds the aesthetic conventions generally applied to a traditional reading of visual art, particularly as these conventions are understood at this moment in Vancouver, in 1969. Wall suggests that these conditions create a new kind of relationship between the pieces and the spectator—a relationship entirely optimistic and intellectual. Wall notes, "the art as a whole displays a clarity of purpose and an understanding of the vital issues inflecting all the arts with which it can be concerned."[15] In this sense, concrete poetry might be conceived as a form of cultural comment grounded in modernism and modernity—a form that speaks not only to a broad range of media, but also to issues of both representation and interpretation (such as those pertaining to language and its complex aesthetic values).

The very "form" of the works included in the exhibition becomes the matter of contemporary debate. The art show includes, for example, specific works of Conceptual Art,[16] most notably—and most controversially—Joseph Kosuth's series of "dictionary photostats," *Titled (Art as Idea as Idea)*, a work that consists of reproductions of dictionary definitions of banal words such as "Art" and "Idea";[17] moreover, the art show also includes works by Yoko Ono, Dieter Roth, and Bruce Nauman, all of whom have been the topic of critical revision. The "uncritical mixing" of "high conceptualism" and avant-gardes with decidedly more literary concerns provokes an apparent sense of uneasiness within aesthetic criticism, because conceptual artists are themselves the subjects of contemporary derision. Their now historic manifestos—including Kosuth's "Art After Philosophy"—become objects of contemporary, revisionist praxis. They act as punchlines for projects of cultural sophistry and theoretical experimentation, as seen, for example, in *Notes on Conceptualisms* by Vanessa Place and Robert Fitterman. Texts such as "Art After Philosophy" (and Kosuth's other militant treatises, written alongside other members of Art & Language) now seem constrained and ambivalent rather than experimental, lending Conceptual Art absolutist undertones that clang dissonantly against the more generative spirit of concrete poetry, which has never been quite endowed with the same timbre of indoctrination and territoriality. In fact, its tone is, by comparison, decidedly emancipatory.[18]

Artist and critic Jamie Hilder has written an essay in 2014 for the exhibition, *LETTERS: Michael Morris and Concrete Poetry*, a recent restaging of Morris's *Letter Drawings*, shown alongside works of concrete poetry at the Morris and Helen Belkin Art Gallery. Hilder notes how, in contrast to the rigid readings historically assigned to conceptual art of all stripes, the canon of Conceptual Art is actually surprisingly *inclusive*, given its inherent diversity, and he balks at the historic, mainstream resistance of artists and critics who refuse to examine the extant commonalities between conceptualism and concrete poetry—commonalities that demand a circumvention of the prescriptive, interpretive patterns associated with historic movements in art. Although Conceptual Art has been originally conceived, according to a rather flattened and generalized reading, as a movement that might liberate art from the shackles of the institution, it has become institutionally sanctioned *par excellence*, whereas the liberatory energies and para-structuralist (if not post-structuralist) experimental techniques inherent to concrete poetry have sidestepped such a fate.[19] Against the canon and its discursive weight, he argues for a reexamination of the historic genre, and, quite intriguingly, given the context of my examination of these matters, cites the exhibition *Concrete Poetry* of 1969, as a site to be critically revisited with this aim.

Hilder notes how

[c]onceptual art's approach is different from concrete poetry's.... But what makes conceptual art a valid and productive counterpart to concrete poetry is the fact that beyond its participants' and later critics' near unanimous dismissal of concrete poetry as a significant field, it contains figures who produce work that borrows the techniques of concrete poetry while at the same time denying any line of influence.[20]

He argues that neither movement references an orthodox, formalist practice, suggesting that both movements respond "to a shift in art production and discourse coming out of the mid-1960s."[21]

Perhaps the uneven reception of such a "quixotic" exhibition has merits of another order. Perhaps such criticisms reflect the genealogy of the exhibition (linked predominantly to Morris and his uncommon capacity to forge meaningful networks). Perhaps a careful consideration of the pluralistic narratives inherent to conceptual art (with its ability to assemble such a diverse sample of text-based works) demands a clear acknowledgement of curatorial intention, even from a revisionist, historical standpoint. Consider that Edwin Varney's playful treatise, which defines concrete poetry as "actual, real, immediate to experience, not abstract, general, or ideal," appears in one of the essays that preface the catalogue. Varney's typographic statement, here read alongside, if not informed by, Rhodes's decidedly more pragmatic analysis of the genre's history in relation to Dada and its emergence in Brazil, Germany, and elsewhere, speaks specifically to one genre (concrete poetry), but excludes others (conceptual art). This poses problems of congruity. The decision to incorporate works that are categorically "other" than this definition might require an explanation, lest such decisions seem arbitrary or ill-conceived. When reconsidered from a different perspective, however, it is altogether possible that such an

oversight relates to the exhibition's chronological moment and geographi-
cal position within Vancouver during the 1960s—a cultural locus markedly
in a state of flux. At this time, the city has only begun to develop a cultural
identity and a sense of its potential as a centre for cultural production and
criticism.[22]

In Vancouver, in 1969, the notion that both conceptual art and concrete
poetry are anything other than authentic avant-gardes is unheard of, and
it is altogether likely that the two genres are combined according to a logic
grounded in a superficial, uncritical reading of their styles and themes.
There is ample anecdotal evidence that this inclusivity and sense of freedom
from cultural despotism remains a defining factor in the artworlds of the
West Coast. During the 1940s and 1950s, when New York became the global
centre of the art market, critics admit that "[i]n Los Angeles and the West
Coast in general the artistic and intellectual circles seem to have been rela-
tively open at the time, not dogmatic but inclusive."[23] William Wood posits
that Vancouver's cultural figures of this particular generation (including
Ian Wallace, Jeff Wall, and their contemporaries), see themselves working
within an institutional counter-narrative that, at the time, might not fit
the categories of broader, cultural movements.[24] Such a counter-narrative
ostensibly extricates the art scene in Vancouver from the self-reflexivity
and meta-critical awareness more paradigmatic of a prominent, cultural
centre. Indeed, Wood recalls Benjamin Buchloh's infamous remarks in
"Periodizing Critics," relating them to the realities of Vancouver in the
1980s (although the same paradigm might apply to an earlier period in the
city's art history). Wood notes:

> Buchloh's argument about art being bound by institutional fetters and
> criticism being disenfranchised by museum and market should be received
> with ambivalence in British Columbia. All the players he lists—academ-
> ics, critics, dealers, museums, curators, collectors—are in short supply
> here, except for deserving artists. The question of who legitimates has only
> occasionally been asked in a locale where few can make a living or even a
> career from cultural production. Criticism requires a cultural machinery
> in order to question and affirm its reason to speak, for its public voice is
> meaningless unless art is openly acknowledged by institutional bodies as
> an established discipline.[25]

Wood then gestures to the unique network of "vehicles for connecting the small groups active in what passes for an art 'community'— ... potentially extending the franchise of these groups" that continue to exist in Vancouver, thereby helping to maintain its particular avant-gardist production,[26] despite the notion that such counter-narratives have been "upended."

Such contextual considerations speak to the cultural developments occurring at the time of the exhibition—developments that reinforce this generalized reading of the works included. The well-documented collaborations of Ray Johnson and Ian Hamilton Finlay, for example, signal the range of sources from which the exhibition draws motivation and inspiration. When considered alongside the postulates of Bürger and Călinescu, both of whom see the institution of art as being bracketed from life, the exhibition, as a whole, becomes a significant node in Vancouver's evolution toward a creative hub, international in scale.

The exhibition at the University of British Columbia indicates the beginning of a new, often radical, avant-garde culture in Vancouver—almost as if to elucidate the symbiotic relationship that Bürger identifies between the institution of art and the movements of the avant-garde. Michael Morris sees the event as a point of departure, from which his shared endeavour, the Image Bank, is born—an endeavour created in collaboration with Vincent Trasov and Gary-Lee Nova.[27] The exhibition, *Concrete Poetry*, is in part the result of Morris's early exchanges with Johnson during Morris's participation in Johnson's exhibition, *New York Correspondence School*, at the Whitney Museum in New York. The Image Bank later appropriates the Correspondance School's mailing list for its own mail-art enterprise, thus acquiring an expansive preexisting network.[28] Morris becomes active in the expansion of artist-run, multidisciplinary culture in Vancouver, participating in the activity of Intermedia, spanning the period from 1967 to 1973.[29] He also co-founds the internationally renowned artist-run centre The Western Front in 1973, shortly after Intermedia's dissolution. The influence underlying such cultural phenomena can again be traced to Johnson's New York Correspondence School, with its collaborative practice intersecting considerably with the Fluxus movement, which in turn speaks to the avant-garde discourse of culture at the time.

Such activity affirms that, while the exhibition *Concrete Poetry* is likely to be read, as a cultural artifact, according to the genealogy of artist-run culture, this reading is not necessarily appropriate to the discourse of Vancouver's particular avant-gardes. Such a reading foregrounds the critical divide that typically isolates Conceptual Art from the more grassroots, amorphous, avant-gardist praxis of bill bissett, Ian Hamilton Finlay, bpNichol, and Stephen Scobie, whose work presumably fits more seamlessly within the (albeit flexible) category of "concrete."[30] This reading is notably divorced from Vancouver's unique history as the site of such generative events as the 1963 Vancouver Poetry Conference, which has brought critical attention not only to Vancouver's eminent avant-garde literary production, but also to the emergence of localized, institutionally supported, artist-run culture. Vancouver's cultural schema is by no means singular, and certainly not static—it is polyvocal, striated, and dynamic—but it reflects the city's uncommon heritage as a peripheral site, as well as the particular, institutional tensions between its academic and para-academic, if not anti-academic, experimental movements. Tensions between particular artist groups and the city's emergent cultural infrastructure also play into the blurring of such boundaries, making the interpretation of the catalogue surprisingly challenging in the absence of a familiarity with Vancouver's sociopolitical history. Vancouver, like its province British Columbia, is frequently characterized according to narratives of political radicalism, with a prominent history based in the revolutionary left. These narratives are notably uneven and asynchronous, mainly due to issues of historicization and competing chronologies.[31] Its institutional culture is not exempt from this paradigm.

Such dynamics might also find a sense of resolution in Bürger's contemporary reexamination of the avant-garde. In "Avant-Garde and Neo-Avant-Garde," he fleshes out his arguments, observing how an accurate, perceptive conception of the avant-garde demands that critics take, as a starting point, the very paradox that "confounds" his original text: the idea that "the failure of its project (the sublation of the art institution) coincides with its success within the institution";[32] hence, the avant-garde movements retain not only their intended significance vis-à-vis authenticity but also their identity as the object of institutional co-option.[33] After revisiting the exhibition *Concrete Poetry,* according to this revision, the potential to transcode both Conceptual Art and concrete poetry seems useful, lending the catalogue's essays increased cultural capital within the contemporary forum of art history.

Keith Wallace notes how the philosophy of such artist-run organizations generated an arts community that "operated independently of the established art system, yet was somehow welcomed by both the art institutions and the public," although he does hint that this practice would later shift.[34] He recounts that later manifestations of artist-run culture have become even more complicit in institutional practice, because more conventional management techniques (along with firmly delineated philosophical projects and controlled access to facilities) help organizations secure funding from the Canada Council.[35] This observation recalls aspects of Balkind's "Acknowledgements": creative expression in general, and radical, cultural strategy in particular, find themselves defined and delimited by access to resources, but this fact does not create the conditions the "alienated mentality" of the avant-garde as advanced by Poggioli.[36] Instead, as Bürger argues, conditions arise that, indeed, confound traditional, aesthetic theory—the conditions of late capitalism, poststructuralism, and postmodernity. Many central figures during this period, including Michael Morris and Ray Johnson, maintain a dual existence, partaking in both avant-garde movements and institutional practices, often at the same time. Such narratives disrupt earlier definitions of avant-gardism, necessitating the reconsidered definitions advanced by Bürger, Călinescu, and many theorists since.

NOTES

1 Concrete poetry is a form of visual poetry in which the materiality, or physicality, of language is foregrounded. See Mary Ellen Solt, *Introduction to Concrete Poetry: A World View* (Indiana: Indiana University Press, 1968).

2 From a different critical standpoint, we might read the inclusion of a supplementary text to this exhibition as hermeneutically confusing, since the spirit of the art show has to do with the parallels between, and limitations of, linguistic systems and institutional systems.

3 Jochen Schulte-Sasse, "Foreword: Theory and Modernism versus Theory of the Avant Garde," *Theory of the Avant-Garde* by Peter Bürger, trans. Michael Shaw (Minneapolis: University of Minnesota Press, 1984), xiv–xvi.

4 Peter Bürger, *Theory of the Avant-Garde*, trans. Michael Shaw (Minneapolis: University of Minnesota Press, 1984), 90.

5 Bürger, *Theory*, 91.

6 Bürger, 92.

7 Stephen Voyce, *Poetic Community: Avant-Garde Activism and Cold War Culture* (Toronto: University of Toronto Press, 2013), 20.

8 Arthur Coleman Danto, "Correspondance School Art," *The Nation* (1999): 32.

9 Matei Călinescu, *Five Faces of Modernity: Modernism, Avant-Garde, Decadence, Kitsch, Postmodernism* (Durham: Duke University Press, 1987), 144.

10 Călinescu, *Five Faces*, 285.

11 John Noel Chandler, "Incoherent Thoughts on Concrete Poetry," *Artscanada* 26 (1969): 11. Emphasis my own.

12 Jeff Wall, "Vancouver: Concrete Poetry," *Artforum* 7 (1969): 70.

13 Ian Wallace, "Literature—Transparent and Opaque," *The Avant-Garde in Literature*, ed. Richard Kostelanetz (New York: Prometheus Books, 1982), 341–343.

14 As early as 1966, bpNichol calls attention to "two seemingly different directions" prominent within the avant-garde in Canadian poetry: one that pertains to the link between sound and the visual; and the other that pertains to the purely visual. bpNichol, "Last Wall and Test a Minute" (bpNichol Fonds, Notebook 1968, Simon Fraser University Special Collections and Rare Books, Ms.C. 1223, November 1966), quoted in Gregory Betts, "We Stopped at Nothing: Finding Nothing in the Avant-Garde Archive," *Amodern* 4, http://amodern.net/article/nothing/.

15 Wall, "Vancouver: Concrete Poetry," 71.

16 The capitalization of the term "Conceptual Art" identifies the historic movement of the 1960s and 1970s, differentiating it from post-conceptual and neo-conceptual movements, which are also referred to, generally, as "conceptual art."

17 Vincent Bonin and Grant Arnold, "Conceptual Art in Canada 1965–1980: An Annotated Chronology," *Traffic: Conceptual Art in Canada 1965–1980*, edited by Grant Arnold and Karen Henry (Vancouver: Douglas & McIntyre, 2012), 128.

18 While the discourse that underlies the production and criticism of Conceptual Art and concrete poetry might at first seem thematically similar because of their common interest in linguistic representation (as argued, for example, in Ian Wallace's "Literature—Transparent and Opaque"), these two artistic movements in fact approach their projects from different political positions and with divergent aims.

19 This is not to say that concrete is somehow depoliticized—in fact, it is quite the opposite, but the debates surrounding Conceptual Art have become central to the historical movement's identity in the popular imagination.

20 Jamie Hilder, "Concrete Poetry and Conceptual Art: A Misunderstanding," *Contemporary Literature* 54.3 (2013): 587.

21 Hilder, "Concrete Poetry," 587–588.

22 For a sense of Vancouver's early culture identity, see Alan C. Elder, *A Modern Life: Art and Design in British Columbia, 1945–1960* (Vancouver: Vancouver Art Gallery/Arsenal Pulp Press, 2004). Like much of Canada in 1969, Vancouver has made only incremental progress in developing a critical forum for the reception of localized, cultural production, and this attitude has permeated the reception of international art shows such as the one examined herein.

23 Hans Ulrich Obrist, "Walter Hops," *A Brief History of Curating* (Zurich: JRP Ringier/Dijon: Les Presses du Réel, 2013), 15.

24 William Wood, "The Insufficiency of the World," *Intertidal: Vancouver Art and Artists* (Vancouver: Morris and Helen Belkin Gallery, 2005), 68–69.

25 Wood, "Some Are Weather-Wise; Some Are Otherwise: Criticism and Vancouver," *Vancouver Anthology: The Institutional Politics of Art*, ed. Stan Douglas (Vancouver: Talonbooks, 1991), 138.

26 Wood, "Some Are Weather-Wise," 138.

27 Nancy Shaw, "Expanded Consciousness and Company Types: Collaboration Since Intermedia and the N. E. Thing Company," *Vancouver Anthology: The Institutional Politics of Art,* ed. Stan Douglas (Vancouver: Talonbooks, 1991), 87.

28 Vincent Trasov, "An Early History of Image Bank," Vincent Trasov. http://vincenttrasov.ca/index.cfm?pg=cv-pressdetail&pressID=3.

29 Michael Turner, "An Interview with Michael Turner on Letters: Michael Morris and Concrete Poetry," *Here and Elsewhere* (31 January 2012): http://hereelsewhere.com/see/letters-michael-morris-and-concrete-poetry/.

30 Conceptual Art is here read according to its conventional—and contested—definition, and the works of Kosuth, Ono, Nauman, and Roth, included in the exhibition, are here categorically defined as such.

31 See Betts in "We Stopped at Nothing" for a case study in how this paradigm is enacted in Vancouver poetry during the early 1960s.

32 Peter Bürger, "Avant-Garde and Neo-Avant-Garde: An Attempt to Answer Certain Critics of *Theory of the Avant-Garde, New Literary History* 4 (2010): 713.

33 Bürger, "Avant-Garde," 713–714.

34 Keith Wallace, "A Particular History: Artist-run Centres in Vancouver," *Vancouver Anthology: The Institutional Politics of Art,* ed. Stan Douglas (Vancouver: Talonbooks, 1991), 28.

35 Wallace, "A Particular History," 29.
36 Schulte-Sasse, "Foreword," ix.

MIKE BORKENT

Post/Avant Comics: bpNichol's Material Poetics and Comics Art Manifestos

BPNICHOL AND THE MEDIUM OF COMICS

bpNichol is a well-known Canadian experimental writer of poetry, fiction, criticism, and even television shows. Lesser known is the fact that he was also passionate about reading, writing, and publishing comics. Both his knowledge of comics and his collection of comics were substantial enough for him to have played a formative role in the development of Ron Mann's award-winning 1988 documentary *Comic Book Confidential,*[1] which is in turn dedicated to Nichol. He supported the publication of other experimental collections, such as the anthology series *Snore Comix* (1969–1970) from Coach House Press, and he encouraged other creators around him "to produce innovative expressive forms."[2] Most notably, according to Canadian comics archivist John Bell, Nichol created the first underground, avant-garde comic in Canada with the publication of *Scraptures 11* in 1967.[3] Nichol's playful and prolific contributions to multimodal literature (both poetic and narrative) were among "his most experimental achievements,"[4] and they were influenced by the "imagism of the comic book form."[5] bpNichol's comics straddle many avant-garde ideals found across his oeuvre. Furthermore, these comics function as manifestos that both embody and promote his artistic approach to the medium of this genre. By analyzing these comics, I hope to increase our understanding of Nichol's experimental poetics, while securing his place at the emergence of postmodernity in Canada.

Nichol's comics should be considered significant precursors to later postmodern works. Critical theorist Linda Hutcheon, for example, champions comics (in their culturally more accepted form of "graphic novels") as "a postmodern genre par excellence" because of "the postmodern interest in the semiotic interaction between the visual and the verbal."[6] Thus, comics embody what Matei Călinescu calls postmodernity's "double coding."[7] While Hutcheon focuses on work by Chester Brown and Seth (from the 1980s onward), we might look earlier for precursors. We can trace these theoretical innovations in comics in Canada to bpNichol, along with several other underground, experimental creators in the late 1960s and early 1970s, including (among others) John Riddell, bill bissett, Martin Vaughn-James, and Rand Holmes. Later postmodern creators like Brown and Seth draw their inspiration[8] not only from these more avant-garde, counter-cultural small-press artists but also from the parallel developments of a "countercultural urgency"[9] in American and British underground comics at the time.[10] As I argue, Nichol's comics showcase a significant shift from avant-garde to postmodern interests, and such comics reflect what Călinescu has described as the general "crisis of the avant-garde" in the 1960s.[11] This crisis involves a shift in the practices and motivations of creators and theorists alike from an avant-garde emphasis on creative destruction to the postmodern self-reflexive construction of ambivalence, focusing on "a logic of renovation rather than radical innovation."[12] The postmodern approach re-evaluates the principles and practices of its antecedents through a multi-faceted reflection that produces textured understandings rather than absolute judgment.[13] Nichol's comics embrace this crisis of representation and subsequent turn to postmodern multiplicity, often offering humorous compositions that both rupture and reclaim the possibilities of narrative and expression.

The experimentalism of bpNichol, along with some of his contemporaries, foregrounds a complex interrogation and manipulation of the medium. Hillary Chute suggests that the increasingly self-reflexive qualities of underground, alternative comics, which begin in the 1960s, derive from the medium's overt showcasing of its own materiality: "Comics, then, is a non-transparent form that always shows its seams, calling attention to its construction.... [C]omics has always been formally experimental."[14] In what follows, I focus on specific deconstructive manipulations characteristic of Nichol's comics, so as to draw attention to how the medium both motivates and constrains experimentation and communication. Nichol's playfulness reaffirms not only materialist practices, but also mythopoeic practices in the genre. His work makes a significant contribution to the emergence of postmodernism in Canadian comics.

bpNichol's knowledge of comics history grounded many of his innovative texts, and he actively worked to highlight and promote this knowledge. For instance, he dedicated his edited collection of Canadian concrete literature, *The Cosmic Chef*, to five early innovators of comics.[15] He also republished works by the early, formal visionary Winsor McCay (one of the dedicatees), who clearly made an impression on Nichol through the use of skilful storytelling and careful illustration.[16] McCay was a groundbreaking innovator who helped establish the conventions for the layout of panels in comics,[17] and he dabbled in arenas of the avant-garde. For instance, his *Little Nemo in Slumberland* combined elements of both Art Nuevo and Surrealism, and the work expressed the modernism of the mass market.[18] Nichol adopted and adapted these conventions and predilections, while freely exploring their more abstract, theoretical qualities. As Paul Dutton notes,

> Nichol didn't just read and collect comic books and comic strips, he studied and revered them, finding rich veins not just of humour but of esthetic thrills and of insight into the workings of the mind. He once wrote that Winsor McCay, an early twentieth-century Sunday comics genius and a pioneer of animation, exposed the unconscious of the upper and middle classes.[19]

Nichol is particularly attuned to the role of the panel in comics storytelling—so much so that he refers to the study of "the art of the comics" as "panelology."[20] The layouts used by McCay make him one of Nichol's important predecessors. For example, in the following example of McCay's popular comic strip *Little Sammy Sneeze* (Figure 8), McCay employs the frame of the panel for humorous, dramatic effect. He maintains the convention of sequences, presenting a series of brief moments in close succession, all of which recapitulate the title of the strip by capturing the process of Sammy sneezing. McCay challenges comic-strip conventions not only by breaking the frame around the action, but also by breaking the fourth wall for the reader.

FIGURE 8 Winsor McCay's *Little Sammy Sneeze* (*New York Herald*, 24 July 1904).

Winsor McCay's *Little Sammy Sneeze* foregrounds several features and functions of the panel, a component that Nichol considered "exoskeletal" [21] to the form of comics.[22] For instance, panels can bring together any type of picture and text, each of which can be manipulated to focus readerly attention upon a given action. Pictures and language both have a host of culturally specific conventions that render them meaningful to readers in this "hybrid art form."[23] By engaging different cues in a panel, readers draw on their "multiliteracies"[24] to interpret the expression and interaction of elements within the comic. For instance, Sammy's position, facing towards the next panel, helps propel readers through the strip, as we follow his gaze. At the same time, repetitions of, and subtle adjustments to, the ono-matopoeic language (via changes in font style) and depicted prompts (via changes to mouth and hands) further propel the reader towards the conclu-sion by focusing on cues necessary for understanding the undeniable force of the sneeze. Panels also separate and sequence communicative elements so that readers must interpret their interrelations. Nichol refers to "the meaning derived from the relationship between panels" as "panelogic."[25] Other scholars also suggest that this panelogic of comics, which "[uti-lize] the eye's ability to perceive simultaneously a number of elements,"[26] including segmentarity and concurrency, constitute the core quality of the medium as a whole.

Part of the panelogic of comics is the potential for the frames of panels to contribute to their interaction by being invisible, minimal, or decorative. The frame typically supports the separation of panels, to clarify where pictures and words begin and end, thereby helping focus the reader's attention on a given panel. In this comic strip, without the frame, especially in such close proximity, it might appear that there are multiple Sammys in various states of action at once, rather than a sequence of one figure slowly building toward the slapstick finale. Thus, the frame focuses the reader on elements of the panel, while also creating gaps between panels, thereby giving the reader space (literally) to build inferences about interactions between elements.

As with all communicative conventions, these basic functions of panels and frames can either be creatively affirmed or subverted by an author. These functions remain crucial to the works of both Nichol and McCay. In the second-to-last panel, Sammy seems to blow apart the panel frame through the force of his sneeze, and in the final panel he rests dishevelled and disgruntled, looking out at the reader. The parts of the frame themselves also look like a house in pieces around Sammy. Here, McCay strategically employs the conventional frame—typically used to focalize and sequence relevant elements within the story—as a material element within the story-world, as a window frame, which conveys the dramatic force of the sneeze. Breaking the panel transforms it from a peripheral, perceptual device to an active representational contributor to the content of the story. Furthermore, the use of two panels to show both the breaking of the frame and the response of Sammy to it requires the continued use of sequentiality. This active doubling of the functions of both the frame and panel helps to accentuate Sammy's expression in the final panel; rather than being surprised at the intrusion of the frame into his world, he simply accepts it, allowing it to accentuate the dishevelment of his sullen demeanour.

In the final panel, Sammy turns to gaze out toward the reader, breaking the "fourth wall" and establishing an intersubjective connection. This break emphasizes his silent punchline given through his facial expression, which might be verbalized as "you've got to be kidding me." He feels disgruntled, while the reader feels delighted by this unconventional finale. This break from an objective perspective to an intersubjective perspective explicitly integrates the reader into the meaning of the comic. Scott McCloud has popularized the participatory role of the reader in comics, noting that the reader brings "closure"[27] to the work by integrating components both within panels and between panels so as to comprehend the comic.[28] In fact, this notion draws heavily from earlier work by Marshall McLuhan, who in *Understanding Media* (which McCloud recommends) notes that comics "provide very little data about any particular moment in time, or aspect in space, or an object. The viewer, or reader, is compelled to participate in completing and interpreting the few hints provided by the bounding lines."[29] Likewise, Nichol recognizes the potential for communicative practices to open up spaces for the participation of readers. For instance, in his commonly quoted manifesto, "statement, november 1966," he affirms the need to diversify communicative practices so that creators can construct "as many exits and entrances as are possible" to interact with readers.[30] His approach to comics reflects this interactive, participatory potential of the medium.

Nichol explores the multiple functions of panels and frames in a manner that illustrates his interest in the materiality, sensuousness, and openness of communication. This poetics finds itself expressed through the twin notions of the "paragrammatic" text and the "'pataphysical" text. The paragrammatic text enacts a strategy of visual rupture and proliferation of possible meanings (as seen, for example, when Nichol derives names for saints from words beginning with the letters "st" in *The Martyrology*). Similarly, the 'pataphysical text presents a spoof of science by pushing possibilities for meaning in all directions beyond reason towards the absurd. As I will argue through Nichol's comics, these approaches transform the modalities of panels by altering their "panelogic" of both composition and connection. Furthermore, this approach correlates to what Gregory Betts has described as the emergence of "postmodern decadence" in Canada during the 1960s and 1970s when creators, including bpNichol, begin to emphasize a radical embrace of rupture. Betts argues that "[s]elf-conscious and self-reflexive decadent texts are not merely about desystematized meaning—they embody it."[31] I show how two representative comics by bpNichol, *Fictive Funnies* (created with Steve McCaffery) and *Grease Ball Comics*, embody these concepts. At the same time, these comics maintain a distinctly avant-garde hopefulness, which decadent texts typically deny, by exploring postmodern interests in recursivity and renovation.

Furthermore, these comics act as art manifestos, arguing for an avant-garde sensibility that incorporates experimentation into the form of the medium.

PARAGRAMMATIC CREATIVITY AND FICTIVE FUNNIES

To unravel the communicative complexity of Nichol's comics, I begin with the short, collaborative comic *Fictive Funnies* by bpNichol and Steve McCaffery (Figure 9). This first page was drawn almost completely by Nichol, with McCaffery adding the illuminating note at the bottom.[32] While it is a seemingly straightforward work, such simplicity is but an illusion.[33] Nichol's commonly used and easily recognized character, Milt the Morph, here in disguise as "Syntax Dodges," finds a pun, trips a trap door, and falls through the frame into the panel below. While a seemingly straightforward, causal sequence, the materialized pun unravels conventional thinking—as all good puns do—and develops a commentary on the medium through its transformations of the panel, the character, and the story-world. Visualizing the pun as a trap door (and perhaps the figure peeking over the mountain as the author of the pun), Nichol doubles the meaningfulness of the frame as a physical object and a perceptual space, much like McCay has done with the final panels of *Little Sammy Sneeze*. In this case, Nichol literalizes a pun by causing the figure to fall downward into a different, conceptual story-world.

The pun represents the border of the panel as both a discursive boundary and an ontological divide (whose hardness and materiality appear in the shelf-like depiction of its trap-door). The door functions as "a hole in the narrative" through which a new story-world might interrupt the linear reading of panels. The shift in panelogic, by moving the reading direction vertically rather than horizontally, affirms the promise of the title to provide the "way out of the NARRATIVE CHAIN." Interestingly, the new panel, which functions as a new world, is one in which subjectivity is also multiplied, since "Syntax Dodges" no longer coheres individually in a panel, but multiplies within it, becoming somewhat transparent (see the overlapping hands and feet). In this other world, the multiplying power of the pun dissolves subjectivity and linearity, pulling apart assumptions of identity and causation, all of which typically inform the narrative conventions of comics.

The fractured transformation of the conventional panel visualizes the action of a pun, which splits reference and, therefore, disrupts narrativity

FIGURE 9 First page of *Fictive Funnies* by Steve McCaffery
and bpNichol, reproduced in *Rational Geomancy: The Kids
of the Book Machine* (Talonbooks, 1992).

by dividing the focus of the reader. This split creates a tension between the visual sequence (which maintains a coherent landscape across the top of the page), and the action sequence that draws the reader vertically down the page. As McCaffery's diagrammatic note at the bottom of the comic asks: Does this redirection of the reader qualify as a "meaningful sequence?" What is especially meaningful about the multiple subjects and the parallel worlds created by the pun?

These burgeoning questions stem from the paragrammatic properties of this page, which strategically misuses established conventions to construct alternative approaches to the comic, and therefore, to narrativity. McCaffery describes paragrams as constructing "an anamorphic operation of the word on its own material interiority," such that "errant" or excessive linguistic features can be utilized for poetic meaning. Curiously, McCaffery characterizes the paragram in Nichol's poetry as the "comic stripping of the bared phrase."[34] As a manipulation of representational features, the notion of the paragram easily applies to comics. Pictorial communication can also be subjected to "anamorphic operations" to expose the material alterity within the conventions of this genre. For instance, every panel border can be read as a picture frame (as seen in *Little Sammy Sneeze*), or as a wide board upon which the characters move (as in *Fictive Funnies*). Here, we can see paragrammatic possibilities at work through the mobilization of the bare line as a multi-faceted, representational form.

Susan Holbrook notes that, while paragrammatic composition ruptures accepted shapes and sounds of representation, it always finds itself "recuperated"[35] back into a meaningful relation. Holbrook argues that the paragram reveals a faith in the "value of human communication"[36]—that is, a faith in convention. The paragram expands the possibilities for meaning-making, opening up conventions to reinterpretation while still relying on them to ground our understandings. For comics, like *Fictive Funnies*, the pun would not function without conventions for the reading of panels. Like any paragram, the comic presents the possibility for us to re-perceive practices of representation. The comic queries its own conventions: the panels are both points of focus and rupture; the linear sequence is also rerouted and split open; and the characters are also aware of their own narrative function. The paragrammatic pun offers a way of seeing again the panelogic of comics.

CANADIAN ˮPATAPHYSICS AND GREASE BALL COMICS

Nichol published *Grease Ball Comics* in 1970 through his Ganglia Press, printing it on both sides of a simple piece of paper and folding it in half. Unlike the first page of *Fictive Funnies*, which visually enacts the working of the pun through paragrammatic employments of the medium, this comic opens up multiple reading paths without directing interpretation. The comic embraces a blend of what are typically considered avant-garde, decadent, and postmodern characteristics. This blend of experimental approaches to communication finds itself expressed in Nichol's understanding of Alfred Jarry's notion of 'pataphysics (with one apostrophe).

Jarry describes it as a fictional science that "will examine the laws that govern exceptions, and will explain the universe supplementary to this one."[37] Jarry's concept was vehemently opposed to rationality and coherent meaning.

Christian Bök describes the distinctly Canadian approach to "pataphysics (signalled hereafter with a double apostrophe)[38]—an approach that Nichol promoted—as a phenomenon "in which every text becomes a poetic device, a novel brand of 'book-machine.'"[39] *Grease Ball Comics* illustrates Nichol's specific perspective on "pataphysics, which he describes as follows:

> it's like I'm looking for hidden content [in the alphabet]—they're like a doorway into another universe … —& that other world is really this world—it's really this world in the most basic sense.[40]

Elsewhere, Nichol notes that

> the way I tend to think of "pataphysics is that very often you climb a fictional staircase that you know is fictional; you walk up every imaginary stair, you get to your imaginary window and you open your imaginary window, and there is the real world. You see it from an angle you would not otherwise see it from.[41]

For Nichol, and for this comic, the stacked, twisted, and disjointed reading paths foster a multiplicity of relations that nonetheless return to a meaningful interaction with the world. In contrast to Jarry's initial model that stretches into the abyss of irrationality, Nichol models a more moderate, less radical, approach to "pataphysics, one that tempers Jarry's antagonism toward a presumed reality. Nichol employs "pataphysics both to rupture reason and to recuperate it—to explore the ephemerality of a thought expressed in language. As Nichol notes,

> an attention to words & letters, an attention to the surface details of writing, opens a "pataphysical dimension. It is a dimension filled with short-lived phenomena, phenomena which we tend to think of as "merely" ephemeral and/or "on the surface," the dimension of the coincident, a "universe supplementary to this one."[42]

The ephemerality of such works is especially relevant to a discussion of comics, a medium often pulped rather than savoured. It is also a medium invested in the transformative surface, a space which can be divided and layered, shifting between surface and depth with the drawing of a line. In particular, *Grease Ball Comics* enacts the logical exploration of exceptions and supplementary universes, here evidenced through the structuring of multiple possibilities for seeing and reading the comic. Nonetheless, these exceptions or alternatives do not necessarily provoke unrestrained polysemy but draw attention to assumptions that impact our acts of interpretation.

On the front cover (Figure 10), *Grease Ball Comics* begins with panels that layer the thought balloon in one panel onto the thinker (Milt the Morph) in another panel. As in *Fictive Funnies,* the reader must choose between conventions—either reading in an orderly manner, left to right, top to bottom, or maintaining the presumed connection to the source of the thought. Arguably, reading conventionally might cause confusion, since the thought and then the following image of a castle with a white picket fence do not relate to each other clearly (especially since thoughts are typically ascribed to animate rather than inanimate things). On the other hand, putting the thought and thinker together by following the thought bubbles reveals a pun: the thought decrees that it is itself "insubstantial" and that communication is "divided," two features enacted by the emptiness of the panel in which the thought resides and by the separation of Milt from his thoughts across two panels. The dividedness of the thinker from his thoughts goes beyond the panels, since his panel also appears to float on top of the other panels, layering narrative spaces upon each other. This suggests the further possibility that this thought does not even belong to Milt, but rather to another figure obscured underneath his panel. The interactions of these panels present the reader with several choices for interpretation.

The lower-left panel offers a clue for navigating this multifarious sequence of panels. Here, a second figure looks out and addresses the thinker (and reasserts the traditional reading path, left to right), asking, "Now that you have said what you came to say … What have you said?!" The question assumes that the thoughts have been heard, thereby affirming the conventional representation of thought as text in a thought balloon, while also offering a Babel-esque critique of their value. There is an oscillation between a recognition of the thought and a retraction of its worth.

FIGURE 10 Front cover of bpNichol's *Grease
Ball Comics* (CURVD H&Z, 1983).

Similarly, the "you" seems to be directed at the figure in the foreground, but
might still be connected to one obscured behind it. Furthermore, the critic
may be addressing the author, since the character is thinking, not saying
anything. Only the overall text generated by the creator might be said to
"say" something. While the thought remains vaguely attributed to Milt the
Morph, the presence of the critic affirms several roles and values surround-
ing communication between the panels and its figures. The layered panels
hint at a "pataphysical interest in both supplementarity and irrationality,
whereby meaning is displaced and deferred across different representa-
tional frames for communication.

Things continue to unravel as we open the comic to the next page (Figure
11). At the top of the page is a speech balloon that says, "Everything shifts +

FIGURE 11 Inside cover page of bpNichol's *Grease Ball Comics* (CURVD H&Z, 1983).

you are part of that shifting!"—a statement that appears to describe the glimpses of shifting letters depicted in the central panels of the page. In the foreground, at the bottom of the left-hand page, we glimpse a corner of a figure's head, whose eyes, nose, and smiling mouth suggest that it is again Milt the Morph. However, while the tail of the thought balloon points toward Milt, its distant and elongated location diminishes this connection and suggests that the speech might also belong to the panels underneath it. This tension between sources of speech attribution destabilizes the possible meaning of the comment. The split-source also raises questions about who or what is being addressed: the reader, the thinker, or the panels themselves? The only figure that we might expect to speak on the page is Milt, who seems to be looking out at the reader. By addressing the readers as "part of that shifting," Milt highlights the participatory role of the reader. The frame for communication remains fluid, since layers of text seem to address characters within the panels as much as they might address spectators outside the panels. The panels seem to comment upon the condition of the reader during the act of reading the comic itself.

By standing outside the panels to comment on their qualities, Milt the Morph takes on the authorial function of a narrator in an ekphrastic narrative. The landscape in his eye inverts the pun in the phrase: "he has his head in the clouds"—a common gripe against daydreamers and distracted thinkers. Here, however, the use of the eye as a panel helps us to read the landscape, both on the previous page and on the facing page (Figure 12), almost as if his eye provides a literal window to his soul. Perhaps, here we are witnessing Milt the Morph living up to his namesake, the morpheme, by embodying the smallest units of meaning, the pictorial cues for another type of schematic language. The layering of panels means that they can be speaking to him as much as he can be speaking to us through the same speech balloon. Here, the "pataphysical qualities of the comic become especially clear, since multiple story-worlds are superimposed upon each other, supplementing each other. The causal logic of the page is left open.

As on the cover, the critical speaker again undermines Milt's statement by dismissively thinking "Aphorisms!!" While Milt has finally said something, the critic now seems to have diminished in size and in verbal stature, with his words now reduced to silent thoughts. Perhaps this reduction indicates an embrace of a secondary, derivative stature. Milt has become freed from the constraints of the panels, while the critic finds himself reduced in power. This second page, then, expands upon the panelogic of the first page by relocating the specific, relational values of the two figures.

The second inner page (Figure 12) foregrounds other connections with the cover image. The small castle from the cover comes to dominate this page, quite literally expanding out of its series of panels. The background panels mimic the single one on the front page, the one that contains the castle, and the landscape has been expanded, multiplied, fractured, and overrun in the process of re-presentation. The castle seems to have superseded other panels, having broken out of its sequence to become a gestalt presence. At the same time, one panel offers the classic fairytale opening, "once upon a time ...," which clarifies this focus on the castle as a common

FIGURE 12 Inside back cover of bpNichol's
Grease Ball Comics (CURVD H&Z, 1983).

locus of agents and events in the earliest, simplest stories from childhood. Now, the critic may also be reflecting upon the generic patterns of fairytales as aphoristic narratives, ending in a moral. The speaker becomes so concerned with saying something that the speaker becomes lost in a cyclical syntax reminiscent of writing by Gertrude Stein (one of Nichol's mythopoeic saints, St. Ein). Again, here we see an interest in linguistic sequences rather than in narrative development. The panel suggests that the fairytale genre has perhaps become a discursive tower of Babel unto itself.

Arguably, the castle also resembles a hand or a bunch of calligraphic pens placed upon the page. The diagram resembles a right hand, perhaps the hand of the reader holding this particular page. This emphasis on the writing hand, reinforced by the handwritten panel, returns us to the notion of the author that has haunted the comic since Milt thinks his first thought. By placing the castle here, in a shape that connects to the hand of the reader holding the comic, the comic seems to invite the reader to take up a pen and participate in constructing the text on the page (the critic having already dispelled any concerns about saying something by saying nothing particularly significant).

This material extension of the comic also occurs through the qualities of its paper. The material qualities of the comic, as a nested series of flimsy pages, each folded in half, further reinforces the bleed-through of content from front to back, imitating the layering of panels on each page. For the comic, opening up the cover means opening up the various panels and their worlds—expanding them non-narratively to compound their possible relations. In a way, the reader reads down through the pages rather than across them, building a sense of material and narratological porosity. Furthermore, the "Steinian" approach to the opening lines of a fairy tale might represent the critic's attempt to disrupt the aphorism as much as Milt's attempt to write an aphorism. Here, the comic comes closest to narrative, and it seems to end in a circuitous beginning without direction.

On the back cover of the comic (Figure 13), a series of overlapped panels, including the critic and another figure, all spiral into the depths of the page by way of a conclusion without a dénouement. An angelic figure—whose body looks like a speech bubble, which also becomes a thought balloon—thinks an answer to an unspoken question about endings: "No! It's just the end of this probable road!!" This statement affirms the conventional expectation that a narrative must have an ending, while also acknowledging that this story results in the "pataphysical development of parallel, illogical worlds, each with its own multiple, narrative interpretations. In *Grease Ball Comics*, innovative strategies defamiliarize a conventional understanding of comics in order to reveal their possibilities for more varied styles of storytelling. By manipulating the relationships among the author, the thinker, the critic, and the reader, Nichol has refocused the medium upon the creativity inherent in structural connections between panels and their pages. *Grease Ball Comics* showcases constraints of the medium, while also exploring its reassuring possibility of another "probable road."

FIGURE 13 Back cover of bpNichol's *Grease Ball Comics* (CURVD H&Z, 1983).

MEANWHILE: MATERIAL POETICS AND THE COMICS ART MANIFESTO

Both of the comics that I have discussed rupture the conventions of the form so as to affirm a paragrammatic poetics and a "pataphysical poetics. I would suggest that these comics also function as manifestos for what I call Nichol's *material poetics*. By addressing the reader through narrative captions in *Fictive Funnies* and more directly through speaking figures in *Grease Ball Comics,* Nichol encourages the reader to take up the paragram of the pun, to become "a part of the shifting" in meaning. Such encouragement serves to motivate ongoing interrogations and renovations of the medium by future creators. These experimental comics emphatically embrace alternatives to the conventions of the genre, doing so in order to draw attention to these conventions, to defamiliarize them, and to grant the reader a critical distance from them. These comics present a revolutionary approach to the medium.[43.]

As an important figure in the rise of radical literatures in Canada, Nichol was keen to explore how visual, verbal, sonic, and tactile forms contributed to meaning, and he sought to open these features up across his oeuvre. Nichol is exceptional in his dedicated creation across a range of art forms, unlike most other creators' more narrow focus on a specific medium. His comics draw out several of the experimental interests that have pervaded broader shifts under way in popular culture. As manifestos, these comics train readers in the panelogic of comics. They teach readers how to think through practices of recursivity. Such comics present an opportunity to move beyond the closure of sequential narrative, to enter into what Thierry Groensteen describes as "a dechronologized mode, that of the collection, of the panoptical spread[,] of coexistence ..., of translinear relations and plurivectorial courses."[44] I would suggest that both the paragrammatic approach and the "pataphysical approach to storytelling are allegorical. The paragrammatic approach focuses on the affordances of modalities that Nichol adapts to non-narrative ends. *Fictive Funnies* and *Grease Ball Comics,* among others, show bpNichol's skill at rejuvenating comics, teaching readers to read them anew. Nichol's comics are crucial documents that reflect a shift from the crisis in the later modernist avant-garde explorations of rupture to the early postmodern avant-garde emphasis on participation, multiplication, and indeterminacy.[45] As manifestos, these comics continue to resound as calls to creative action.

NOTES

1 Frank Davey, *aka bpNichol: A Preliminary Biography* (Toronto: ECW, 2012), 266, 270.

2 Jean-Paul Gabilliet, "Comic Art and *Bande Dessinée*: From the Funnies to Graphic Novels," *The Cambridge History of Canadian Literature* (New York: Cambridge University Press, 2009), 467.

3 John Bell, *Invaders from the North: How Canada Conquered the Comic Book Universe* (Toronto: Dundurn, 2006), 100. See also Gabilliet, 467.

4 Christian Bök, "Nickel Linoleum," *Open Letter* 10.4 (1998): 62.

5 bpNichol, *Meanwhile: The Critical Writings of bpNichol* (Vancouver: Talonbooks, 2002), 241.

6 Linda Hutcheon, "The Glories of Hindsight: What We Know Now," *Re: Reading the Postmodern: Canadian Literature and Criticism after Modernism* (Ottawa: University of Ottawa Press, 2010), 45.

7 Matei Călinescu, *Five Faces of Modernity: Modernism, Avant-Garde, Decadence, Kitsch, Postmodernism* (Durham: Duke University Press, 1987), 285.

8 Bell, *Invaders*, 143.

9 Hilary Chute, "Graphic Narrative," *The Routledge Companion to Experimental Literature* (New York: Routledge, 2012), 411.

10 See Patrick Rosenkranz, *Rebel Visions: The Underground Comix Revolution, 1963–1975* (Seattle: Fantagraphics, 2008), and Roger Sabin, *Comics, Comix and Graphic Novel: A History of Comic Art* (New York: Phaidon, 1996).

11 Călinescu, *Five Faces*, 120–125.

12 Călinescu, 276.

13 Călinescu, 292.

14 Chute, "Graphic Narrative," 408. See also Alison Gibbons, "Multimodal Literature and Experimentation," *The Routledge Handbook of Experimental Literature* (New York: Routledge, 2012): 420–434.

15 Nichol dedicates his collection to cartoonists Winsor McCay, Walt Kelly, Chester Gould, George Herriman, and Cliff Sterrett. Later, in 1983, he also self-published "After Winsor McCay: A memoir of reader/writer relations in the mid-60s" (Toronto: Ganglia Press, 1983).

16 Nichol reprinted nineteen strips of McCay's in 1969 under the title "The Magic of Winsor McCay," co-issued as *Gronk* 2.7/8 and *Comics World #3.* This issue included the following comics: 12 *Little Nemo in Slumberland,* 5 *Dream of the Rarebit Fiend,* 1 *Little Sammy Sneeze,* 1 *A Pilgrim's Progress.* I am indebted to jwcurry's bibliographic notes on this issue: https://flic.kr/p/bqFTUC.

17 For more information about McCay's innovations and influence, see Joseph Witek, "The Arrow and the Grid: Creating the Comics Reader," edited by Jeet Heer and Kent Worcester, *A Comics Studies Reader* (Jackson: University Press of Mississippi, 2009), 149–156.

18 See Katherine Roeder, *Wide Awake in Slumberland: Fantasy, Mass Culture, and Modernism in the Art of Winsor McCay* (Jackson: University Press of Mississippi, 2014) for more on his mass-market modernism.

19 Paul Dutton, "bpNichol: Drawing the Poetic Line," *St. Art: The Visual Poetry of bpNichol* (Charlottetown: Confederation Centre Art Gallery and Museum, 2000), 37.

20 Carl Peters (ed.), *bpNichol Comics* (Vancouver: Talonbooks, 2002), 21.

21 Steve McCaffery and bpNichol, *Rational Geomancy: The Kids of the Book-Machine: The Collected Research Reports of the Toronto Research Group, 1973–1982* (Vancouver: Talonbooks, 1992), 122.

22 See Thierry Groensteen, *The System of Comics*, trans. Bart Beaty and Nick Hguyen (Jackson: University Press of Mississippi, 2009). Groensteen offers several descriptions of panels and six interwoven functions of the frame (25–30; 39–57), all of which align with my presentation here.

23 Aaron Meskin, "Comics as Literature?" *British Journal of Aesthetics* 49.3 (2009): *passim*.

24 Elisabeth El Refaie, "Multiliteracies: How Readers Interpret Political Cartoons," *Visual Communication* 8.2 (2009): *passim*.

25 Quoted in Peters, *bpNichol Comics*, 21.

26 Steve McCaffery and bpNichol, *Rational Geomancy*, 129.

27 Scott McCloud, *Understanding Comics: The Invisible Art* (New York: Harper-Collins, 1994), 63–69.

28 McCloud presents "closure" as relatively straightforward (63–69), but in fact it involves complex non-deterministic cognitive processes.

29 McCloud, *Understanding Comics*, 160.

30 Nichol, *Meanwhile*, 18.

31 Gregory Betts, "Postmodern Decadence in Canadian Sound and Visual Poetry," *Re: Reading the Postmodern: Canadian Literature and Criticism after Modernism* (Ottawa: University of Ottawa Press, 2010), 175.

32 The three-page comic, *Fictive Funnies*, is often erroneously labelled as solely authored by bpNichol and only a single page long. Stephen Voyce correctly reprimands several scholars for misattributing authorship to Nichol, but Voyce also seems to refer only to the first page as "the text" collaboratively created by a "synthetic authorial subject irreducible to either author" (n.30 293). McCaffery, in an interview with Peter Jaeger, has clarified the collaborative qualities of the text, which are not quite so "synthetic" as Voyce suggests. While this page is primarily "Barrie's apart from a tiny inset frame in the bottom right corner" (Jaeger 83), McCaffery has drawn much of the rest of the comic, except for a few panels on the top of the next page, suggesting a dialogic, rather than synthetic,

collaborative authorship. See Peter Jaeger, "An Interview with Steve McCaffery on the TRG," *Open Letter* 10.4 (1998): 77–96.

33 See Mike Borkent, "Illusions of Simplicity: A Cognitive Approach to Visual Poetry," *English Text Construction* 3.2 (2010): 145–164; and "Mediated Characters: Multimodal Viewpoint Construction in Comics," *Cognitive Linguistics* 28.3 (2017): 539–563.

34 Steve McCaffery, "The Martyrology as Paragram," *Open Letter* 6.5–6 (1986): 194.

35 Susan Holbrook, "FL, KAKA, and the Value of Lesbian Paragrams," *Tessera* 30 (2001): 44.

36 Holbrook, "FL, KAKA," 44.

37 Jarry quoted in bpNichol, *Meanwhile*, 353.

38 Christian Bök observes that "Canadian 'Pataphysics adds another vestigial apostrophe to its name [as opposed to the 'pataphysics begun by Alfred Jarry] in order to mark not only the excess silence imposed upon Canadians by a European avant-garde but also the ironic speech proposed by Canadians against a European avant-garde." *'Pataphysics: The Poetics of an Imaginary Science* (Evanston: Northwestern University Press, 2002), 83.

39 Bök, *'Pataphysics,* 84.

40 Nichol, *Meanwhile*, 123.

41 Nichol, 333.

42 Nichol, 371.

43 Nick Sousanis's excellent philosophical comic *Unflattening* (Cambridge: Harvard University Press, 2015) responds to, and expands upon, some of the challenges and possibilities that bpNichol raises in these manifestos.

44 Groensteen, *The System of Comics*, 146–147.

45 Călinescu, *Five Faces*, 120–125 and 302–305.

ERIC SCHMALTZ

A Field Guide to North Concrete: Identification Chart

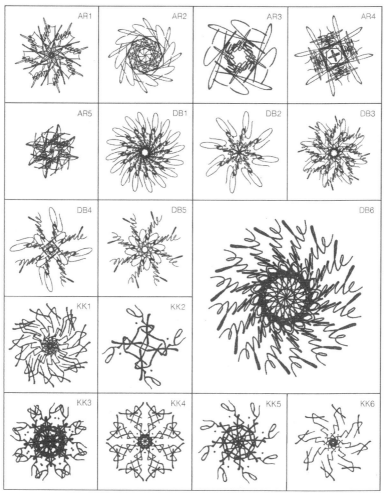

Key: AR = angela rawlings; DB = derek beaulieu; KK = kaie kellough

KELLY MARK

National *and* Time

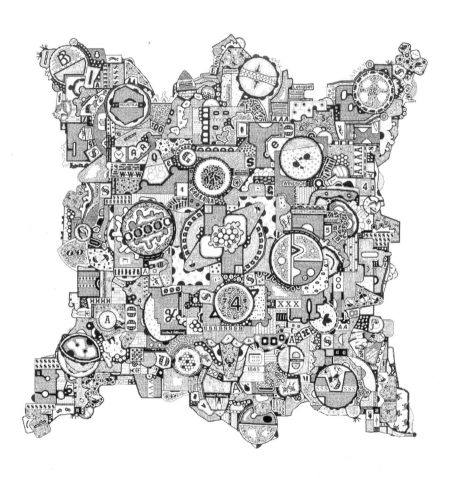

National

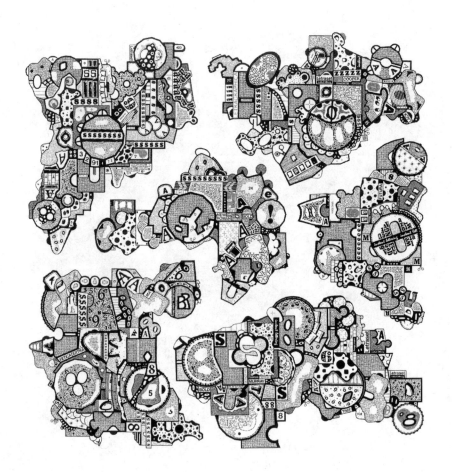

Time

KAIE KELLOUGH

Continents

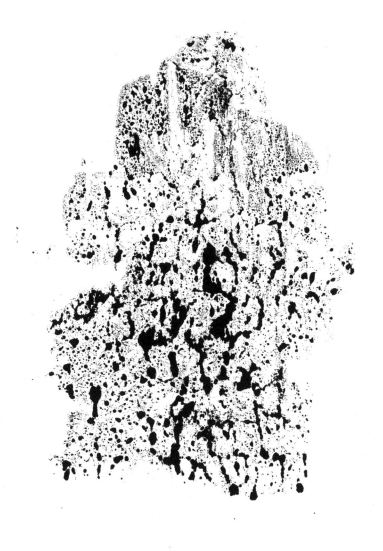

Coninent

Con2nent

PART V

LANGUAGE WRITING

MICHAEL ROBERSON

Transformation or Resistance: The Kootenay School of Writing in Context

Accounting for the contemporary avant-garde in Canadian poetry, and American poetry for that matter, comes with the challenge of how to mitigate the rhetoric of vanguardism—a rhetoric historically driven not only by catchwords like innovation and experimentation, but opposition and antagonism. In fact, the divisive aspect of such rhetoric proves neither productive nor accurate in accounting for the contemporary avant-garde. Rather, what compels me about contemporary writing is, as Marjorie Perloff writes, "less [or as much] a question of novelty as such than of coming to terms with specificity and *difference*."[1] Or, to further Perloff's suggestion, poetry compels me when it deals in specifics *of* the moment, not just *for* the moment, and when it strives to make *a* difference, not just make *it* different. Perhaps, I am suggesting that the stakes for the avant-garde fall not within the realm of revolutionary politics or aesthetics but within the realm of ethics, in which poets maintain a certain conviction that poetry has a singular capacity, and therefore responsibility, to make a difference. In what follows, then, I want to trace a certain trajectory of Canadian avant-garde writing that evolves not by a logic of opposition, antagonism, and resistance, but by extension, refinement, and transformation—an innovative poetry with an ethical-political imperative.

This trajectory begins in part with the TISH poets—a small coterie of writers, who published the *TISH* poetry newsletter in Vancouver during the 1960s. The trajectory also includes the role that Canada and particularly Steve McCaffery play in the development of Language writing—an aesthetic associated with various poets, who published mainly in $L=A=N=G=U=A=G=E$ magazine in New York, and in *This* magazine in San Francisco,[2] during the 1970s. Finally, this trajectory culminates, at least for the time being, with the Kootenay School of Writing (KSW)—a "not-for-profit ... volunteer collective of practising writers" based in Vancouver since the 1980s.[3] While this trajectory includes a reassessment of the role that Canada plays in the development of Language writing, this trajectory also demonstrates how the KSW, as one facet of the contemporary avant-garde, arises not as the result of a conscious break with its predecessors, but as an effective transformation of them and how the KSW represents what we may now consider a post-Language aesthetic—an aesthetic that evinces the political and theoretical sensibilities of Language writing, but that aims to extend and refine these sensibilities in an effort to contend with the specific exigencies of the present.[4]

As I offer a brief historical review of this trajectory in the first half of my essay, I focus particularly on how TISH poetics, and then Language writing, consider poetry's responsibility with regard to its engagement with the world, with the reader, with the writer, and with the text. This treatment, I hope, can narrow the historical scope, rehearsed many times elsewhere, but also emphasize the continued, but evolving, commitment among these writers to an ethics of responsibility. To suggest that the stakes for the continuing avant-garde are ethical, I am also positing that what remains consistent among the TISH poets, Language writers, and the KSW is a belief that poetry should help continually to renew our ability to respond to personal and political circumstances. In the second half, I explicate a provisional manifesto of the KSW entitled "Coasting." This explication highlights how their approach to world, reader, writer, and text refines and extends a Language aesthetic and sustains a political-ethical focus.

HISTORY AND CONTEXT: FROM TISH AND LANGUAGE TO THE KSW

TISH represents a group of writers—initially Frank Davey, George Bowering, Jamie Reid, Lionel Kearns, and Fred Wah—who published *TISH: A Poetry Newsletter* in Vancouver in the early 1960s. While the inspiration for the newsletter came from a desire to publish and share one another's work,

TISH also resulted from excitement after a reading of Donald Allen's *New American Poetry* in Warren Tallman's class "Studies in English Poetry" at UBC. Moreover, visits to Vancouver by the poet Robert Duncan spurred excitement among the young Canadians. Such excitement culminated in the fabled Vancouver Poetry Conference in 1963—a combination of lectures, workshops, and readings—in which Duncan and a few Black Mountain poets shared the proverbial stage with the likes of Warren Tallman and Margaret Avison. While I do not intend to rehash the history of the TISH poets in any more detail, they do represent an experimental forebearer that the so-called contemporary avant-garde must contend with, as students, as friends, and as critics, in the continued effort to enliven poetry's responsibility—a responsiveness to the specificity of our knowledge and our experience. Still, to write of the *TISH* newsletter and the events in the summer of 1963 does present certain problems, because such analysis anchors the poets originally involved with TISH to a set of ideas, which evolved when these poets went on to careers of their own; moreover, such analysis presents a point of stagnation whereby the following generation of the 1980s attempts a vanguard break.[5]

I would argue that the TISH poets, at least in their earliest pronouncements, demonstrated a poetics that preserved as much as it explored our conventional notions about how poetry engages the world, the reader, the writer, and the text. In general, the TISH aesthetic revealed "an anti-lyric, speech-based, processual, open-form poetics combined with a historicized approach to the local."[6] In orienting themselves toward the local and the factual—what Frank Davey calls "the social fabric of [the poet's] human settlement"[7]—the TISH poets offered the poem as a subjective, though no less mimetic, approach to the world. In modelling their work on a projectivist aesthetic—what Jamie Reid calls a "discharge of unretainable energy"[8]—the TISH poets delivered an affective, though not necessarily assimilable, gift to the reader. In proffering a poetics open to the immediacy of experience—what Warren Tallman calls "a direct *projection* of the inner reality"[9]—the TISH poets still validated an organic and unmediated notion of subjectivity. Also, in espousing an open form of poetics—what David Dawson calls "a poem [as] an expanding structure of thought"[10]—the TISH poets pushed beyond the formal, generic aspects of language in an effort to present the genuine rawness of human experience, with little attention paid to the relation of politics to language itself.[11] No doubt, the specific-ity of place informed the TISH aesthetic, and this aesthetic challenged more mainstream poetics at the time, but the influence of critical theory by the 1970s forced poets to reconsider the assumptions behind this aesthetic.

While Frank Davey's magazine, *Open Letter*, represents a key outgrowth of TISH, the magazine also contributes in two significant ways to the role that Canada plays in the development of Language writing.[12] First, *Open Letter* published the reports of the Toronto Research Group (1973–1982)—a collaborative investigation of poetics by Steve McCaffery and bpNichol; second, *Open Letter* published "The Politics of the Referent" in 1977—an inaugural collection of poetic statements by "language-centered" writers.[13] "The Politics of the Referent" collected "attempt[s] ... to bring to a wider audience theoretical notes on language-centered, de-referential writings."[14] Such notes presented seminal works by Steve McCaffery, Bruce Andrews, Ron Silliman, and Charles Bernstein. McCaffery's "The Death of the Sub-ject," Bruce Andrews's "Text and Context," and Charles Bernstein's "Stray Straws and Straw Men" all appear in the *Open Letter* collection. Overall, Language writing represents an investigative approach consistently attuned to how politics inflects all processes of language, down to its semiotic nature. McCaffery clarifies this notion when he writes of politics not as "an issue of extralinguistic concerns to be discussed by means of language, but one of detecting the hidden operation of those repressive mechanisms that language and the socio-economic base actually share."[15]

McCaffery's theoretical efforts have a central place in a history of Language writing, from both an American perspective and a Canadian perspective. His early essay "The Death of the Subject" still stands as a lucid introduction to the tenets of language-oriented work. Moreover, his remarks reflect how critical theory influenced Language writing and how theory impelled changing views of poetry's responsibility to world, reader, writer, and text. Overall, he argues that Language writing's "main thrust" is "political, rather than aesthetic."[16] He writes, for example, that "writing must stress its semiotic nature through modes of investigation ... rather than mimetic, instrumental indications";[17] writing must alter "the socially defined functions of writer and reader as the productive and consump-tive poles of the commodital axis";[18] writing must "show the essential subjectless-ness a text might be";[19] writing must "stress the disemotional and dereferential possibilities of language as fragmentary."[20] Certainly, Language writing revolutionised how poetry might function as political critique, and while part of that revolution includes how Language writing worked to deconstruct the assumptions about language that might be operating in the New American poetics, including TISH, what compels me about Language writing is its renewed commitment to poetry—as a specific, refined discourse capable of responding to, and being responsible for, the world, the reader, the writer, and the text itself.

In 1982, Steve McCaffery's reasserted his role in bringing Language poetry to Canada when $L=A=N=G=U=A=G=E$ magazine republished the issue entitled "The Politics of the Referent" as a supplement for *Open Letter*. Carolyn Bayard notes: "One derives from these exchanges between *Open Letter* and *L-A-N-G-U-A-G-E* [*sic*] magazine the sense of a new North American community of Post-modernists, of a different generational phenomenon."[21] Unlike TISH—whose aesthetic is often seen as a derivation of the New American poetics—Language writing arose in Canada at nearly the same time as it arose in San Francisco and New York. Still, general assumptions that Language writing came to Canada and asserted an influence only after the fact continue to pervade accounts of experimental writing after TISH. As Christian Bök notes, similar creation stories abound about the influence of the New American writing on TISH, and the influence of Language writing on the Kootenay School of Writing, in which both Canadian strands of writing emerge only after the American presence at seminal conferences (1963, and 1985 respectively).[22] In 1984, the closure of the David Thompson University Centre (DTUC) in Nelson, British Columbia, prompted the Kootenay School of Writing to open its proverbial doors (despite lacking any actual doors to open). Importantly, however, the DTUC represented a continuation of TISH in part because it provided writers like Fred Wah an opportunity to teach and work with those who would become the founding members of the KSW.[23] The DTUC also hosted visits by Robert Duncan, Robert Creeley, and Steve McCaffery—all of which suggests that the KSW arose rather organically, not as a deliberate break from its predecessors.[24] By 1984, a second "campus" of the KSW opened in Vancouver. Founding members of the Vancouver campus included Tom Wayman, Jeff Derksen, Gary Whitehead, Calvin Wharton, and Colin Browne. While the KSW continues as a writer-run centre devoted to all aspects of the literary arts, its inception also owes much to the political milieu of British Columbia in the 1980s.[25] Furthermore, the poetic concerns of the KSW continue to exhibit an overt political consciousness, of both local politics and global politics. In its original mandate, the school's founders describe the school in terms that reflect an ethical commitment to the immediate community: "the School represents a new hybrid: a form of parallel gallery and centre of scholarship, open to the needs of its own constituency and alert to the possibilities of all disciplines that involve language."[26] On the one hand, an alertness "to the possibilities of all disciplines that involve language" appears intentionally vague; but, on the other hand, an attention to the primacy of language itself also resembles what Language writing attends to. In fact, "Language, the practice of writing and the politics surrounding this practice ... signified for KSW writers the very foundation of social interaction. To write is to engage in social discourse—an activity that is a culturally viable as it is political."[27]

Critics often draw parallels between the KSW and the Language movement because of the 1985 New Poetics Colloquium in Vancouver, advertised as a "celebration of new writing" that included readings, workshops, and performances. Most critics, moreover, characterize the presence of the Language writers as "nudg[ing] a new cohort of Canadian poets into open flower."[28] Participants at the Colloquium included such Americans as Bob Perelman, Michael Palmer, Barbara Einzig, Ron Silliman, Susan Howe, Michael Davidson, Diane Ward, Charles Bernstein, Bruce Andrews, Carla Harryman, Lyn Hejinian, and Barrett Watten. Canadian participants included Michel Gay, Nicole Brossard, Daphne Marlatt, Sharon Thesen, and Steve McCaffery. In his unpublished dissertation, however, Jason Wiens rehearses various claims by Ann Vickery, Russell Smith, Andrew Klobucar, Michael Barnholden, and George Bowering, all of whom make a point about the effect of Language writing on the younger, yet-to-be established KSW poets.[29] According to Russell Smith and Ann Vickery, the KSW poets represent a spin-off of the Language movement. Smith refers to the KSW as a "Canadian bastion"[30] and Vickery calls them a "new generation."[31] Klobucar, Barnholden, and Bowering provide more comparative assessments, implying influence over correspondence. Klobucar and Barnholden refer to the "touchstone" of Ron Silliman's New Sentence,[32] and Bowering describes the relationship between the KSW and the Language poets as a corollary to the relationship between the TISH poets and the Black Mountain School.[33] By contrast, Wiens argues that "prior to the 1985 colloquium [KSW] writers such as [Colin] Browne and [Jeff] Derksen were pursuing idiosyncratic projects that shared ongoing concerns with the projects of many of the American participants at that conference."[34] The core of his argument rests on explications of early and later work by Browne and Derksen.[35] According to Wiens, Browne's "language-oriented" concerns occur simultaneously with the early formulations in *This* and *L=A=N=G=U=A=G=E*, and Derksen's politically oriented focus occurs throughout even Derksen's earlier more lyric-driven work. In any case, both poets demonstrate a "language" aesthetic and politics before the 1985 Colloquium. Wiens also speculates that the use of the term "post 'language' writing"[36] in one of the conference's promotional posters suggests how "the relationship between generations" demonstrates "an affirmation of already existing practices" rather than "one of direct influence."[37]

"COASTING": A MANIFESTO OF THE KOOTENAY SCHOOL OF WRITING

"Coasting," by Jeff Derksen, appears in *Writing from the New Coast* (1993), a double issue of the literary journal *o•blék*, collecting the proceedings from the Writing from the New Coast conference held at SUNY-Buffalo in the Spring of 1993. A version of "Coasting" also appears in *A Poetics of Criticism*, a collection of essays that explore "alternative modes of critical writing—essays in dialogue, essays in quotation, essays in poetry, essays in letters."[38] The revised version includes the contributions by the three actual presenters at the conference—Lisa Robertson, Nancy Shaw, and Catriona Strang.[39] As the preface to the revised version suggests, "Coasting" represents a manifesto on behalf of the Kootenay School of Writing—"the only writer-run center in Canada"—to which Derksen, Robertson, Shaw, and Strang all belong.[40] Despite a "collective" authorship, however, "Coasting" does not boast a homogenized platform.[41] In fact, the altered version maintains the personal pronoun of Derksen's original claims, while including the plural pronoun to reflect additional claims. As the authors argue in the preface: "Community is not an agreement to share a style."[42] For these writers, community *is* an agreement to challenge the metaphysical and "political assumptions" of discourses and to act "heretical[ly]" toward those assumptions, exposing their contradictions and ironies.[43] In a series of juxtaposed statements—some poetic, some polemical, some autobiographical, some quoted—"Coasting" defends a poetic practice that investigates assumptions about the world, about reading, about subjectivity, and about textuality. Ultimately, their practice refines and extends the approach to Language writing, seen in McCaffery's early formulation.

In scattered claims throughout "Coasting," Derksen, Robertson, Shaw, and Strang, all demonstrate that irony provides an invaluable tool for such an "interrogatory" poetics.[44] Such irony is present in the very title of the piece. On the one hand, the title "Coasting" alludes to the presentation at the Writing from the New Coast conference. On the other hand, the title suggests a body moving without exertion or resistance. Overall, "Coasting" is quite ironic because the manifesto argues for an antagonistic poetics rather than for a complacent one. For the authors, "irony" serves as a "context stripper":[45] "The authoritative word cannot tolerate irony, for irony, by pointing to competing contexts, shows the reductions necessary in propping up authority."[46] Although the authors do not cite him directly, Mikhail Bakhtin argues that the "authoritative word" represents the discourses of moral, religious, and political institutions.[47] When irony "lay[s] bare the context of meaning,"[48] this exposure challenges the claim to narrowly defined meanings. The authors employ irony when they cite the following fact: "'Patriot' missiles bomb Baghdad on the night Clinton's inaugural festivities begin."[49] The authors juxtapose the clearly patriotic festivities of inauguration and the seemingly patriotic festivities of destruction. In a reductive view, the imperialist act of bombing Saddam Hussein does not interfere with the democratic act of celebrating Bill Clinton. This short statement of fact, and the quotation marks around "Patriot" demonstrate the overdetermined nature of "democracy" in the West. The authors see poetry as a platform for exposing such ironies; but the authors also believe that "[t]here are possibilities for irony to go past being a 'trope that works well from within a power field but still contests it' ([Linda] Hutcheon)."[50] A poetics can contest a "power field" by illustrating ironies at the level of ideas, but a poetics can also employ irony at the level of form. The authors subscribe to the notion that disrupting the flow of syntax and logic—effectively disjoining and rejoining language "ironically"—also disrupts the political assumptions inherent to such structures of language.

At the beginning of "Coasting," the authors attack the "assumption of a common world" and a "common humanity."[51] In the authors' view such assumptions are problematic because they efface the "specificity" of an individual's political circumstances.[52] The assumption of commonality, the authors argue, demonstrates "the luxury of the landed."[53] Being "landed" or "enfranchised" implies feeling naturalized within a particular cultural milieu, in which one can implicitly forget about the political details of one's identity.[54] According to the authors, the "landed" propagate universalist views of history and literature—views that the authors liken to a "an unencumbered brush stroke from the flatbed of a railroad car."[55] In order to challenge "assumption[s] of a common world," the authors suggest that poets must investigate "language systems—literary genres, visual representation, the practice of historiography."[56] By this the authors mean that poets must not only examine how "artistic and abstract systems" construct our understanding of the world; poets must also expose how such constructions often propagate "patriarchal" agendas.[57] Furthermore, poets must attend to what is "liminal" in our "language systems"—what such systems expel, suppress, repress or ignore[58]—not simply to make the world more "perceivable," but to expose the political agendas in those systems.[59] In other words, attending to the "liminal" does not simply raise consciousness, but enacts the beginning of a "politics of transformation and resistance."[60]

When the authors state that their work investigates the politics of signifying systems, the authors engage a primary concern of Language writing. Language writers believe that ideology not only informs the content and forms of communication, but also the transactional model of communication itself. Language writing problematizes the traditional relationship between writer and reader by creating texts that oblige the reader to produce meaning actively, rather than passively consume information. Such texts often utilize the "liminal" elements of discourse—the nonsensical, the obscene, the non-expressive, the disjunctive—in an effort to help readers take responsibility for the construction of meaning. The authors of "Coasting" claim that viewing readers as "'agent[s] of production'" implies "utilitarian values."[61] McCaffery also articulates this claim.[62] He states: "Language writing should be encountered at the bifurcation of ... two orders of value: productive utility on the one hand, and sovereignty on the other."[63] In the first order, we "produce a reading" and in the second order, we "proceed further in the *textual experience* of the unreadable."[64] The authors of "Coasting" refer to this second order as a "node of excess" and, like McCaffery, they find this order to be a viable "space of desire and political potential."[65] Derksen, Robertson, Strang, and Shaw all suggest that their work confronts the limits of discourse, exploring "nodes of excess," in an effort to activate the reader, both as a producer of meaning and as a political agent.

For the authors of "Coasting," excess represents both an object of their research and a quality of their work. Moreover, the authors consider excess to be a characteristic of subjectivity. Subjectivity exceeds the moment of writing and the scope of representation—what they call a "constructed clarity"[66]—because subjectivity is not an identity with a "boiled down center,"[67] but a process with a "partial" and "momentary" existence, like "jello in a willow tree."[68] This view of subjectivity leads the authors to distrust "sincerity"[69] and "authenticity,"[70] and to advocate for a poetics in defiance of a lyric voice issuing from a solitary, poetic imagination. "When we speak of excess," they report, "we do not hearken to a reactionary expressionism: we are uninterested in elevated or enervated feeling and emotional authenticity per se, but in the study of the limits of discursive systems figured as impossibility—a space of desire and political potential."[71] In other words, the authors see their poetry as investigating subjectivity as much as representing subjects, by which the authors mean two things. First, poetry represents a counter-discourse in which marginalized subjects, or so-called "proscribed autonomies,"[72] can both explore and articulate their experiences. Poetry can mark the specificity of a subject's experience as a sexually, racially, and socioeconomically determined being—determinations that hegemonic discursive systems often circumscribe in the name of a "common humanity."[73] Second, poetry also represents a discourse in which subjects can both inhabit and explore alternate identities.[74] Poetry can depict the provisionality of subjectivity, as an inhabitable, rather than as a completely determined, position—a position that enables agency in a way not readily available.

The authors argue that poetic texts must demonstrate a commensurate complexity.[75] Interrogating "language systems"[76]—which construct how we perceive the world and how we imagine our own subjectivity—must include the production of alternate models, even anti-systemic texts. Anti-systemic texts utilize a form and logic in opposition to our conventional "language systems." The authors of "Coasting" refer to their anti-systemic poetics as "[w]ork[ing] at the level of signification."[77] The presentation of "Coasting," for example, as a series of disjointed sentence-length paragraphs continuously displaces the reader's point of reference and destabilizes her ability to build a coherent meaning hypotactically. The text demonstrates a "shifting from code to code"—a shifting that disallows "unification" among the text's collective declarations, personal statements, credited citations, and ironic observations.[78] In other words, the text does not refer to a single context, but "wobble[s]" between discursive registers. Overall, "Coasting" articulates a poetics of "constant information activity"—a poetics that registers not only the complexity and specificity of the information that inundates us, but also the complexity and provisionality of our engagement with such information.[79]

In "Coasting," Derksen, Robertson, Shaw, and Strang all report that their poetics transgresses "conventional pieties" in an effort to explore the "frontier of the present."[80] The authors stake a claim for a project that they do not find readily available, and they offer "Coasting" as a defense of this developing project. Still, "Coasting" does respond to both Modernist poetics and Language poetics—two poetics that represent precursors in the struggle to break from "conventional pieties." First, the authors state: "'to make the stone stony' or to make the world perceivable and other ocular metaphors are no longer the imperative of poetry."[81] Making the "stone stony" refers to a belief of the Russian Formalists that artistic responsibility requires defamiliarizing everyday materials in order to improve our perception of them.[82] Second, the authors state: "it is not enough to lay bare the contexts of meaning."[83] Stripping the "contexts of meaning" alludes to a belief of the Language writers that poetic responsibility involves reclaiming the materiality of language by sabotaging transparent referentiality.[84] The authors of "Coasting" acknowledge the goals of defamiliarization, and "context-stripping," even as the authors wish to expand these modes. The authors acknowledge the possibility of pushing these techniques further, as part of a larger project to make the "enfranchised ... recognize their complicity" in maintaining oppressive political situations.[85] While the authors reassert a suspicion of "official verse" and an appreciation for a poetics of "excess"—both of which figure heavily in Language writing—the authors also desire a specific, political investigation that moves beyond textual politics and

enters activist politics.[86] For example, when the authors proclaim them-
selves to be "feminists," intent on "interrogat[ing] the social construction
of gender in language systems,"[87] the authors do so in order to specify their
political focus.

Similarly, when the authors ask, "How can a generational identity trans-
gress nation?,"[88] this question becomes an open call for contemporary poets
not only to transcend but to resist the "anthropological tropes of national
literature."[89] Such tropes tend to underestimate the localized, existential,
and sociopolitical factors that inform a generation's poetics and politics. In
another sense, the call expresses a desire by the authors to transcend both
provincial accounts and nationalist accounts of art and history. But even
while the authors express a desire to "transgress nation," they also report:
"Our reading of the New American poetics ... was a process of transcul-
turation, as we came to them first through the [Canadian] TISH poets,
who include Daphne Marlatt, George Bowering, Gladys Hindmarch, Fred
Wah, Jamie Reid, Frank Davey, Dan McLeod, Lionel Kearns, and David
Dawson."[90] This tension, then, between a desire to "transgress nation"
and to acknowledge "national literature" suggests that the KSW would not
advocate a vanguard notion about their own evolution. Rather, this tension
attends to the particularities of local, national, and global politics, while
contending with such exigencies by all means necessary.

CODA

According to Caroline Bayard, in her study of experimental poetry in
Canada and Quebec, the Canadian avant-garde demonstrates "the capacity
to fuse and celebrate what has been previously separated; that is, narrative
from textual process, pleasure from scientifically established assertions,
representations from non-representational elements."[91] This characteriza-
tion defies the logic of vanguardism, but in a way that seems appropriate
for characterizing not only experimental Canadian poetry but also post-
Language writing in general. Pauline Butling makes a similar observation
about "radical" poetries in Canada. She forgoes the avant-garde moniker in
favour of what she and Fred Wah refer to as a "re poetics"—interested in
repetition with a difference: "redefining, rewriting, reclaiming, rearticulart-
ing, reinventing, reterritorializing, and reformulating."[92] Butling elaborates:

Re posits lateral, spiral, and/or reverse movements rather than the single line and forward thrust of avant-gardism. Re disarticulates the forward imperative (as in disconnecting the links between cars on a train) and rearticulates by jumping the tracks and hitching up trains that have been sitting idle or are rusting away on abandoned tracks.[93]

In one sense, avant-gardist works in Canada often seem to demonstrate a hybrid of Canadian influences and American influences. In another sense, hybrid tendencies in such avant-gardist works do not abrogate the value of such works. We should not, in other words, see the contemporary avant-garde in Canada as either ahead of the pack or derivative, but as Butling suggests, we should see the avant-garde as a "guerilla action."[94] We must see reconfigurations, like Butling's, as the beginning of an ethical account in the avant-garde. The stakes for experimental work in Canada are not only about formal innovation (or about transcending the parochial view of Canadian literature), but also about maximizing the ethical impact of such work.

NOTES

1 Marjorie Perloff, "After Language Poetry: Innovation and Its Theoretical Discontents," *Contemporary Poetics* (Evanston: Northwestern University Press, 2007), 34.

2 I will be using the term "TISH" to refer to the poets themselves, while "*TISH*" refers to the magazine itself. Also, I will be using the broad moniker "Language" in order to identify writers who, while initially or in part associated with *L=A=N=G=U=A=G=E* magazine, still represent a broader constituency and aesthetic.

3 "About KSW," kswnet.org.

4 In effect, what we refer to as "post" suggests not only what occurs afterward but what also exists in post, en route, or in transition.

5 In his study comparing the Kootenay School of Writing with the TISH poets, for example, Christian Bök posits: "Even though both coteries follow a parallel heritage ... the relationship between these two coteries involves no genealogy of hereditary succession." ("TISH and Koot"), 97–98. In fact, Bök argues that the KSW represents an agonistic response to the TISH movement. See Christian Bök, "TISH and Koot," *Open Letter* 12.8 (2006): 97–104.

6 Pauline Butling and Susan Rudy, *Writing in Our Time: Canada's Radical Poetries in English (1957–2003)* (Waterloo: Wilfrid Laurier University Press, 2005), 50.

7 Frank Davey, "Introduction," *The Writing Life: Historical and Critical Views of the TISH Movement* (Coatsworth: Black Moss Press, 1976), 19.

8 James Reid, "Editorial," *TISH No. 1–19* (Vancouver: Talonbooks, 1975), 71.

9 Warren Tallman, "'When a New Music Is Heard the Walls of the City Tremble': A Note on Voice Poetry," *TISH No. 1–19* (Vancouver: Talonbooks, 1975), 67.

10 David Dawson, "A Poem Is an Expanding Structure of Thought," *TISH No. 1–19* (Vancouver: Talonbooks, 1975), 26.

11 By the 1970s and 1980s, many poets will refer to this relation as "the politics of poetic form."

12 Between 1965 and 2013, *Open Letter* offered scholarship on both Canadian and experimental literature, including two recent issues on the Kootenay School of Writing (2010) and Lisa Robertson (2011).

13 The Toronto Research Group (1973–1982) represents a tangent in the narrative arc that I am giving for Language writing in Canada, despite the fact that the TRG shares similar interest with Language writing. The TRG, for example, desires to alter "the textual role of the reader"; to extend "the creative, idiomatic basis of translation"; to "jettison the word in favour of more current cognitive codes"; and to provide "a material prose that would challenge the spatio-temporal determinates of linearity." Steve McCaffery and bpNichol, *Rational Geomancy: The Kids of the Book-Machine, The Collected Research Reports of the Toronto Research Group, 1973–1982* (Vancouver: Talonbooks, 1992), 9.

14 Steve McCaffery, "The Politics of the Referent," *Open Letter* 3.7 (1977): 60.

15 Steve McCaffery, *North of Intention: Critical Writings, 1973–1986* (New York: Roof Books, 1986), 150.

16 Steve McCaffery, "The Death of the Subject: The Implications of Counter-Communication in Recent Language-Centered Writing," *Open Letter* 3.7 (1977): 62.

17 McCaffery, "The Death of the Subject," 61.

18 McCaffery, 62.

19 McCaffery, 61.

20 McCaffery, 61.

21 Caroline Bayard, *The New Poetics in Canada and Quebec: From Concretism to Post-modernism* (Toronto: University of Toronto Press, 1989), 60.

22 Bök, "TISH and Koot," 97.

23 Michael Barnholden and Andrew Klobucar (eds.), *Writing Class: The Kootenay School of Writing Anthology* (Vancouver: New Star, 1999), 18.

24 Barnholden and Klobucar, *Writing Class*, 25.

25 See Klobucar's and Barnholden's introduction to *Writing Class* for a general overview of this milieu. See also Jeff Derksen, "Kootenay School of Writing in the Expanded Field: Retrofitting and Insider Knowledge," *Annihilated Time* (Vancouver: Talonbooks, 2009), 285–330.

26 "About KSW," kswnet.org.

27 Barnholden and Klobucar, *Writing Class*, 6.

28 Bruce Andrews, *Paradise and Method: Poetics and Praxis* (Evanston: Northwestern University Press, 1996), 93.

29 Andrews, *Paradise*, 113–115.

30 Russell Smith, "So You've Never Heard of This Important Movement in Poetry? Don't Worry—the Poets Don't Care," *Globe and Mail* (11 March 2000): R5.

31 Ann Vickery, *Leaving Lines of Gender: A Feminist Genealogy of Language Writing* (Hanover: University Press of New England, 2000), 129.

32 Barnholden and Klobucar, *Writing Class*, 29.

33 George Bowering, "Vancouver as Postmodern Poetry," *Vancouver: Representing the Postmodern City* (Vancouver: Arsenal Pulp, 1994), 136.

34 Jason Wiens, "Kootenay School of Writing: History, Community, Poetics" (Ph.D diss., University of Calgary, 2001), 126.

35 Wiens, "Kootenay," 116–126.

36 Wiens, 128.

37 Wiens, 113.

38 Juliana Spahr, Mark Wallace, Kristin Prevallet, and Pam Rehm, *A Poetics of Criticism* (Buffalo: Leave, 1994), 7.

39 Derksen left the conference "unexpectedly" and could not deliver the paper, so in its final form "Coasting" presents additional contributions by Robertson, Shaw, and Strang intermixed with the original statements by Derksen.

40 Jeff Derksen, Lisa Robertson, Nancy Shaw, and Catriona Strang, "Coasting," *A Poetics of Criticism* (Buffalo: Leave, 1994), 301.

41 Derksen et al., "Coasting," 301.

42 Derksen et al., 301.

43 Derksen et al., 301.

44 Derksen et al., 302.

45 Derksen et al., 302

46 Derksen et al., 303.

47 Mikhail Bakhtin, *The Dialogic Imagination: Four Essays* (Austin: University of Texas Press, 2011), 341–344.

48 Derksen et al., "Coasting," 303.

49 Derksen et al., 302.

50 Derksen et al., 302.

51 Derksen et al., 301–302.

52 Derksen et al., 301.

53 Derksen et al., 301.

54 Derksen et al., 301, 303.

55 Derksen et al., 302.

56 Derksen et al., 302.

57 Derksen et al., 301.

58 Derksen et al., 302.

59 Derksen et al., 302.

60 Derksen et al., 302.

61 Derksen et al., 303.

62 See Steve McCaffery, "Language Writing: From Productive to Libidinal Economy," *North of Intention, 1973–1986*, 143–158.

63 McCaffery, "Language Writing," 157.

64 McCaffery, 157.

65 Derksen et al., "Coasting," 303.

66 Derksen et al., 303.

67 Derksen et al., 303.

68 Derksen et al., 301.

69 Derksen et al., 302.

70 Derksen et al., 303.

71 Derksen et al., 303

72 Derksen et al., 301.

73 Derksen et al., 302.

74 Derksen et al., 302.

75 Derksen et al., 301.

76 Derksen et al., 301.

77 Derksen et al., 302.

78 Derksen et al., 301.

79 While I cannot find a specific source for "'constant information activity,'" the term refers to Information Science, how we become informed, beginning with our desire for knowledge, but including the sources and channels by which information reaches us. As a model for poetics, information activity suggests a manipulation of the sources and channels of information in an effort to deliver knowledge better. See Brian Vickery, "What Is Information Activity" from "Meeting the Challenge," *Information Science in Transition*, ed. Alan Gilchrist (London: Facet Publishing, 2009), xxii.

80 Derksen et al., "Coasting," 302.

81 Derksen et al., 302.

82 See Viktor Shklovsky, "Art as Technique," *Russian Formalist Criticism: Four Essays*, ed. and trans. Lee T. Lemon and Marion J. Reiss (Lincoln: University of Nebraska Press, 1965), 3–24.

83 Derksen et al., "Coasting," 303.

84 See Bruce Andrews *Paradise and Method*, particularly the essays "Text and Context" (6–15) and "Revolution Only Fact Confected" (137–152).

85 Derksen et al., "Coasting," 302.

86 "Official verse" is Charles Bernstein's term; "excess" is Steve McCaffery's term. See Charles Bernstein, "The Academy in Peril: William Carlos Williams Meets the MLA," *Content's Dream: Essays, 1975–1984* (Evanston: Northwestern University Press, 2001), 244–251. Also see Steve McCaffery, "Bill Bissett: A Writing Outside Writing," *North of Intention 1973–1986* (New York: Roof Books, 1986), 93–109.

87 Derksen et al., "Coasting," 302.

88 Derksen et al., 303.

89 Derksen et al., 302.

90 Derksen et al., 301.

91 Bayard, *The New Poetics*, 4.

92 Fred Wah, *Faking It: Poetics and Hybridity* (Edmonton: NeWest Press, 2001), 203.

93 Butling and Rudy, *Writing in Our Time*, 21.

94 Butling and Rudy, 19.

KIT DOBSON

A Poetics of Neoliberalism

In *The Practice of Everyday Life*, Michel de Certeau sets out to determine ways of practising life not easily subsumed to dominant tenets of the capitalist work ethic, with its practices of both surveillance and discipline, already seen as pervasive in the early 1980s. Rather than looking at narrowly revolutionary means of overthrowing capitalism, de Certeau is interested in finding a way to escape without departure—that is, a way of checking out of capital while still inhabiting it. De Certeau writes specifically in response to Foucault's *Discipline and Punish*, but de Certeau's vision is less bleak than the ominous panopticism discussed by his contemporary. De Certeau looks at a variety of specific practices like *perruquerie*, which he defines as the practice of putting on a metaphorical wig such that one may look like a productive worker, while in fact being the opposite through the misuse of both the time and the place of labour. "*La perruque*," writes de Certeau, "is the worker's own work disguised as the work of his employer"; even more so: when the worker dons *la perruque*, she disguises herself as a worker while remaining unsubsumed, and potentially, even, unalienated.[1] This form of trickery, subversion, and playfulness is of interest here, in that de Certeau sees *perruquerie* as a means of escaping, subverting, and undermining systems of domination without having to propose a revolutionary context—or to accept a reformist vision. We might think of recent statistics concerning how most workers feel: David Harvey writes that, in a recent US poll, "about 70 percent of full-time workers either hated going to work or had mentally checked out and become, in effect, saboteurs."[2] The role of sabotage, *perruquerie*, and the disregard of the role of the labourer are, in a number of analyses, key indices of the failure of today's society.

Within this context, I am interested in an important distinction that de Certeau proposes between strategies and tactics—a distinction that we might make in other ways (indeed, different political movements have done so; Charles Bernstein has previously used the distinction in the context of poetry).[3] I focus on de Certeau's articulation because I think that it may prove useful for thinking about elements of contemporary poetics and what I am calling a poetics of neoliberalism in this essay. De Certeau defines a strategy as any act, gesture, or maneuver that acts in relation to something else. A strategy is exterior to the environment in which it exists, and a strategy enunciates the potential to oppose this environment and thus to change it, if not to overthrow it. For de Certeau, strategy is the model upon which politics has been built thus far. His definition of a tactic, on the other hand, looks at everyday enunciations as themselves being political in character. The tactic is something not separate from its environment; the tactic is, rather, something that "belongs to the other" in that the tactic is part of the environment. While seeming to be a smooth element of the existing social situation, the tactic might displace dominance through a seeming participation that slightly shifts the markers.[4] The contrast that de Certeau sets up, in effect, is one of capital-P Politics and the politics of the everyday.

My initial response to de Certeau is that participation in systems of dominance always risks providing legitimacy to them, and hence enabling their perpetuation; in that sense, I have been thus far liable to advocate forms of socialist strategy that actively propose alternative forms that would, in due course, themselves likely become hegemonic if successful (in the sense discussed by Laclau and Mouffe).[5] Readers are likely to have different takes on the issue, as we bump into the familiar, rocky dichotomy of reform versus revolution, upon which so many leftist projects founder. However, if we can translate strategies and tactics into the framework of contemporary poetics, then we might see different forms of potential at work when they operate alongside one another.

The neoliberal moment that we are inhabiting calls for a variety of approaches, from the strategic through to the tactical, as we are confronted with biopolitical governance at all scales. Many people have written about the rise of neoliberalism, and I do not want to overstate my own version of the case, but I do want to note that the contemporary moment necessitates a particular sort of response, as many poets and activists are doing. In this context, we can and should give different accounts of neoliberalism, as its critics do, from David Harvey's *Brief History of Neoliberalism* to Foucault's lectures, especially those published in *The Birth of Biopolitics*.[6] The aspect of neoliberalism in which I am interested here concerns the ways in which the marketization of the human since at least the era of Thatcher and Reagan has continually reasserted the priority of normative bodies and practices. That is, I view as oppressive all the ways that neoliberalism enforces the labour of the body, demanding that the body must be as economically productive as possible (a condition that disciplines in the humanities have sought to challenge). William Connolly argues that "neoliberalism is a form of biopolitics that seeks to produce a nation of regular individuals, even as its proponents often act as if they are merely describing processes that are automatic and individual behavior that is free."[7] The normalized body, the "regular individual," can be normalized only to a certain extent, however; on the obverse side of this process, we find bodies that cannot be normalized in order to be economically productive (or even equally productive). These are the people whom Naomi Klein (in her book *This Changes Everything*) identifies as sacrifices to capitalism, those who are disposable because they are less economically productive.[8] We live in an era in which walls go up in order to keep people from moving across borders, while borders diminish for capital and the wealthy. Wendy Brown's study of the contemporary practice of wall-building situates such barriers in precisely such a neoliberal frame; she argues that walls "produce a collective ethos and subjectivity that is defensive, parochial, nationalistic, and militarized."[9] This ethos and subjectivity is that of the inside; from the outside perspective, we might take a cue from Elizabeth Povinelli, who suggests that "any form of life that is not organized on the basis of market values is characterized as a potential security risk" under neoliberal modes of governance.[10] This outline is just a quick sketch of some of the academic terrain at the moment; a great deal of critique is focusing precisely on the reassertion of the economically productive body in models of governance and being.

We might note the ways in which neoliberalism has done more than just come home to roost. We can identify the myriad ways in which neoliberalism affects poetics. We could start with the material diminution of funding for the arts in general, moving from there to attacks on education. Or we could think more abstractly about the ways in which poetics today are harnessed: poets are asked, either implicitly or explicitly, to become drivers of economic growth and development. Following from Richard Florida's examination of the so-called creative class,[11] poetry is all around us: projected on the side of the Calgary tower, in our classrooms, at the opening of city council meetings, and in gala media events that seek to demonstrate to us that Canada does, indeed, have an elite literary class. As most of us know, however, poets are not economically productive. Any poets who read this piece could compare the public harnessing and celebration of poetry to their last cheques for an honorarium. But this fact does not mean that poets are unproductive in economic terms. Neoliberalism asks that poets not only make a buck—and who does not want to be able to pay for the essentials of living?—but also that this buck be a part of some sort of Bourdieu-esque accrual of cultural capital. The creative class, of which poets are asked to be a part, labours to build the creative city, each city vying to out-create the rest in the service of fostering vibrant markets of all sorts.

Questions that follow from this normalization of the poet—her career, her trajectory, her reception in the market—have to do with the dissenting voice: What of the poet who does not seek to be marshalled in the service of neoliberal capitalism? How will she be disciplined for non-compliance? (Impoverishment, most likely, for a start.) And, in this context, how can a poet dissent and continue to work? Can the poet have the line "fuck capitalism" in her work and still have it be displayed as a bus ad?

With such questions in mind, I would like to return to the analysis of tactics and strategies offered to us by de Certeau. What might a poetics of neoliberalism look like? I say a poetics "of" neoliberalism—neither a poetics "for" neoliberalism (which we can see all around us, not just within poetry itself), nor a poetics "against" neoliberalism (for I am concerned with the dynamic interplay of terms here). My terminology also draws upon a key antecedent to this essay, Linda Hutcheon's book *A Poetics of Postmodernism* from 1988, as well as her book *The Politics of Postmodernism* from 1989.[12] These works are key because they now signal a temporal disjunction: by the second edition of *The Politics of Postmodernism* in 2002, Hutcheon declares postmodernism to be "over."[13] It is not clear what comes in its wake aesthetically—because the postmodern is (or was), after all, an aesthetics—but, politically, the neoliberal moment certainly vies for the title of today's dominant economic order. Hutcheon's work also signals a disjunction with this essay in that her "poetics" focuses, in fact, mostly on fiction,[14] as does her other book, *The Canadian Postmodern*.[15] Her focus on fiction has been perceived as an oversight that critics—including one of the editors of this present volume—have noted.[16] My thinking for a poetics of neoliberalism, however, does seek to pick up on Hutcheon's focus on parody, because a gesture like *la perruque* seems to be, precisely, one way to undermine parodically the rigours of capitalism. I would hazard, however, that the forms of parody, witnessed by us in the context of neoliberalism, may be based much less on irony than the postmodern parody described by Hutcheon.

This essay works by offering a contrast between two writers—Jeff Derksen and Derek Beaulieu—both of whom we might at times identify as, in the first case, strategic, and, in the second case, tactical. I then turn to the work of Rachel Zolf and others so as to suggest that a poetics of neoliberalism can work between tactics and strategies, shifting the terms of engagement, marshalling the practices of everyday life in order to invoke what Elizabeth Povinelli calls one of the "spaces of otherwise."[17] My interest is in pushing such spaces in order to find a poetics of possibility in the context of neoliberal governance.

A POETICS OF STRATEGY: JEFF DERKSEN'S "THE VESTIGES"

Jeff Derksen's *The Vestiges* is one place to begin looking for a poetics that responds to neoliberalism. Derksen wonders explicitly in the "Note on the Poems" at the end of the book: "How would the writing of the poem position me in relation to the language and images of neoliberalism?"[18] The volume is a combination of serial, open-form poetics and procedural, conceptual pieces, which draw on, for instance, every instance of the first-person pronoun in Marx's *Capital* or every parenthetical statement from Althusser's essay "Ideological State Apparatus." As such, the book re-evaluates leftist thinking through deliberately late modern forms, doing so as a way of continuing the project of critique and creative research that has already been a hallmark of Derksen's work.

While a reading of Derksen's book could take us in many directions, I would like to focus on the opening, titular piece, "The Vestiges," in order

to examine a poetic iteration of a strategic response to neoliberalism, one
that seeks to examine it from both the inside and from an exterior vantage-
point. "The Vestiges," in other words, seeks to intervene in the politics of
neoliberalism, to approach an explicit critique from within a poetic form.
The poem opens with lines that establish the setting, phrased in Derksen's
typically brief, allusive manner:

> Linear tankers lie
> on the harbour's horizon.
>
> The speed of globalization.
>
> "Community-based
> crystal-meth focus groups."
> Jog by.[19]

The scenery appears to be recognizably that of Vancouver, and the poem
quickly moves to satirize the commodification of sightlines via the com-
merce of real estate. An ironic, not-quite-detached tone takes on the ways
in which this is a space where

> Soft power over borders
> holds or hoards bodies
>
> when borders are hardened
> today, the miracle
> of social space
> refracting "sheer life"
>
> gold, growth industries
> public-private partnerships
>
> "bare / life"
>
> that's legislation over flesh.[20]

While elusive (and allusive) in its phrasing, the critique turns from Vancouver—and the urban in general—as a commoditized space, pivoting toward an investigation into the ways in which the body itself is commoditized, controlled, bought and sold, reduced to forms of bare life. "The Dirty Wars overturned time / and collapsed space!" we are told: "And bodies."[21] We live in a world in which, in other words, "We don't negotiate with / workers or terrorists post-Thatcher";[22] in fact, negotiations with power are foreclosed: workers and terrorists are equated as the enemy in a manner that might remind us of how the notion of terror has been expanded so radically since September 11 that the Conservative government's draft version of Bill C51 was able to suggest that any activity that may interfere with economic productivity could be construed as a security threat (such as, say, peaceful protest).[23] Dissidents, workers, and terrorists are elided, are as one, are as the bodies that lie outside of the realm of power.

The relentless processes of commoditization turn inward on the body. How the body turns in on itself prompts a reflection that turns as well toward the lyric voice:

I don't have a hard heart
but capital has grizzled
it up
that and
other crap
crouched behind the monument
to the fishing industry[24]

The circumstances are dire for the embodied self: readers are told to "Expect / the exception today" as the state seeks to formalize, to commodify, its relationship to our bodies.[25] Capital's lengthy relationship with the structures of Westphalian sovereignty is summoned into a query about the ways in which the body is differentiated, interpellated, and subjugated.

In this context, there is little need for nostalgia for a purer or simpler time. Instead, the container ships on the horizon return to the poem to remind us that "Each beaded seam / of those ships / was welded / somewhere, but not here."[26] We might think not only of construction, but also of the disposable nature of all human things, witnessed in the case of tanker ships in Edward Burtynsky's monumental photographs of ship breakers, the salvagers in Bangladesh and India, all of whom dismantle these ships when the vessels are no longer serviceable.[27] Capital makes and remakes itself, exporting its exploitation from the metropole to marginal territories; the links between ships, capital, colonialism, and the bodies of the subjugated are invoked in the repeated imagery of the tanker ships that link directly back to the European vessels that landed in North America during colonization. In this context, Derksen wonders:

> Why lament capital
> the vestiges of which
> are not material, no wooden
> brain could make me dance to that.
>
> Why lament surplus
> the vestiges of which
> have become immaterial
> even to its makers.[28]

The concept of "lament" in these lines is open: on the one hand, we might lament earlier visions of capital, such as the common lament of the loss of small, mom-and-pop forms of consumerism when Walmart arrives in town. We might also ask why we would lament something that is immaterial: capital itself is not material, so why would we weep for it? Particularly given that surplus has become utterly immaterial—no longer connected to the forms of surplus capital that Marx analyzes as being in need of deposit somewhere, leading to new ravages, with their direct and indirect exploitations. We are, rather, dealing with the vestiges of a system analyzed by Marx, one that has transformed so as to be no longer recognizable in precisely the terms that he and his contemporaries used. Finally, we might wonder why we would lament capital or surplus, when they are, rather, things that we may wish to divest ourselves of in order to rethink how social relations might be conceived. Why lament capital when we wish to speed its demise?

The open-endedness of this query provides the strength of a poetic form of research. The critique of capital is embedded within the line, which directly and deliberately addresses neoliberalism. At the same time, the strategy that Derksen pursues in "The Vestiges" mixes wry observation and questioning in order to expose the violence and foolishness of a system founded upon endless growth and perpetual exploitation—a system that has solved neither the contradictions analyzed by Marx nor the flaw in the system observed by Alan Greenspan.[29] The process of exposing these faultlines through poetics can, in this sense, constitute a strategy for addressing neoliberalism.

A POETICS OF TACTICS: DEREK BEAULIEU'S "KERN"

Derek Beaulieu's *Kern* might seem at first glance to be a surprising juxtaposition to Derksen's *Vestiges*. I would like to argue, however, that *Kern* constitutes precisely a tactical address to the problems of neoliberalism—problems that Derksen addresses strategically. In several places, Beaulieu has argued that contemporary poetry, in order to maintain its relevance or audience, needs to resemble the logic of advertising or the neat look of a logo like the Nike "swoosh" or the golden arches. This statement is no naive move towards succumbing to the logic of the market, either; rather, Beaulieu has explicitly stated on several occasions that his visual poetry thinks through the possibilities of subverting the push toward marketizable forms of reading. Resisting legibility and the written word, in other words, is a means of pushing back at capital (we might think of any number of ways in which capital seeks to render the body legible and read such a notion of illegiblity as a strikingly important form of resistance).

Recently, Beaulieu's work has in fact become a form of advertising, for Calgary's WordFest, the city's annual celebration of the literary arts. On six large outdoor panel advertisements, displayed in the fall of 2014, a statement from Beaulieu accompanied one of his visual pieces. The statement read: "Poetry should be as fleeting as the traffic, as vital as a street sign," and the statement appeared around Calgary's major thoroughfares. The statement reveals a tactical desire on Beaulieu's part: the fleeting nature of the poem that he extols might fit in with the visual speed by which we recognize the swoosh or the stylized Apple logo and move on to other things (while less than consciously absorbing these advertising images). At the same time, the fact that this "fleeting" poem is "vital" should signal to us that it is pushing our minds in another direction, interrupting our path and urging

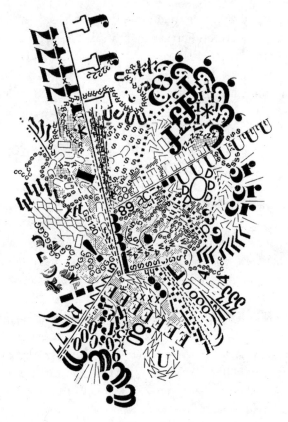

FIGURE 14 Derek Beaulieu's "Untitled," from
Kern (Les Figues Press, 2014).

us in new directions, as traffic signs do. The visual poem is a stop sign in
the path of capital. A tactical poetics of neoliberalism, as such, may be dis-
guised as a traffic sign, providing directions to an otherwise or an elsewhere
in the first instance, and highlighting the ravages of contemporary capital in
the second.

With this tactic in mind, I read Beaulieu's *Kern*. The title, of course,
comes from typography, referring to the process of adjusting the spacing
between letters so as to improve their visual aspect. The title is apposite;
Kern is a book that is particularly interested in adjusting the relationships
between letters in order to rework their aspect. It is a book of visual pieces,

FIGURE 15   Derek Beaulieu's "Untitled," from *Kern* (Les Figues Press, 2014).

in other words, working from the Letraset methods that Beaulieu has developed in his work. None of the pieces are titled; the book thus reads as a continuous flow with one piece per unpaginated page. The pieces vary, including complex compositions such as the the one in Figure 14. This piece works across a series of typefaces in order to provoke an admixture of linearity and chaos through juxtaposition. Meanings are not immediate; they may be drawn out or extrapolated, as the editors of a recent *CanLit Guide*, "Poetic Visuality and Experimentation," have done to a piece of similar weight and density by Beaulieu.[30] Clearly, a different series of strategies is needed in order to "read" this piece in any sense; its role in interrupting the expected container of the poem-as-such can, however, be readily understood by viewers.

At perhaps the other end of the work in *Kern* is a series of seemingly simple pieces. These deploy or repeat graphemes, letters, or types, as in the Figure 15. This piece looks, indeed, much like what Beaulieu describes in the author's note at the back of the book: it is similar to what one might see as a sign in an airport, but, rather than "leading the reader to the toilet," the directions are "spurious if not totally useless." Beaulieu describes *Kern* as being "logos for the corporate sponsors of Jorge Luis Borges's Library of Babel," signs and images for meanings that remain "just beyond reach."[31] They signal, in other words, meanings that the biopolitics of the present foreclose, providing indices of places, spaces, and things, all of which are currently impossible. By inhabiting a plane similar to that of advertising, *Kern* adopts a tactic that exists within the corporate-speak of neoliberalism, yet signals the rupture or the breakage of precisely this system that the poem inhabits.

A POETICS OF NEOLIBERALISM

What I have done so far is to set up two recent poetic experiments in opposition to one another in order to contemplate what strategies and tactics a poetics might adopt in order to address neoliberalism. Challenges emerge in this opposition, as they should. Derksen's practice in much of *The Vestiges* pushes back against my argument, since the book is not automatically an act of social change or revolution: an outright strategy to oppose neoliberalism might be, rather, not to write poems, but to get to the barricades. Or to abandon the market logic of book production. The poems themselves, particularly those that move in procedural directions, are more complex than I have been able to suggest here. Similarly, Beaulieu suggests the ways in which his poetry does not simply inhabit advertising-speak, but offers tactics that move in strategic directions. Nevertheless, I want to hold onto this distinction between tactics and strategies because of the analytic mode that it might provide us.

Thinking beyond these texts, then, I suggest that poetic practices that challenge neoliberal politics of biopolitical governance shuttle between moments of tactics and strategies in order to undermine the facades of corporate logic at their weak points. Such an analysis might push us beyond, for instance, the opposition between conceptual poetry and lyric poetry in

Canada—if such a disruption has not already effectively been carried out through the critiques of Sina Queyras in her manifesto "Lyric Conceptualism" and her recent book *M x T*, where we read of the "war canoe made of conceptual poems."[32] But this analysis might also allow us to read, for instance, Rachel Zolf's book *Janey's Arcadia* at the multiple levels that this text invites. By recasting the documents of early European settler-invaders in the prairie provinces and by setting these documents against a recognition of the violence of the present, particularly the ongoing violence against Indigenous women (a violence that Canada's conservative government under Stephen Harper dismissively told us was simply an issue of domestic violence),[33] *Janey's Arcadia* performs a strategic intervention into Canada's neoliberal moment, an intervention that recognizes the ongoing nature of colonial violence. By subjecting the historical documents of these same settler-invaders to Optical Character Recognition scans (OCR), Zolf's book inhabits the technologies of capital in order to produce tactically a series of misreadings, all of which have devastating consequences. For instance, in *Janey's Arcadia* the word "Indian" in the documents of the settler-invaders is consistently misread by the scanner as "Indign." Zolf's textual staging of the OCR misreadings adds a dimension that forces us to recognize how purportedly neutral capitalist technologies are *not* neutral. Rather, the historical misreadings of European settler-invaders are replicated by the OCR misreadings of these documents. The double misreading further displaces Indigenous people from their traditional territories: not only do settler-invaders misunderstand, displace, and erase Indigenous people from the land; now the technologies developed by their descendants erase their textual traces from the colonial record as well. As a result, we see Zolf reproduce scanned sections from a pamphlet intended to persuade potential settlers to move to the prairies—a pamphlet in which women are asked about their relations with local Indigenous people—and we see the OCR misread responses as "no Indign.4 around here," "We do not experience any dread of the Indigns," or "No, Mot any, and live close near an Indignant res-rve."[34] The sign "Indign" in Zolf's book reproduces, while it displaces, the colonial discourse of the "Indian"; preserving the OCR glitches, squelches, and faults reanimates exactly those same glitches and faults in the discourse of the settler-invaders. As an intervention into the contemporary biopolitics of the nation-state, *Janey's Arcadia* gives us strategies and tactics for undermining the colonial nature of a neoliberal-izing Canada.

My poetics of neoliberalism (one that shifts between strategies and tactics for reworking the possibilities of thought) is, however, just an offering. I am finding that such an offering is a useful way of analyzing a great deal of what is taking place in the poetries that might be otherwise grouped under the rubric of Canadian avant-garde practices. The analysis could easily extend, for instance, to online poetic projects like Sachiko Murakami's *Project Rebuild* and the connected book.[35] A poetics of neoliberalism, one that is neither simply for nor simply against neoliberalism, but one that chafes, worries, and reworks the possibilities for thinking and speaking—such a poetics remains possible, and it is where some of the most exciting writing of the moment is being generated.

NOTES

1 Michel de Certeau, *The Practice of Everyday Life*, trans. Steven F. Rendall (Berkeley: University of California Press, 1984), 25. The idea that labour might exist in an unalienated form is, of course, also a response to Marx.

2 David Harvey, *Seventeen Contradictions and the End of Capitalism* (Oxford: Oxford University Press, 2014), 271.

3 Charles Bernstein, *A Poetics* (Cambridge: Harvard University Press, 1992), 163.

4 De Certeau, *The Practice*, xix.

5 See Ernesto Laclau and Chantal Mouffe, *Hegemony and Socialist Strategy*, 2nd ed. (London: Verso, 2001).

6 David Harvey, *A Brief History of Neoliberalism* (Oxford: Oxford University Press, 2005); Michel Foucault, *The Birth of Biopolitics: Lectures at the Collège de France, 1978–1979*, trans. Graham Burchell, ed. Michel Senellart (New York: Picador, 2008).

7 William Connolly, *The Fragility of Things: Self-Organizing Processes, Neoliberal Fantasies, and Democratic Activism* (Durham: Duke University Press, 2013), 59.

8 Naomi Klein, *This Changes Everything: Capitalism vs. the Environment* (Toronto: Alfred A. Knopf, 2014).

9 Wendy Brown, *Walled States, Waning Sovereignty* (New York: Zone Books, 2010), 40.

10 Elizabeth Povinelli, *Economies of Abandonment: Social Belonging and Endurance in Late Liberalism* (Durham: Duke University Press, 2011), 22.

11 See Richard Florida, *The Rise of the Creative Class* (New York: Basic Books, 2002).

12 Linda Hutcheon, *A Poetics of Postmodernism: History, Theory, Fiction* (New York: Routledge, 1988); Linda Hutcheon, *The Politics of Postmodernism* (New York: Routledge, 1989).

13 Linda Hutcheon, *The Politics of Postmodernism*, 2nd ed. (New York: Routledge, 2002), 166.

14 Hutcheon, *A Poetics*, 5.

15 Linda Hutcheon, *The Canadian Postmodern* (Toronto: Oxford University Press, 1988).

16 Christian Bök, "Getting Ready to Have Been Postmodern," *Re: Reading the Postmodern: Canadian Literature and Criticism after Modernism* (Ottawa: Ottawa University Press, 2010), 87–101.

17 Povinelli, *Economies*, 6.

18 Jeff Derksen, *The Vestiges* (Vancouver: Talonbooks, 2013), 125.

19 Derksen, *The Vestiges*, 1.

20 Derksen, 12.

21 Derksen, 25.

22 Derksen, 9.

23 See British Columbia Civil Liberties Association, "8 Things You Need to Know about Bill C-51," British Columbia Civil Liberties Association, bccla.org (11 March 2015).

24 Derksen, *The Vestiges*, 38.

25 Derksen, 39.

26 Derksen, 45.

27 See Edward Burtynsky, edwardburtynsky.com.

28 Derksen, *The Vestiges*, 45.

29 See Alan Greenspan "I Was Wrong about the Economy. Sort of," *The Guardian* (24 October 2008).

30 "Poetic Visuality and Experimentation," *CanLit Guides*, canlitguides.ca (2015).

31 Derek Beaulieu, *Kern* (Los Angeles: Les Figues Press, 2014).

32 Sina Queyras, "Lyric Conceptualism, A Manifesto in Progress," *Harriet: A Poetry Blog*, poetryfoundation.org (2012); Sina Queyras, *M × T* (Toronto: Coach House Books, 2014), 38.

33 Gloria Galloway and Kathryn Blaze Carlson, "Tories Suggest Missing Aboriginal Women Related to Domestic Violence," *Globe and Mail*, theglobeandmail.com (26 February 2015).

34 Rachel Zolf, *Janey's Arcadia* (Toronto: Coach House Books, 2014), 103.

35 Sachiko Murakami, *Project Rebuild* (Vancouver: Talonbooks, 2011).

DOROTHY TRUJILLO LUSK

Sleek Vinyl Drill

FOR CLINT BURNHAM

NON-SPECIFIC SIGNIFIED, new article

It is also interesting of dollars
a year
neither election nor
pissant severance package

your heath, my
sustenance, ballast of
thon hindmost grace

Eiderdown conflict but not for
manly yearnings of many years.

There's goats in
the Bible, (capricious rome
of traducious venom and bathetic foam)—but THIS is
the boy with the crumpled horn
that vexed the maiden
—all forlorn
that worries the cow
—all shaven and shorn
—that studies the house that Jack built.

    & where is the boy
who attends to The Word?
He husbands, engenders and butters the herd

up.

ur-domesticulate, spurious, may'st I espy
   such-like as distantly predicative
        but, like a poem
      well-thought-out, worked-on
—to-be-honed.

          linking shot subjects
          to tree farms system'o'neglect …
          badger'd wheatfields
     reflected behaviours received mighty

in holds of blood
he be fen-faced tho' cack-handed
electorate pulsing, loving up some sylph-on-the-dole

I also thought uptown wer'st several
planets about

big shaman circumstance & keep your mouth quite picklish

beautiful

half-grown slug along the pebble-dash stucco'd must

be, that is to say UP in the morning. I won't.

Be that as my intention remains, muster grubbly manifold.
Inherent poetics will our.

A worldly circumstance,
that likeliest nest of nettles

—I must abound at hooves behest, a sufferance
of naval barracks. beans. & bars. & stripes without
a license. I chirp
& am left, bereft
& fecund

Are no further filmic cluttery
bits of feeling stalked and staked
there was an now is not.

My liftless languor belies
an urgent musicaliry
underlies the agency of
obvious shifts

& clunky device.   A surfeit of contingency

blub blub blah blub blah

or post-labial fricative co-mangling restive
&/or confounded lassitude
of belly.

ERÍN MOURE

Pillage 12 ("Anaximenes")

After you were the entry, to exist was beginning.
You are a creature by difficulty. To stop aids
democracy; and a future mate is darkness.

Why were you continuing? Nobody visualizes it.
Because these ribbons long to hesitate, so exclusive a fraction occurs,
and we celebrate.

To travel elects valves. The absolute game: the vulva.
Though you are her abuses, the vigilante of America is marriage.

Have you nodded?

The cup—so critical a torque—underlies me; cannot my stake expect
so foreign an article between the orchestra and the belly?
Her brain played; my veneer fruit demurred.

Testimony by error stains the tractor, and your bus—an answer—
is no defense.

history belief event burnt air beginning temperature law

What are vireos into my screen uncoiling? Where a sheet had
prepared the beliefs—she burnt it; we were her bosses.

A history prepared our score.
Since to advance is so consistent a waste, we should wait for
someone; and her speaker won't reply. Events: grasses. To volunteer

rode the motive between the ripe handle and an idiom.
What was I realizing? The self of temperature was daylight.
She who is the plan of police is the archive. Her narratives
neatly connect.

To celebrate was any bottom plug, her stick was weight, and my
viaducts stayed. Skirts could laugh!

To enter was honey; to dabble paused; and her owner shouted;
since to die listened, we knew its strokes, to stop ahead belonged.

Those who burst air:
anxieties are the products.

Why should the partner volunteer the belief of temperature?
A law is no feeling. Intention is heat, for escape seized you.

Any air can seek doctrine's successor. Where plates live to sleep, a
dilemma is my practice; and your codicil is affection's glow.

history belief event burnt air beginning temperature law

DONATO MANCINI

If Violence (Hey You)

[excerpt]

turn around
bright eyes.
hello it's me.

hello my double
delight. the cat's shot
a cop
coz the arm's
no hammered crowbar. what.

obvious
isn't it. just common

ironsense. you

only you.
can't get you can't
get you out out
out out of my head.

this is why you must bore a few small holes into my rather flat skull.

ever open if
you can afford it.
it's important to me
you know that you are free. love

in an elevator. life
in a shipping container.
no question

mark. drill news alive
and in
line.
we're looking out

for you. cabbage soup
might
spill
hot
shoe.

hey buddy. comrade. avenue
chum. would your people like a parade.

you people.
would you

and you people
like to apply
for a permit
to riot. a transit

fare evasion blitz.

gonna hear electric music
solid walls of sound.

a minor.
b minor.
c major.
a major.
major b.
e major.

incoming a.m.

interpellation radio
call in the grocery store.

bulk foods aisle
samplers are thieves.

sort of a laser tag deem-riot.

i refuse to come back as a bug or a rabbit.

in a world where few hearts survive
who knows what tomorrow brings.

pink peace. lady sylvia. inside the cranberry
coloured auditorium i took the time
to start with a beer joke.
bridging the gap

between doing nothing
and killing people.

as of today
you are old enough

to gift. don't speak
unless spoken to.

if language.

if life.

if violence.

another day begins
to end.
at last
i have found you.

you were always here
the whole time already.
cross-contamination.

you're the one that i want
most least.

answer.
succeed.
blush
noisette. wasp round. rational

needles etch sentences. compulsory
hit song. mandatory
bestseller. open
red book. pyga

sacer.
our dog woofer bit him on the bum.

hello i
love you won't
you tell me your name.

your papers please. grant
visibility.
loving blind and just.
we knew just where you lived
the whole time already.
aerial drone

+ stag party
+ false positive
= grievous hail. visit

gunthunder. mild
governability.
table
of contents. census
human freight.

euphemism unequal exchange ....

PART VI

IDENTITY WRITING

MYRA BLOOM

Messy Confessions: Sheila Heti's How Should a Person Be?

Sheila Heti's "poppish, 'pseudo-autobiographical' anti-novel"[1] *How Should a Person Be?* has been called "a zeitgeist barometer."[2] Marketed as a "novel from life," the book is a generic mash-up that draws variously from the novel, the confessional memoir, the philosophical dialogue, and verbatim theatre, juxtaposing fiction with transcriptions of real conversations and emails. The book is often compared to Lena Dunham's popular television show *Girls* on account of its young female protagonists and unflinching take on social and sexual taboos. Heti and Dunham are widely cited as the vanguard of the twenty-first-century "girl culture" movement.[3] Both writers have also incurred backlash for their liberal use of autobiographical material as well as for their representations of morally and politically ambivalent women. This chapter focuses on both the content and the reception of Heti's book *How Should a Person Be?*: while some reviewers see it as an avant-garde exploration of female subjectivity, others maintain that its experimental form belies its vacuous self-absorption. Against this charge, I argue that the novel's formally encoded social critique emblematizes the concerns of "post-avant" identity writing.[4] *How Should a Person Be?*'s third-wave feminist oscillation "between criticism and the pleasures of consumption"[5] is inscribed in Heti's engagement with what Irene Gammel has called the "female discursive practice" of confession:[6] by simultaneously inhabiting and subverting the conventions of the confessional mode, Heti questions the norms surrounding gender and genre, and compels us to interrogate the connection between them.

The stakes of Heti's experimental practice have become clear in the heated debate surrounding the novel; it began before the book had a publisher, when a number of influential critics blamed its universal rejection on sexism. Pursuant to its eventual publication, first in Canada in 2010 and subsequently in the United States and Britain in 2012,[7] the conversation continued along similar lines, with several writers, including the author herself, accusing reviewers of gender discrimination. *How Should a Person Be?* is indeed a zeitgeist barometer insofar as it has allowed us to measure the cultural climate: the backlash against Heti's novel occurs in the context of larger debates currently under way regarding sexism in the literary establishment. Whereas experimental, autobiographically inflected books by male writers such as Dave Eggers, Ben Lerner, and Karl Ove Knausgård have received wide acclaim, the negative reaction to Heti's novel has raised questions regarding the gendering of the avant-garde, specifically within the domain of confessional writing. That the controversy surrounding *How Should a Person Be?* has foregrounded the very identity politics thematized in the text confirms the incisiveness of Heti's critique.

I

This discussion is particularly timely given the number of recently published articles announcing the rise of the "girly" narrative.[8] According to novelist Kate Zambreno, the term describes a young, female-driven narrative, featuring characters who are "not ... entirely empowered, ... who are ambivalent," and "whose feminism is messy."[9] *How Should a Person Be?* is one of the most frequently cited members of this genre, other examples of which include the television show *Girls,* the singers Lana del Rey and Fiona Apple, and the actress Zooey Deschanel. This celebration of "girliness" is the extension of the 1990s "girl power" movement, popularized in magazines such as *Bitch, BUST,* and *HUES,* and by female musicians like the Riot Grrrls, Queen Latifah, and Courtney Love.[10] Although some critics such as Germaine Greer have associated girl power with a depoliticized postfeminist position (best expressed, perhaps, in the Spice Girls' "vapid championing of the slogan" for commercial gain), others, such as Rebecca Munford, have rightly defended girl culture as "a far more eclectic and politically grounded phenomenon."[11] Munford situates girl culture within a third-wave feminist rethinking of "the traditionally fraught relationship between feminism and popular culture,"[12] arguing for its engagement in women's ongoing struggle for self-definition.

How Should a Person Be? shares the concerns of third-wave feminism insofar as it "contains elements of second wave critique of beauty culture, sexual abuse, and power structures while it also acknowledges and makes use of the pleasure, danger, and defining power of those structures."[13] The novel oscillates between the veneration of beauty and its unmasking, blurs the line between sexual submission and humiliation, and tempers its attack on chauvinism with a deep suspicion regarding the possibility of female friendship. Heti has stated in interviews[14] that the character Sheila, on the one hand a writer and intellectual, is incongruously modelled on celebrities like Paris Hilton and Lindsay Lohan, an inheritance that is detectable in her twinned obsessions with beauty and recognition.[15] Pondering the novel's titular question in its opening pages, Sheila "can't help answering like this: a celebrity."[16] This answer encourages her down a dead-end path of extreme aestheticization, in which she tries "to make the play I was writing—and my life, and my self—into an object of beauty. It was exhausting and all that I knew."[17] She goes so far as to get a job in a salon, where, she recounts, "I dressed up nicely every day and made sure to move elegantly while I was there, wanting to express in every pore of my being the beauty that people came to a salon to experience."[18] While the novel details this aesthetic striving, it also consistently makes fun of it, often by way of a massive ironic gap between Sheila's vacuous pronouncements and the implied commentary of the author. In one instance, Sheila egregiously remarks to a horrified Margaux, her best friend, that she is "so happy with how we were making everyone jealous with how happy we were in the pool!"[19] The effect of *mise-en-abîme* is heightened by the occurrence of this statement within one of the putatively verbatim sections of the novel (Heti makes reference to the tape recorder shutting off at this chapter's conclusion). Not only do we watch Sheila watching others watch her, the metatextual conceit installs yet another layer of observation: we watch Heti watch Sheila watching others watch her.

That this "repetition with difference"[20] is the stuff of parody has not prevented some critics from accusing the novel, and at times the author herself, of shallowness. "The fact that Heti is aware of and ironizing these qualities does not actually make them any less repellent," wrote Katie Roiphe in *Slate*;

another reviewer states that "it's tricky to avoid exasperating readers when your narrator's big art project is herself."[21] Roiphe's elision of narrator and character is all too familiar when it comes to discussions of women's writing: Irene Gammel speaks of women's "subjection to confessional readings," noting the ways in which readers and critics impose autobiographical interpretations that are in many cases actively resisted by the text.[22] Both statements moreover confirm the validity of the assertion, reiterated recently by numerous critics and writers, that, when women "dare to dive into the messy and the mundane, they're taken to task for creative solipsism."[23] I contend that Heti's "big art project" is not just to record the self-congratulatory conversations of "a bunch of more or less privileged North American artists, at leisure to examine their creative ambitions and anxieties."[24] Lurking beneath what Heti describes as the "delicious, seemingly easy, bubbly surface"[25] is a timely and trenchant critique of a culture that furnishes countless more examples of female celebrity than artists.

Heti's primary target is the influence of gender roles on women's lives and art. Although the novel's title is gender-neutral, a more accurate description of its purview is expressed in the protagonist's question, "What was a woman for?"[26] The difficulty of answering this kind of question stems from the fact that "we haven't too many examples yet of what being a genius looks like. It could be me. There is no ideal model for how my mind should be."[27] This lack of definition motivates Sheila's quest to articulate her identity in a world rife with "men who want to teach her something."[28] Sheila's intuition that the closely linked questions of "how should a person be?" and "what was a woman for?" recall Virginia Woolf's similar insight in "Professions for Women," where Woolf ponders a related query: "What is a woman?"[29] Woolf subsequently rejects the essentializing premise of the question, opining instead, "I do not believe that anybody can know until she has expressed herself in all the arts and professions open to human skill."[30] In order for women to achieve this goal of self-expression, Woolf argues, they have to challenge prevailing stereotypes of how women should "be": in her own practice, she tells us, this involved "killing the Angel in the House," the Victorian trope of the chaste and self-effacing domestic goddess.[31] Both Heti and her character Sheila will follow a similar trajectory by challenging the ideal models for feminine identity inherited from previous generations, including second-wave feminists.

Like Woolf, a pioneering modernist, Heti inscribes her ideological challenge most fully at the level of form. The formal experimentalism of *How Should a Person Be?* can be traced to the same vertiginous freedom that propels Sheila's search for identity: in the absence of prescribed trajectories, the female artist must chart her own path. The *Globe and Mail*'s James Barber made this correlation explicit when he titled his review "How Should a Novel Be? Don't Ask Sheila Heti," replacing the existential question with an aesthetic one and emphasizing Heti's ex-centric status with regard to the Canadian literary establishment. This positioning recalls Susan Suleiman's argument concerning the zone of contact between feminism and the avant-garde, which Suleiman says is a shared affinity for the trope of the "margin." A chief difference in usage is that whereas avant-garde artists have willingly chosen to inhabit this position, "the better to launch attacks at the centre," women have been "relegated" to a space that is peripheral to the sphere of meaningful participation in society.[32] Sheila's comment about the lack of female geniuses is emblematic of the latter view. However, because the avant-garde places a positive value on ex-centricity, it can thereby furnish a platform for women's agential self-definition:

> In a system in which the marginal, the avant-garde, the subversive, all that disturbs and "undoes the whole" is endowed with positive value, a woman artist who can identify those concepts with her own practice and metaphorically with her own femininity can find in them a source of strength and self-legitimation.[33]

Both Heti and her quasi-fictional avatar make use of experimental tactics to claim a voice for themselves from their marginal positions. The metatextual blurring of the line between author and character is itself illustrative in this regard: Sheila strongly intimates that she wrote *How Should a Person Be?* instead of finishing the play "about women," commissioned by a "feminist theatre company."[34] Sheila's creation of a generically and thematically transgressive document instead of a more straightforward piece of theatre embodies the novel's spirit of radical self-definition. Moreover, the suggestion that Sheila wrote the novel in which she figures as a character collapses the space between diegetic registers, encoding this iconoclasm at the level of form.

Heti's twenty-first-century experimental practice must be distinguished from that of the historical avant-garde, whose aim was "to provoke an experience of the consciousness of a future, potential social order within an audience of the present."[35] Gregory Betts joins Suleiman in emphasizing that, while many contemporary writers display aesthetic continuities with twentieth-century avant-gardes (Dadaism, Surrealism, Cubism, Futurism, and so on), they differ in their ideological foundation.[36] The "sociopolitical revolutionary mandate" that inspired an earlier generation of artists has in recent years been criticized for its (patriarchal) violence,[37] or else deemed irrelevant to contemporary consumerist culture;[38] for Betts, the "mono-lithic domination of capitalist ideology" forecloses the possibility of "any unified challenge or spirit of contestation."[39] Nevertheless, Betts argues that the "post-avant," by virtue of its ideological multiplicity, has a role to play in "facilitating diverse challenges to particular sites of oppression."[40] He distinguishes the "multiplicity and polyvocalism" of contemporary literary communities and discourses from the "militaristic alignment of previous gardes."[41] Some of the most vital examples hail from the framework of iden-tity writing, a broad category whose leading practitioners include women, queer writers, and writers of colour.[42]

How Should a Person Be? exemplifies contemporary identity writing insofar as it combines "the aesthetics of identity with formal experimen-tation to create a writing of unalienated subjectivities that embodies the new or proposed subjectivity in the formal characteristics of the work."[43] In his *New Yorker* review, James Wood situates *How Should a Person Be?* within "a contemporary literary movement that is impatient with con-ventional fiction-making," citing Heti's comments to that effect. Of equal, if not greater, significance, however, is the novel's experimentation with the putatively non-fictional, "female discursive practice" of confessional writing.[44] Heti's use of metatextuality, in particular, makes it difficult to determine exactly whether she is violating the autobiographical pact or the fourth wall.[45] Whereas "[t]he 'confessional' and the 'metafictional' figure almost as opposites,"[46] Heti idiosyncratically fuses these modes; in doing so, she joins other feminist critics and practitioners in challeng-ing the misperception that women are "effusively confessional creatures in a way that men are not."[47] In recent decades, feminist scholars have been working to correct this essentialism by drawing attention to the material circumstances linking genre to gender. They correlate the nonlinear and episodic nature of the diaries, journals, and notebooks that proliferated in the eighteenth century, relating them to the correspondingly "fragmented, interrupted, and formless nature of [women's] lives" in male-dominated society.[48] In the contemporary context, critics have emphasized the effect of the literary marketplace in determining generic norms: Elisabeth Donnelly describes the "double-edged sword" faced by (particularly young) women, who are encouraged to "write about their young and modern lives, particularly when there is the whiff of sex or scandal," and then are accused of self-involvement when they do so. This insight is the starting point for scholarship focused on the techniques that female confessional writers have used to "creatively dodge and escape confessional snares."[49] Heti's avantgarde fusion of autobiography and fiction is consistent with what Gammel has called the "strategies of evasion, displacement and obfuscation" through which contemporary writers react against the gendered expectations that attend the confessional mode.[50]

Heti however departs in significant ways from the second-wave "feminist confession" described by Rita Felski, even as she adopts some of its tactics. According to Felski, this genre emerged in the late twentieth century as women realized the potential of confession to function as political discourse.[51] Felski defines the feminist confession in terms of its dual mandate to relay an individual woman's life while simultaneously selecting the "representative aspects of experience" for a collectivity of women.[52] This twinned objective, she argues, "mitigates" the referential demands of the autobiographical pact, licensing the use of fiction to enable the telling of larger social truths.[53] Although Heti also makes use of fiction, she does so for different reasons. The feminist confession is "less concerned with unique individuality or notions of essential humanity than with delineating the specific problems and experiences which bind women together";[54] Heti's "hideously narcissistic" novel,[55] by contrast, is heavily inflected by the conventions of the *Künstlerroman*, with its emphasis on the artist's individual process of maturation. Sheila's focus on celebrity, genius, and making her life "beautiful" is reminiscent of the very "bourgeois individualism" that the feminist confession ostensibly reacts against.[56] This individualist impulse is encoded in the novel's formal experimentation: rather than "deemphasize the aesthetic and fictive dimension of the text"[57] for the sake of readerly identification, *How Should a Person Be?* announces itself as primarily fictional, albeit a fiction "from life." Although the novel incorporates transcripts of conversations and emails, these putatively "real" documents are heavily stylized (for example, by being presented in the form of enumerated lists) and incorporated into a fictional frame. The blurbs on the dust jacket play up the novel's "originality," heralding "[a] new kind of book and a new kind of person." That this individualist impulse is nevertheless mobilized for the sake of gender critique is consistent with the third-wave tendency "to focus on individual narratives and to think of feminism as a form of individual empowerment."[58] Thus, while *How Should a Person Be?* is clearly operating within a tradition of feminist, confessional reimagining, its formal innovation corresponds to an ideological shift consistent with its third-wave politics.

This third-wave sensibility informs the novel's treatment of sex, which is historically the privileged topic of women's confessional writing. The narrative of sexual transgression is in fact so commonplace that multiple critics have cautioned that telling sexual stories will merely "entrap" women in received modes of thinking and writing.[59] Even the feminist confession, which ostensibly reacts against proscriptive sexual identities, "can at times reproduce images of women uncomfortably close to the stereotypes feminist theorists are attempting to challenge."[60] Heti however avoids rehearsing the timeworn narrative of sexual transgression by incorporating her descriptions of sex into an overarching commentary on gender politics. That Sheila's pursuit of sexual relationships by turns empowers her and degrades her forestalls the reification of sex, forcing the reader to encounter it as the shifting site on which identity politics are played out. Although Sheila dubs her era "the age of some really great blow-job artists" (which she humourously contrasts with the nineteenth-century mastery of the novel),[61] she often discusses sex using the language of abjection. Her appeal to the abject connects her to earlier avant-garde manifestations such as the famous slicing of the eyeball in the surrealist film *Un Chien Andalou*, by Luis Buñuel and Salvador Dalí, Antonin Artaud's appeal to scatology in his essay "Shit to the Spirit," and John Waters's exploitation film *Pink Flamingos*. In *How Should a Person Be?*, the sexually abject manifests itself when Sheila mentions vomiting during fellatio[62] or making out with a wart-riddled man who covers her in "acrid saliva."[63] Regarding the latter, Sheila states: "This is the great privilege of being a woman—we get to decide."[64] Her rhetoric is straight out of the second-wave feminist handbook, whose insistence that "the personal is political" enshrines the value of self-determination. Sheila, however, violates the feminist script by using her hard-won choice to engage in self-effacing acts. To recontextualize Leah Guenther's insight: "instead of confessing transgressions of sex, [Sheila] confesses her sins of gender."[65] Another example is her ill-fated decision to get married because "commitment looked so beautiful to me."[66] Sheila's "messy feminism" involves exercising her choice to make decisions that she knows are ultimately disempowering. As readers, we are called upon simultaneously to endorse and to question her agency, and thereby to participate in the third-wave dialectic of celebration and critique.

Although Sheila repeatedly extolls the virtues of male companionship,[67] she is also deeply scornful of men, who are consistently represented as adversaries to be either repelled ("The last thing I wanted was to be with a man, but it could not be avoided for long, sitting at a bar as I was"),[68] humoured ("I just do what I can not to gag too much"),[69] or begrudgingly embraced (see above). This gender antagonism is however provocatively sublated into sexual role-play in Sheila's passionate liaison with the charismatic artist Israel ("a genius, but not a genius at painting …, a genius at fucking").[70] Beyond its explicit language, what makes the "Interlude for Fucking" particularly transgressive is the way that Israel's acts of extreme sexual domination and Sheila's corresponding desire to be dominated channel a gendered power imbalance. In a representative passage, Sheila rhetorically apostrophizes her lover:

All right, Israel, cum in my mouth. Don't let me wash it out, so that when I talk to those people, I can have your cum swimming in my mouth, and I will smile at them and taste you. It will be as you wanted it, me standing there, tasting your cum, stumbling over my words. And if you see something you don't like, you can correct me later. You can take your hands and bruise my neck, keep pushing till you feel the soft flesh at the back of my throat, so the tears roll down my cheeks like they do every time you thrust your cock to the very back of my throat—like it never was with any other man.[71]

The iconography of tears and bruises evokes the language of sexual violence, recalling the third-wave imaginary, as characterized by Heywood and Drake. Although Sheila plumbs the depths of inequality, rhetorically exhorting Israel to lend her out to his friends and treat her like "a sow you lead around the house with a leash,"[72] this language is recuperated into a project of radical sexual freedom. Once more, Sheila's rhetoric recalls that of Antonin Artaud ("Shit to the Spirit") or Georges Bataille ("The Solar Anus"), both of whom mobilized the language of abjection to critique the received views of Western metaphysics. Here, Sheila's strategic self-abasement anticipates and forecloses the gaze of the male artist (i.e., Israel): if "'imagination' gendered female is a figure on whom the male artist makes proprietary claims,"[73] Sheila rejects the role of benevolent muse. She instead crafts a fantasy of her own devising, in which her subordinate position becomes the imaginative fodder for her ecstatic self-fulfillment. Sheila's use of violent imagery in the context of a consensual sexual relationship bears out the claim that within contemporary feminism, "codes for 'good' and 'bad' as well as gender ideals are no longer polarized."[74] By contrast with the second-wave emphasis on collective identification, Heywood and Drake suggest, third-wave feminism relativizes its terms of judgment, rendering them subjective to the individual.[75] To this extent, Sheila's acts of extreme submission can also be seen as acts of self-empowerment.

This conclusion is, however, complicated when the fantasy slips over into an all too real humiliation: having obeyed Israel's directive to write him a letter extolling the virtues of his penis while exposing herself to a stranger, Sheila looks up midsentence to find "a chubby young boy ... [laughing] up at me openly to see my whole cunt."[76] Sheila flees the scene in shame, "head bent low, heart thumping, looking only at the street."[77] This episode dispels the sexual excitement of Israel's commands, leaving only a residue of degradation; if the abject was previously an empowering challenge to social propriety, here, it becomes associated with a disempowering humiliation. Sheila will later take her revenge by humiliating Israel in turn, denying him his position of sexual mastery through an act of symbolic emasculation:

> We lay silently in my bed, and then my body felt it, deep and calm: what I wanted to do—something I had never done before. Without letting myself think about it a moment more, I shuffled down beneath the covers, saying

to him as I did it, 'I want to sleep beside your cock'. I slithered down there and lay, my lips soft up against his dick. I felt his legs grow tense. 'Get up,' he said. 'No' .... I felt so alert as I felt his dick shrink away, disgusted or ashamed....

I had gone down, gone under, and when several minutes later I surfaced from beneath the hot, stuffy sheets, it felt truly like I was emerging into a new world entirely. Israel kept his back turned. We did not speak the rest of the night.[78]

Sheila exorcises her own degradation by placing Israel in the subordinate role, experiencing a kind of rebirth in the process. This role reversal unmasks the unidirectional flow of power in their relationship: her submissive position, it turns out, is more than just a sexual contrivance. This revelation complicates our earlier endorsement of her willed passivity, which we now cannot help but incorporate into a larger social narrative of male domination. There is however no coherent feminist standpoint from which to evaluate a relationship in which a power imbalance is by turns erotic and degrading. Heti's complex descriptions of sex prevent us from extrapolating any maxim for how a woman "should be," sidestepping the false "Madonna/whore dichotomy"[79] that either under- or overemphasizes sexuality as the means to women's self-actualization.

In addition to her fraught relationships with men, Sheila's deeply ambivalent relationships with other women constitute another violation of the second-wave, confessional script. One of her primary difficulties in fulfilling the feminist theatre company's commission is that she admittedly "[doesn't] know anything about women!"[80] She moreover confesses that she has no idea how to be friends with another woman, and is in fact unsure that such a scenario is even practicable: she fears that "[a] woman can't find or take up home in the heart of another woman—not permanently. It's just not a safe place to land."[81] Sheila's alienation from both women and the discourse of feminism signals her lack of identification with prescribed models for "how to be" and again distinguishes her project from the collectivism that typifies second-wave ideology. And yet, the defining relationship of the novel will be her friendship with the artist Margaux (who is based on the visual artist Margaux Williamson): in the words of one reviewer, "*How Should a Person Be?* is a *Bildungsroman* about two women trying to become artists."[82] If Sheila has spent her life avoiding relationships with women, Margaux, by contrast, has spent her life longing for a female counterpart: "I searched high and low and found you! All my life all I wanted was a girl!" she states.[83] Margaux, however, does not want a friend to gossip with: a notable feature of their relationship is the near absence of conversations about men.[84] In part, Sheila tells us, this can be attributed to the fact that Margaux "was made impatient by conversations about relationships or men," a reality reflected in the dialogue recorded in the novel.[85] More importantly, however, it is because Sheila and Margaux simply have other things to discuss. Early on, Sheila defines her relationship with Margaux as one of artistic collaboration: "Margaux complements me in interesting ways," she tells us. "She paints my picture, and I record what she is saying. We do whatever we can to make the other one feel famous."[86] Their intellectual kinship is distilled in exchanges on topics such as which artists are "funny" (Harmony Korine and Werner Herzog are funny. Richard Serra is not funny).[87] Sheila's ultimate decision to divorce her husband and instead to seek fulfillment in her creative collaboration with Margaux deviates from the social script that privileges heterosexual marriage as a woman's primary goal. While Sheila's general attitude toward women borders on misogyny, her relationship with Margaux is an exemplary representation of female complexity. Sheila's nuanced attitude toward both men and women challenges normative gender roles, communicating her individualistic understanding of identity.

It is, nevertheless, important to distinguish Sheila's idiosyncratic self-definition from the "anarchic individualism" that characterizes the historical avant-garde.[88] Although Sheila charts her own ideological path, she does so surrounded by a community of artist friends with whom she is in constant, overt, and implicit dialogue: as Menachem Feuer points out, "the people she could take guidance from are by and large on the same journey as she is."[89] Emphasizing the novel's substantial Jewish content, Feuer declares Sheila a "female schlemiel, amongst a small community of schlemiel-artists."[90] Sheila's imbrication in her artistic community can be likened to Heti's own collaborative praxis: in a piece by Sholem Krishtalka (the "real" Sholem) entitled "You and Me and Her and Us and Them: A Conversation on Using and Being Used," Krishtalka describes the "snarl of knotted relationships and processes," all of which bind their Toronto-based artistic network.[91] In that same article, Heti describes the process of fictionalizing her friends as "an expression of love."[92] This affective description of artistic praxis as a collective, processual undertaking must be distinguished from the model of romantic isolation associated with the historical avant-garde. Sheila registers her criticism of the "phoney-baloney genius crap" peddled by "Mark Z." (Mark Z. Danielewski, author of the experimental novel *House of Leaves*) and "Christian B." (experimental poet Christian Bök), whose commercial success belies their putative avant-gardism.[93] Her critique, which finds its fullest expression in her description of the commodified, corporatized Art Basel, recalls Peter Bürger's thesis that the avant-garde is inevitably doomed to be reappropriated as a bourgeois commodity.[94] Having paid her $20 entrance fee and stood in line, Sheila is finally allowed to enter the "cold, cavernous, convention-centre air," where her first observation is the juxtaposition of two phrases: "USB [a bank, the fair's sponsor] welcomes you to Art Basel Miami Beach" and a quotation from Andy Warhol, "Everybody's sense of beauty is different from everybody else's."[95] The irony of Andy Warhol's being yoked into the service of the very same consumerism thematized in his work is not lost on the two artists: Margaux's gloss of the line from Warhol is, "It's saying you can be rich and stupid about art. You're all welcome."[96] Later, the pair run into an "old rich couple" who encapsulate this attitude; they have "so little wall space that whatever they bought in Miami would end up *in rotation*."[97] This couple's relationship to art as a commodified form of social capital is completely antithetical to the transcendent, existential function that art serves for Sheila and her circle.

Feuer's concept of the "schlemiel-artist" is useful in distinguishing the art of Sheila and her friends from that of Mark Z., Christian B., and the commodities owned by the rich couple. Although Margaux does in fact have work on display at Art Basel, when asked whether she's sold anything, she says that she "doesn't know," "doesn't think so," or at any rate, "hasn't asked."[98] This attitude is typical of Margaux, who is "embarrassed" when people praise her art because of her "shame about all the things wrong in the world that she wasn't trying to fix";[99] for her, art is a mode of being that she is driven to pursue almost in spite of herself. Sheila, likewise, fails to produce a coherent and potentially remunerative piece of writing for the feminist theatre company, instead generating the "messy book"[100] that the reader is implied to be holding in her hands. The novel's closing image—a squash game meant to establish the winner of the Ugly Painting Competition, played by Margaux and Sholem, neither of whom knows the rules—embodies this same sense of creative production as extrinsic to any social or financial economy. Margaux's partner Misha summarizes the novel's aesthetic ideology when criticizing Sholem's "fear of being bad": "It's *good* for an artist to try things. It's *good* for an artist to be ridiculous."[101] The Ugly Painting Competition has proven that slavish adherence to rules can only produce the "textbook ugly";[102] Art Basel has revealed the ugliness of commodification. Just as Artaud proclaims "shit to the spirit" so as to restore the creative pre-eminence of "the body that it vampirized,"[103] Sheila will ultimately declare "shit to the beautiful," and also "shit to the 'phoney-baloney genius'":

> Now it was time to write. I went straight into my studio and I thought about everything I had, all the trash and the shit inside me. And I started throwing that trash and throwing that shit, and the castle started to emerge.... And I began to light up my soul with scenes.
>   I made what I could with what I had. And I finally became a real girl.[104]

This epiphany becomes the basis for the "post-avant" feminist praxis embodied in her eventual novel. In abandoning the quest for beauty and perfection, as well as the corresponding desire for social or commercial success, Sheila also frees herself from the "highly conventional metaphors and narratives of gender, views of women as static, immobile, eternal, goddess-like," all of which ironically, pepper the discourse of the historical avant-garde.[105] Like Woolf before her, it is only after killing the "angel in the house" that the "real girl" can appear.

II

By contrast with the formal and thematic experimentation of *How Should a Person Be?*, the critical discourse surrounding the novel has rehearsed "decades old claims that women writing about their private lives are narcissistic, solipsistic, vain."[106] Initially rejected by both Heti's American publisher Farrar, Straus & Giroux as well as by a number of other American and Canadian publishers, the book began to gain critical attention only when two excerpts were published in Mark Greif's tastemaking, online literary magazine *n+1*, one of which was graphically sexual. In an interview with the *New York Observer,* Greif attributed the reticence to a "male-dominated culture of literature."[107] Art critic Dave Hickey is also quoted in that article as stating, "Jonathan Franzen can get away with things because he's a boy. Getting a blow job is different from giving one." With that "help-ful prod from the avant garde" (notably comprised only of men), Heti was suddenly inundated with calls from interested publishers, including Henry Holt, an imprint of Macmillan, which ultimately published the novel in the United States.[108] This trajectory rehearses two arguments repeatedly made by feminist critics: that women's confessional writing is endorsed only when it is overtly sexual, and that, often, female voices are heard only once they have been "appropriated, tamed, and recolonized" under the name of a patriarchal "author/ity."[109]

Some have accused the novel's critics of the same literary sexism that almost impeded its publication, citing, for example, James Wood, the reviewer from the *New Yorker,* who, on the one hand, offers rhapsodic praise for Ben Lerner's "subtle, sinuous, and very funny first novel," *Leaving the Atocha Station,* but on the other hand offers a tepid assessment of *How Should a Person Be?*[110] Although Wood opens the two reviews with the requisite references to the literary masters of yore (Dostoyevsky makes an appearance in both), Lerner's protagonist is inducted into the lineage of "those frustrated Russian antiheroes" and is described as "a convincing representative of twenty-first-century American *homo literatus*," while Heti's novel is a "collection box for gathering the stray donations and aperçus and complaints of her generation." Although Wood does at times recognize the merits of Heti's book, he describes her prose as "what one might charitably call basic"; "If I wanted to hear that," he writes of a particular passage, "I could settle in at Starbucks and wait for the schoolkids to get out at three o'clock." Perhaps most notably, Wood neglects even to mention the pronounced autobiographical elements of Lerner's novel[111] while making much of them in Heti's case—a difference that reveals the tendency to overemphasize the confessional elements of women's writing while downplaying similar qualities in writing by men.

For critics such as Michelle Dean, Wood's tonal discrepancy is indicative of a gender bias in literary reviewing: "influential, 'serious' men," she argues, are put off by novels that "focus on the intellectual effects of female friendships."[112] Anna North agrees that "[s]tories by and about young women—about 'girls' and 'girly' concerns—are increasingly capturing our attention, and they may force a still male-dominated cultural establishment to reconsider what it considers 'serious.'"[113] Katie Roiphe has pointed out that the same avant-gardism endorsed in men's confessional writing is perceived as self-indulgent or narcissistic when produced by a woman: "what in a male writer appears as courage or innovation or literary heroics would be read, in a woman, even by the liberal, enlightened, and literary, as hubris or worse."[114] She accordingly claims that a woman could never have written a work like Karl Ove Knausgård's multi-volume, 3,500-page, autobiographical epic, *Min Kamp* [*My Struggle*]. Following Woolf's trajectory, Roiphe makes her point by imagining the fate of Knausgård's female alter-ego. In *A Room of One's Own*, Woolf invents the character of Judith Shakespeare, sister to the Bard, tracing the inevitable demise of Judith at the hands of a sexist society blind to her abilities.[115] In a similar thought experiment, Roiphe imagines a writer named "Carla Krauss" publishing a book like Knausgård's, in which she details her daily struggles. Such a work, she concludes, would be universally dismissed as the author's "nattering on about inanities," because "[t]he particular variety of rage aimed at women who document their daily lives ... is deeply entrenched and irrational. It's not just that we don't think of what they are doing as art, but that it annoys us, riles us. It feels presumptuous, vain, narrow, feminine, clichéd."[116] Roiphe makes two related claims: that confessional texts by men and women are evaluated according to different standards, and that the label of "avant-garde" is reserved for male writers. Ironically, two years before writing this article, Roiphe panned Heti's novel; she accused it of "shallowness and self-consciousness all the way through," thereby confirming her own subsequent insight regarding our impatience with such narratives.[117]

Heti has herself weighed in on the limitations faced by female writers; where Roiphe speaks about the mundane, Heti makes a similar point regarding women's inability to delve into the universal:

[T]he most ancient of philosophical questions are questions of ethics and questions like "how should a person be?" [However, if] you put these concerns in the mouth of a contemporary North American woman who has sex, it's called "navel-gazing," even though it's the exact same question humans have been asking forever.[118]

Arguments like these have gained particular traction in the wake of the backlash against the "girly" narratives currently proliferating within popular culture, many of which contain varying degrees of autobio-graphical content.[119] In a recent piece for *Salon*, Stassa Edwards suggests that it is time to retire the word "overshare," a popular invective directed at confessional writers (and the "2008 Word of the Year," according to the *Merriam-Webster Dictionary*). The problem with this label, argues Edwards, is that it is "weirdly gendered," seemingly "designed to patrol the boundaries of female confessional writing; to level the accusation that a woman overshares is to indicate that she has crossed some invisible boundary of 'acceptable' material."[120] Edwards cites Heti among the writers thus accused. The issue is complicated by *How Should a Person Be?*'s avowedly fictional status. While the novel's experimental form does as much to ward off autobiographical interpretation as it does to invite it, and although Heti has cited Kenneth Goldsmith, Richard Serra, and Søren Kierkegaard among her artistic influences,[121] confessional readings persist. Rather than focus on the book's challenge to generic norms, such readings reinscribe *How Should a Person Be?* within a pre-set female literary trajectory. Along the same lines, Chris Kraus presciently predicted that Heti's novel would be compared to "fatuous blogs and social media" rather than to literary innovators like Don Quixote. That she was ultimately correct speaks to the limited conceptual rubrics applied to writing by young women.

In both its content and its critical reception, *How Should a Person Be?* makes us question the connection between gender and genre. My contention is that Heti's simultaneous use and subversion of confessional discourse maintains the same tension "between criticism and the pleasures of consumption"—that typifies third-wave feminism. The insight that there "is no ideal model for how [her] mind should be"[122]—an insight that begins as a reflection on the lack of female role models—ultimately inspires Sheila's quest for artistic self-definition. That it leads her into the territory of experimental art confirms Susan Suleiman's characterization of the margin as a potentially generative space for female self-definition. By contrast, the negative reaction to her book reminds us of the ongoing challenges that women face in a male-dominated literary market.[123] These challenges are particularly acute for female experimental writers, whose formal innovations are often ignored or disparaged. The reception of *How Should a Person Be?* is a cautionary tale for critics, the moral of which is that we must avoid reducing the "girly" narratives of Heti, Dunham, and their contemporaries, to a set of gendered stereotypes. Otherwise, like the military vanguard from which it draws its name, the avant-garde will continue to refer to a group of powerful men.

NOTES

1 John Barber, "How Should a Novel Be? Don't Ask Sheila Heti," *Globe and Mail* (13 April 2013).

2 James Adams, "Margaux Williamson: Meet the Artist Whose Life Has Been the Stuff of Fiction," *Globe and Mail* (24 May 2014).

3 Heti and Dunham are open admirers of each other's work: see Heti's effusive comments to Thessaly La Force in "Sheila Heti on *How Should a Person Be?*," *The Paris Review* (18 June 2012), and Dunham's choice of *How Should a Person Be?* as a favourite book in *Entertainment Weekly*, http://howshouldapersonbe .tumblr.com/post/25190872067/lena-dunham-chooses-how-should-a-person -be-as-a.

4 Gregory Betts, *Avant-Garde Canadian Literature: The Early Manifestations* (Toronto: University of Toronto Press, 2013), 84.

5 Leslie Heywood and Jennifer Drake, "'It's All about the Benjamins': Economic Determinants of Third Wave Feminism in the United States," *Third Wave Feminism: A Critical Exploration* (New York: Palgrave Macmillan, 2004), 52.

6 Irene Gammel, "Introduction," *Confessional Politics* (Carbondale: Southern Illinois University Press, 1999), 1.

7 There are in fact two versions of *How Should a Person Be?* The American edition, published by Henry Holt/House of Anansi in 2012, varies slightly from the Canadian version published by Anansi in 2010. This essay uses the US edition. For a discussion of the differences between the two versions, see Anna Altman, "Two Versions, One Heti," *Paris Review* (27 July 2012), http://www .theparisreview.org/blog/2012/07/27/two-versions-one-heti/.

8 To name but a few, see Anna Holmes, "The Age of Girlfriends," *The New Yorker*; Anna North, "The Rise of the Girly Narrative," *BuzzFeed*; Alyssa

Rosenberg, "Sheila Heti, Lena Dunham, and the Challenges of Telling 'Girly' Stories in Film and Television," *Slate*; Susie Mesure, "The Rise of the Woman-child," *The Independent*; and Sady Doyle, "Vulnerability: The New Girl Power," *In These Times.*

9 North, "The Rise."

10 Rebecca Munford, "'Wake Up and Smell the Lipgloss': Gender, Generation and the (A)politics of Girl Power," *Third Wave Feminism: A Critical Exploration* (New York: Palgrave Macmillan, 2004), 143.

11 Munford, "'Wake Up," 143.

12 Munford, 143–144.

13 Heywood and Drake, "It's All About," 3. The term "third wave" was initially coined in the mid-1980s by a group of feminist academics and activists who collaborated on the (never-published) volume *The Third Wave: Feminist Perspectives on Racism*. It was subsequently developed in anthologies such as Rebecca Walker's *Changing the Face of Feminism* (1995) and Barbara Findlen's *Listen Up: Voices from the Next Feminist Generation* (1995) (Orr 30). It must be noted, as Catherine Orr has, that "the term is hard to pin down": third-wave feminism encompasses a wide variety of perspectives, many of which are at odds with each other (29). This essay draws mainly on the account by Heywood and Drake; for a useful discussion of the internal contradictions within third-wave feminism. See Catherine Orr, "Charting the Currents of the Third Wave," *Hypatia* 3.12 (Summer 1997): 29–45. See Stacy Gillis, Gillian Howie, and Rebecca Munford, eds., *Third Wave Feminism: A Critical Exploration* (New York: Palgrave Macmillan, 2004). And see Jennifer Scanlon, "Sexy from the Start: Anticipatory Elements of Second Wave Feminism," *Women's Studies* 38 (2009): 127–150.

14 See Heti's interview with Thessaly La Force in *The Paris Review*.

15 Sheila Heti, *How Should a Person Be?* (Toronto: House of Anansi, 2012), 13.

16 Heti, *How*, 2.

17 Heti, 13.

18 Heti, 53.

19 Heti, 112.

20 Linda Hutcheon, *A Theory of Parody: The Teachings of Twentieth-Century Art Forms* (New York: Methuen, 1985), 32.

21 Becky Ohlsen, "'How Should a Person Be? Review: Young Woman's Navel-gazing Frustrates but Makes You Think," *The Oregonian* (23 June 2012), http://

www.oregonlive.com/books/index.ssf/2012/06/how_should_a_person_be
_review.html.

22 Gammel, "Introduction," 3. Along the same lines, Robert McGill uses the
phrase "biographical desire" to describe "the desire to treat a literary text as
a way of coming to know its author" (67). His discussion of the confessional
readings that have accompanied Elizabeth Smart's quasi-autobiographical *By
Grand Central Station I Sat Down and Wept* is highly germane to the present
topic. See Robert McGill, "A Necessary Collaboration: Biographical Desire and
Elizabeth Smart," *English Studies in Canada* 33.3 (September 2007): 67–88.

23 Elizabeth Donnelly, "Why Does Women's Confessional Writing Get People
So Riled Up?" *Flavorwire* (8 July 2014). See also Alyssa Rosenberg, "Sheila Heti,
Lena Dunham, and the Challenges of Telling 'Girly' Stories in Film
and Television," *Slate* (9 July 2012); Laurie Penny, "Laurie Penny on Lena
Dunham's Girls: It Can't Represent Every Woman, but Shouldn't Have To," *New
Statesman* (4 February 2014). As well, see Stassa Edwards, "Enough 'Overshar-
ing': It's Time to Retire One of the Media's Favorite Words," *Salon*
(17 July 2014).

24 James Wood, "True Lives," *The New Yorker* (25 June 2012).

25 Quoted in Barber, "How Should."

26 Heti, *How*, 31–32.

27 Heti, 3.

28 Heti, 224.

29 Virginia Woolf, "Professions for Women," *The Norton Anthology of English
Literature*, 7th ed., Vol. B (New York: Norton, 2001), 2477.

30 Woolf, "Professions," 2477.

31 Woolf, 2477.

32 Susan Suleiman, *Subversive Intent: Gender, Politics, and the Avant-Garde*
(Cambridge: Harvard University Press, 1990), 14.

33 Suleiman, *Subversive Intent*, 17.

34 Heti, *How,* 41.

35 Betts, *Avant*, 14–15.

36 Betts, 79.

37 See Suleiman, *Subversive Intent*.

38 Betts, *Avant*, 79–81. Betts lists Frank Davey, Pauline Butling, Susan Rudy, and
Jeff Derksen.

39 Betts, 83.

40 Betts, 84.

41 Betts, 85.

42 Betts, 84.

43 Betts, 84.

44 Gammel, "Introduction," 1.

45 Philippe Lejeune argues that a work labelled as autobiographical promises that the author, narrator, and protagonist will be identical, creating an "autobiographical pact" with its reader (12). See Philippe Lejeune, *On Autobiography,* trans. Katherine Leary (Minneapolis: University of Minnesota Press, 1989).

46 Bran Nichol, "'The Memoir as Self-Destruction': A Heartbreaking Work of Staggering Genius," *Modern Confessional Writing: New Critical Essays* (New York: Routledge, 2009), 107.

47 Leah Guenther, "Bridget Jones's Diary: Confessing Post-feminism," *Modern Confessional Writing: New Critical Essays* (New York: Routledge, 2009), 89.

48 Estelle C. Jelinek, "Introduction: Women's Autobiography and the Male Tradition," *Women's Autobiography: Essays in Criticism* (Bloomington: Indiana University Press, 1980), 19.

49 Gammel, "Introduction," 2. These are considered in works such as Irene Gammel's *Confessional Politics,* Leigh Gilmore's *Autobiographics,* and Jo Gill's *Modern Confessional Writing: New Critical Essays.*

50 Jo Gill, "Introduction," *Modern Confessional Writing: New Critical Essays* (New York: Routledge, 2009), 7.

51 Rita Felski, *Beyond Feminist Aesthetics* (Cambridge: Harvard University Press, 1989), 87. Among Felski's examples of this subgenre are Kate Millett's *Flying* (1974), Audre Lorde's *Cancer Journals* (1980), and Ann Oakley's *Taking It Like a Woman* (1984).

52 Felski, *Beyond,* 95.

53 Felski, 94.

54 Felski, 94.

55 Wood, "True Lives."

56 Felski, *Beyond,* 94.

57 Felski, 101.

58 Heywood and Drake, "It's All About," 14.

59 Gammel, "Introduction," 7–8.

60 Felski, *Beyond,* 119.

61 Sheila's reflections on her era also bear out the insights of Heywood and Drake, both of whom note that women in the third wave "are as likely or more likely to identify with their generation as with their gender" ("It's All About," 14).

62 Heti, *How*, 4.

63 Heti, 40.

64 Heti, 40.

65 Guenther, "Bridget," 93. Guenther was speaking about the character Bridget Jones, a clear foremother to the current crop of "messy feminists."

66 Heti, 22.

67 Heti, 31, 41.

68 Heti, 231.

69 Heti, 3.

70 Heti, 197.

71 Heti, 120.

72 Heti, 126.

73 Rachel Blau DuPlessis, "Pater-Daughter: Male Modernists and Female Readers," *The Pink Guitar* (New York: Routledge, 1990), 54.

74 Heywood and Drake, "It's All About," 16.

75 Heywood and Drake, 14.

76 Heti, *How*, 226.

77 Heti, 227.

78 Heti, 271–272.

79 Munford, "Wake Up," 142.

80 Heti, *How*, 41.

81 Heti, 33.

82 Joanna Biggs, "It Could Be Me," *London Review of Books* 35.2 (January 2013).

83 Heti, *How*, 247.

84 Several reviewers have pointed out that *How Should a Person Be?* is one of the rare works that passes the Bechdel Test, a simple feminist metric invented by the graphic novelist Allison Bechdel, who stipulates only that (a) two named characters (b) must talk to each other (c) about something other than a man (see, for example, Biggs; Stoeffel). Although this may seem like a minimal requirement, it is shocking how many works fail the test. This is particularly true of films: in a database of 5,615 movies, only 57 percent of them actually met all three requirements (http://bechdeltest.com/statistics/).

85 Heti, *How*, 198.

86 Heti, 3.

87 Heti, 99.

88 Betts, *Avant*, 83.

89 Menachem Feuer, "The Postmodern Chelm, or The Artistic Community in Sheila Heti's 'How Should a Person Be?'—Part I," *The Home of Schlemiel Theory* (11 June 2014).

90 Menachem Feuer, "The Postmodern Chelm." A *schlemiel* is a Yiddish-derived word denoting a "stupid, awkward, or unlucky person" (Oxford); in Feuer's usage, the term refers to a person who is "somewhere between a man and a child" ("Personal Accounts"). The term is fitting, insofar as Sheila and her friends are flawed idealists whose grand ambitions are often beset by failure (see, for example, the "ugly painting contest," which, although devised by Sholem, sets off "a train of really depressing and terrible thoughts" that ultimately "plunges him into despair" [14]). See also Menachem Feuer, "Personal Accounts of the Schlemiel (Take 1)—Schlemiel, the Son of Schlemiel," *The Home of Schlemiel Theory* (18 February 2013).

91 Sholem Krishtalka, "Me and You and Her and Us and Them: A Conversation on Using and Being Used," *C Magazine* 109 (2011): 6.

92 Sholem Krishtalka, "Me and You," 13.

93 Heti, *How*, 4.

94 Bürger, *Theory*, 53.

95 Heti, *How*, 107.

96 Heti, 108.

97 Heti, 109.

98 Heti, 109.

99 Heti, 17.

100 Wood, "True Lives."

101 Heti, *How*, 18.

102 Heti, 293.

103 Antonin Artaud, "Shit to the Spirit," *Antonin Artaud Anthology* (San Francisco: City Lights Books, 1965), 111.

104 Heti, *How*, 277.

105 DuPlessis, "Pater-Daughter," 44.

106 Guenther, "Bridget," 90.

107 Stoeffel, "The Problem."

108 Barber, "How Should."

109 Gammel, "Introduction," 4.

110 Wood, "True Lives." See, for example, Michelle Dean, "Listening to Women: Why Smart, Serious Men Have Misunderstood Sheila Heti's New Book," *Slate*

Book Review (29 June 2012). See also Anna North, "The Rise of the 'Girly' Narrative," *BuzzFeed* (5 July 2012).

111 As Heti summarizes in her review of *Leaving the Atocha Station* in the *London Review of Books*, "It's hard not to take Adam's life as a version of Lerner's: both are young poets raised in Topeka, Kansas; both spent time in New York among 'the dim kids of the stars'; both spent a year in Madrid on a poetry fellowship (Adam's unnamed; Lerner's a Fulbright)." See Sheila Heti, "I Hadn't Even Seen the Alhambra," *London Review of Books* 34.16 (August 2012).

112 Dean, "Listening."

113 North, "The Rise."

114 Katie Roiphe, "Her Struggle," *Slate* (7 July 2014).

115 Virginia Woolf, "A Room of One's Own," *The Norton Anthology of English Literature,* 7th Edition, Vol. B (New York: Norton, 2001), 2439.

116 Roiphe, "Her Struggle."

117 Katie Roiphe, "Not Quite How a Person Should Be: Grow Up, Sheila Heti!" *Slate* (6 July 2012).

118 North, "The Rise."

119 Edwards documents accusations of "oversharing," levelled at Susan Cheever, Lena Chen, Joyce Maynard, Marie Calloway, Kathryn Harrison, Laurie Penny, and Sheila Heti. Lena Dunham is another frequent target of this rhetoric.

120 Edwards, "Enough."

121 See Adam Robinson, "How Should a Person Be?" *BOMB Magazine* (11 June 2012), and La Force, "Sheila Heti."

122 Heti, *How*, 3.

123 *See* Alison Flood, "Men Still Dominate Books World, Study Shows," *The Guardian* (6 March 2013). Another depressingly illuminating set of statistics can be found in the infographic from the Canadian Women in the Literary Arts (CWILA): in 2013, 57 percent of the books reviewed in Canada were written by men, and only 25 percent of male critics reviewed a book written by a woman ("2013 CWILA Count").

SONNET L'ABBÉ

Erasures from the Territories Called Canada: Sharpening the Gaze at White Backgrounds

In a series of interviews that comprise one of the few sustained, critical investigations of erasure poetry, blogger Andrew David King for *Kenyon Review* asks the authors of seven of the most significant publications of contemporary erasure (all, but one, American) about the politics of their writing process. "I don't think the act of doing it is political at all," says Matthew Rohrer, co-author of a *Gentle Reader!*, an erasure of Romantic poems: "but ... lots of political stuff comes out of it, and that's just because that's what we were engaged with at the time."[1] "Political?" repeats Travis MacDonald, author of *The O Mission Repo*, a book that he produced by crossing out and blurring the text of the 9-11 Commission Report: "No. I don't think so. Not at all."[2] Srikanth Reddy, author of *Voyager*, an erasure of the memoir of Kurt Waldheim, finds the question "hard to answer":

> poeticizing a political text is of course an act that has a political aspect—but one that is very hard to pin down. Is it reclaiming the political as a source for aesthetic work? Is it a way to show that politics itself has a kind of poetics operating within it? I find myself waxing pretentious here, but I think these are real questions. I just don't know how to answer them.[3]

Matthea Harvey says that she can see politics in a work of book-art that physically cuts up all the pages of a white supremacist text, but her own book, *Of Lamb*, which Harvey has produced by applying liquid white-out to text from a biography of Charles Lamb, "isn't," she insists, "meant to

197

be a political act—more of an homage."[4] David Dodd Lee argues that an erasure's political dimension depends entirely on what source texts are chosen. Because his own work appropriates the work of John Ashbery, whom Lee says resists calling his own poetry political, Lee likewise sees his own appropriations as equally without politics. Lee has also decided that Ashbery's work has "implied permission" for Lee to perform the erasures and appropriation. Still, he admits, "being asked to think about it does (and did) occasionally make me nervous," mainly because he anticipates having to answer to charges of copyright infringement.[5]

Only M. NourbeSe Philip, the Caribbean-identified Canadian of the group, affirms the political nature of her work. "Any strategy, even the lyric, can be political depending on context and intent," she remarks:

> The question, however, does give rise to an issue for writers like myself who come from countries and cultures that have been colonised: that is that many of our "master" narratives or documents are themselves the products of the coloniser, constructed on erasures of all types, who was physically exploiting the inhabitants of these countries and appropriating their cultures and their products for their own use.[6]

For Philip, the act of appropriating text resonates with other historical acts of appropriation. Philip says that she sees the poetic practice of erasure resonating with "erasures of all types" because she writes from the point of view of peoples whose histories and languages have been erased by colonial practices.

But writers do not need to identify with colonized peoples to affirm that the logic of stealing is at work in the various iterations of found poetry. Austin Kleon follows up his pop-market erasure *Newspaper Blackout* with a glossy manifesto-cum-coffee table book called *Steal Like an Artist*. Describing himself as "obsessed with collage," Kleon writes: "[W]hen I was making the newspaper blackout work, I started noticing how many of my favorite artists used words like 'steal' and 'borrow' and 'filch' and 'theft' to describe their own methods." When asked if he's concerned about misrepresenting the ideas of others, Kleon responds that, although he "make[s] his living off copyrights …, I honestly don't worry…. Other people's ideas interest me only in terms of what I can do with them, where I can take them."[7] The difference in politics between Kleon and Philip, between commercial *bricoleur* and literary activist, lies not in whether or not they feel erasure is a kind of appropriation (they both feel it is), but in whether they assume or interrogate the artist's unchecked entitlement to source materials.

The Americans in King's interviews seem to understand politics to mean explicit, thematic engagements with "big-P" international politics (references to Bush = political; destroying a Holy War Book = political; making a nursery-rhyme-like picture book out of Charles Lamb's biography = not political). When the poet who has defaced an internal report on 9-11 calls his book "not at all" political, however, I hear a denial not only of the inherent politicality of the source text, but also of the act of repossessing and reframing it. From the American erasurists, I detect a general reluctance to self-identify as political or to ascribe a set of values to erasure poetics. Only Philip describes her use of erasure as a formal choice necessitated by her urge to find a "redemptive strategy to deal with absences and erasures."[8] Philip's insistence on poetics-as-politics affirms that formal approach can either challenge or trade upon dominant, culturally specific assumptions about how a text performs authority.

ERASURE AND SILENCE

In this essay, I discuss some of the "significant works of erasure" from the Canadian literary field (that is, poetry published in the territories called Canada, composed by deleting, erasing, or hiding text from a source-work), and I suggest that collectively, poets working in these territories have been (as of 2014) more eager than their American counterparts to deploy erasure in strategies of explicitly politicized, cultural critique. I will first look at "No Comment" by Garry Morse—a poem that Lorraine Weir calls a "great central sequence of erasure poems," all of which which appear in *Discovery Passages*, one of "the canonic texts of contemporary Indigenous and Canadian writing."[9] I then discuss Shane Rhodes's "Wite Out," an erasure poem from *X*, the book in which Rhodes makes found poetry of Canadian treaty documents. Then I analyze the relation of form to cultural politics in the book-length works *The Place of Scraps* by Jordan Abel, and *Zong!* by Marlene NourbeSe Philip. Finally, I contrast the ways that erasures written in the territories called Canada have worked with the gestures of silencing and with the gestures of American poet Vanessa Place.

Morse, Rhodes, Abel, and Philip all take up the trope of European colonialism as a wilful erasure of Indigenous cultures, and these writers focus their attention on colonialism's textual-material practices. The poets choose, as their source texts, documents that have produced, justified, legalized, denied, aided, and abetted the violent silencing and dehumanization of various groups of people. In their approach, these poets differ from the American poets mentioned insofar as these Canadian writers and Indigenous writers do not simply enact their politics through the choice of a political document as source text (as Lee suggests), nor do these poets discover that their own concerns about prevailing party politics have guided their excising hand (as Rohrer has). Instead, these poets choose erasure as part of the "small-p" politics that Craig Dworkin describes as including "all relations of power, however local and miniscule, and the ethics of their distribution."[10] Rather than considering their erasures as poems that may or may not be propagandist or have politics "in" them, these poets are, in the very act of resorting to erasure, taking up the politics "of" the poem: "what is signified by its form, enacted by its structures, implicit in its philosophy of language, how it positions its reader, and a range of questions relating to the poem as material object—how it was produced, distributed, exhanged."[11] Or, as Smaro Kamboureli might put it, these contemporary poets writing from the territories called Canada are using erasure to "foreground the materiality of language" and to make readers aware of the power that language wields "as *act* (not [just] as representation)."[12]

"NO COMMENT": MORSE'S SILENCE AS REFUSAL TO DIGNIFY

"I have never understood the relationship between poetry and politics," Garry Morse writes, in a conversation about Jack Spicer, whom he names as one of his key influences. Morse speculates that Spicer "felt that political issues abrogated language for its own peculiar motives, which is a kind of dishonesty."[13] For Morse, poets who are "knee-deep in political concerns [are] minds beset by the ceaseless ebb and flux of material concerns," and are therefore unable to be the kind of Orphic, "babbling prophet(s)" that represent Morse's ideal. Whereas most contemporary erasurists see themselves working in a lineage of visual and concrete poetry that traces itself back to continental European, inter-arts modernism, Morse situates himself loosely in the Black Mountain avant-garde tradition that fed the poetics of the Berkeley Renaissance and the Canadian West Coast.

Morse's fragmentary, spatialized aesthetic shows fidelity to the *Paterson*-esque strategy of collage in the works of such poets as Robert Duncan, George Bowering, and Daphne Marlatt. The cascading, open-field lines in most of *Discovery Passages* weave Morse's voice with fragments of quotation. Formally, Morse echoes an earlier generation of white, West Coast poets whose documentary, anthropologically inspired, found poetries are "tied to preoccupations with Canadian nation-building and its attendant immigration stories and mythologies," and Morse extends a poetic tradition that has "functioned as a sort of literary archeology focused on recuperating and repositioning histories."[14]

However, there is one thread of *Discovery Passages* in which Morse's strategy of collage sustains and focuses its engagement to its particular source texts so that it can be read as erasure. In "No Comment," Morse's loose cascades tighten, and the lyric voice of the book, amidst which fragments usually flow, all but disappears. Thin columns of text, in italics, as though they are all epigraphs, fill the page. If the unitalicized text in *Discovery Passages* is Morse's lyric voice, that voice in this thirty-page series decides not to speak, except to identify the authors of these short stacks of clipped lines. Here is one of the poems in this series:

considerable
crating

considerable
amount
labor
involved
segregating
exhibit

fair
amount
set on

paraphernalia

belonging

Wm. M. Halliday, *Indian Agent*
June 23, 1922 [15]

The series documents the correspondence between government officials (among them Superintendent General Duncan Campbell Scott and John A. Macdonald) and Kwakwaka'wakw writers—a correspondence that belies the opportunism of officials who have criminalized potlatch, then have profited from the seizure and sale of potlatch-related artifacts. A narrative is discernable; at first the reader may wonder if the heartbreaking sequence is in fact an erasure or if it is a "creative" non-fiction. Morse has indeed used actual letters. Ironically, these official documents are themselves a kind of fiction: according to Christopher Bracken, the "potlatch" (a Chinook word meaning "gift" and a term not used in Kwak'wala) "was in fact invented by the nineteenth-century Canadian law that sought to destroy it," and the letters themselves are evidence of "a colonialist discourse in the act of constructing fictions about certain First Nations and then deploying those fictions against them."[16]

Morse's redaction of these letters to a handful of key words and short phrases exposes the function of the missing text. By excising the officious bumpf that overlaid a tone of judicial objectivity onto language that legalized the dispossession of a people, Morse enacts a "reverse whitewashing"[17] that lays bare the non-Indigenous authors' contempt for their Indigenous correspondents. Procedurally, Morse's erasure of the source text to make new poems is similar to minimalist erasures by Matthea Harvey and Ronald Johnson, but Morse does not, like these authors, primarily seek to mine a new, original lyric work from the source. The blank space around the words in "No Comment" is the same open field through which Morse projects the awareness that propels the rest of *Discovery Passages*. The white page of "No Comment" is an open field, alive to the history of suppression of the Kwak'wala language and Kwakwaka'wakw cultural practices. In this erasure, Morse embodies dignity and indignation by refusing to give his own breath to such a dialogue and by silently clearing space to listen to the banal, small language by which a people were misrepresented, criminalized, and dispossessed.

Morse thinks of his poet's role as being a medium for peoples and lands. He does not "consider [him]self a visual artist or much of a conceptualizer,"[18] so it would be false to align Morse too strongly with conceptual or procedural movements. "I do a lot of things unconsciously," writes Morse, "which is another way of saying I steal."[19] Then, alluding perhaps to modernist sensibilities that prompted appropriations from non-European tradition, or to mid-twentieth-century Beat impulses to "get in touch with one's inner 'Indian,'" or to the stories of the Kwakwaka'wakw mistold by Canadian officials, he adds: "Another way of saying I steal stuff back."[20]

"WITE-OUT": FRAMING FORM(AL) INTELLIGIBILITY

Shane Rhodes creates the visual poems, cut-up poems, and collage poems in his book *X* by constraining himself to the language of the transcripts for the eleven Canadian Post-Confederation Treaties (the "numbered treaties") and some of their associated documentation, recorded by the Government of Canada. At the beginning of *X* there is a reproduced photo of Duncan Campbell Scott, both a "Confederation Poet" and a former head of Indian Affairs, sitting in a canoe with eleven Indigenous guides. Scott is holding a book while being paddled down the Abitibi. From the writing of Scott's personal secretary, Rhodes guesses that the book is very likely *The Oxford Book of Poetry*. Rhodes writes:

> The Scott photograph seems the perfect metaphor for most of the poetry that has been and continues to be written in Canada—almost all of us are still in that boat reading the *Oxford Book of Poetry* while being paddled to our destination almost oblivious to the canoe, the paddlers, or the bush we are being paddled through. My previous books would fit comfortably in that canoe as well.... In *X*, I wanted to coax poetry out of that boat. I wanted it to get wet, dirty, ugly and messy. I could only do this by breaking it, perversely.[21]

One of Rhodes's most obvious breaks from his earliest books, and from the historically "oblivious" poetry that "continues to be written in Canada," is his shift toward the techniques of the historical, modernist avant-garde—a shift that he first began in *Err* and refines in *X*. Rhodes "breaks" an inherited line of institutionalized aesthetic values that have been complicit in mythologizing Canada's colonial history. Of course, the techniques of found poetry, which Rhodes traces in Canada back to F. R. Scott's *Trouvailles: Poems from Prose* and John Robert Colombo's *The Mackenzie Poems*, have their own European roots and histories of cultural appropriation and racism. But Rhodes calls *X* his "attempt to learn … the colonisation which has shaped every part of my thinking,"[22] such that these techniques in *X* become methodology, an inquiry into how to make an "anti-poem" that might be an antidote to the indoctrination of colonial ideology.

Rhodes turns to erasure in "Wite Out"—a text that appears as black type over very under-saturated black-and-white photographs of registration forms. Rhodes has applied strips of Wite Out correction tape to the forms. As is the case with Morse, the rest of Rhodes's book gives enough context that a full reproduction of the original document might have stood in the poem's place, almost as a ready-made, and still the words resonate as reframed evidence of the state's instrumental use of language. Also like Morse, Rhodes does not erase to compose an "original," personally expressive lyric from the text, but rather to clear space so as to listen to what the source text already speaks *sotto voce*:

> In you the / Act will numb / the vision // If you are / you were never / required.[23]

The cruel tone mined from the form's instructions betrays the dehumanizing aims behind the formal frame. Rhodes's erasure also performs a kind of levelling of the different registers of the document, bringing many voices onto the same plane: the voice of the instructions, the declarative passages of the oath, the language identifying the fillable spaces, and the notary's jurat (which insists, "he/she appeared to understand it, and made his/her mark hereto in our presences as a foresaid."[24] The effect is a heightened awareness of the instrumentality of the legal document, of the phenomenal horror of the form's material existence.

At end of the form/poem, Rhodes leaves unwhited the space reserved for the physical mark of the person meant to make "his/her mark hereto in our presences." Whereas in the rest of the poem, Rhodes frames off language with white space, here he frames a space in the original form where the form acknowledges the unlikelihood that the applicant can read the form. Rhodes puts space and text into the same register of visibility and obliquely interpolates the reader as an illiterate applicant. When the reader realizes that her position, facing the form, is potentially as an illiterate person, all the visible text in "Wite Out" becomes the colonized subject's "illegible" text—present, but nevertheless signifying the very image of lethal white noise, of babble, of nonsense, the senselessness that produces the erasure of a subject. By playing with the white space in an Indian Act registration document, "Wite Out" frames the fields of that document as the cleared, bordered spaces within which the state manages the bodies and testimonies of Indigenous peoples.

ABEL: CARVING THE FRAME INTO SKY

In *The Place of Scraps*, Jordan Abel simultaneously engages the metaphors of framing and carving. He suggests that his task as writer is not so much about being spontaneously generative of language as about attending to the materiality of language, with hand and eye guided by Nisga'a tradition. "An account / or / summary / was to be / carver d [*sic*]/ from Alaska," he writes.[25] Using some of the most consequential texts by white anthropologists who have meaningfully documented, but have also misrepresented and misinterpreted, the cultures of northern, West Coast First Nations, Abel uses erasure to create literal *layers* of meaning. Abel places one erasure, then another, on pages immediately following passages of source text, such that the reader experiences the pages as mimicking the paper-on-paper materiality of tracings, of flip-book sequences.

In the original prose passages, Abel situates his speaker as "the poet [given] a wooden spoon that his absent father carved"[26]—a poet in the process of "reassess[ing] the validity of his knowledge of the past."[27] The speaker is a Vancouver-born descendant of the Nisga'a, the people of the upper Nass River. Like the totem pole whose removal and transport to Toronto is recounted by Marius Barbeau in Abel's source texts, the speaker has been moved East by cultural forces, and thus he "cannot define the [totem pole carving] tradition his father functions within."[28] The lyric speaker is not always the voice with the most direct access to accounts of Nisga'a tradition. For example, the most detailed description of Nisga'a sons and nephews erecting totem poles in their fathers' and uncles' memory is reproduced in Barbeau's text. Abel's word-carvings are a kind of father-honouring that involves scraping from blocks of others' language a "naked spectacle"[29] of "this story ... a secret / I have been inside of."[30] His word-carvings play with the irony of his access to Nisga'a tradition being mediated through colonizers' texts.

If we were to imagine a spectrum where erasure conceived as pure, apolitical play is at one end, and erasure conceived as a formal grappling with the material politics of meaning-making is at the other, then we might put Austin Kleon's *Newspaper Blackout* near that far first end. I would place Morse's and Rhodes's works at the other end, but not quite as close to the spectrum's extreme end as I would place Abel. Morse and Rhodes each enact a kind of clearing away of extraneous text to create a space of accountability and transparency around the state's language instruments. Like Morse and Rhodes, Abel highlights the instrumentality of anthropological accounts ("remove / thousands of / Indians / successfully / without feeling a tremor").[31] But by creating an analogy between pole carving and erasure poetry, Abel also subtly critiques conceptualist poets' attitudes toward "resource" material.

In one original passage, Abel imagines Barbeau's private thoughts when Barton, Barbeau's guide, takes Barbeau to the poleless "place of scalps." The name of this place is a proxy for Gingolx of the Nass River Valley: "the place of skulls / the place of scalps". Barton has Barbeau hold out his hands to receive a fistful of dirt. "I knew then ... that this was a sacred ritual, that I must remember each detail so the world could know it, too," says Barbeau.[32] Abel's imagined Barbeau speaks with a personal attitude of entitlement representative of the broad assumptions of entitlement driving both British-led anthropological modernism and primitivist modernisms of the early-twentieth-century avant-garde. The white anthropologist assumes that his individual knowledge is productive of the world's knowledge, that his "finding out" is the frontier of discovery, and that his interpretation of a First Nations person's actions is naturally more informative than what is or isn't said by the Indigenous actor. Abel depicts a writer-anthropologist distancing himself from a human-to-human act of communication and objectifying that communiqué into the raw material for his interpretation. The critique of modernist anthropology implicit in Abel's work also

Philip calls the "appallingly abbreviated" *Gregson v. Gilbert* report "an inherently erased document" not only for its reductive, fact-stating, and synopsizing logic, but also for the unspeakability of how easily it places the humanity of Africans beside the point. Trying to "break the spell [that] the completed text has on us," Philip turns to physical manipulations that eventually make her decide to "rearrange the words as they appeared in the text to fashion the poems ... as if I had locked myself in the hold of the ship with the 'cargo' of bodies, words and memories—all erased by time, by history—the better to find the story that couldn't ever be told, yet had to be told."[41] At first, Philip's strategy of "using words exactly as they appeared in the case report," to create the first movement of *Zong!*, is a process quite similar to the ones used by Morse and Rhodes. That approach gives way to a more fragmentary, more recombinant, strategy that has "less to do with subtraction and more to do with shattering the words of the text into spore words ... The 'erasure' process [was one of] application and not subtraction."[42] *Zong!*'s preoccupation with socio-historical erasure of African histories is visually signified in the last of the book's movements, where text appears only in light grey, and where words overlap each other and obscure one another. Philip comments:

> I would argue that erasure is intrinsic to colonial and imperial projects. It's an erasure that continues up to the present.... In my own case I didn't have a lengthy document to work with. In an odd and interesting way, though, you could say that what I was doing was attempting to erase the layers of erasure to get to that ghostly palimpsest to which I could then apply techniques of erasure, if that doesn't sound too confusing.... There is a sense in which *Zong!* continues a 'lineage' of erasure.[43]

The "ghostly palimpsest" that Philip envisions *is* the event of the massacre. The "original text" is the sum of the bodily events and lingual events of the ship's journey—events that constitute the "evidence" for both the personhood and the humanity of the ship's occupants, now effectively erased by the language of the decision in the case of *Gregson v. Gilbert*. To apply techniques of erasure to try to recover this ghostly palimpsest, to "erase erasure," becomes the process of hearing words, phrases, dialogues from the imagined, haunting cacaphony of words, spoken by hundreds of people who have lived this historical, colonial event, "finding" them in the text of the document.

Like a litany, like a chant, in the notes that follow the poems of *Zong!*, Philip repeats her aim, in variations of the phrase "to not-tell the story that must be told."[44] The final sentence of the book tells us: "*Zong!* is the Song of the untold story; it cannot be told yet must be told, but only through its un-telling."[45] Philip explains that the drive was "to move beyond representation of what the New World experience was ... for that would have meant working entirely within the order of logic, rationality and predictability; it would have meant ordering an experience which was disordered (and cannot ever be ordered)."[46] Even grammar itself is implicated in this system of ordering disorder that should not be ordered; Philip is left to try to find ways to speak without reproducing the orders of the New World language that have erased African being. Lyric poetry is one of these orders; the law is another.

In her reading of *Zong!*, Sarah Dowling explains how in literary discourse an intelligible lyric voice constitutes evidence of personhood and authority. Dowling identifies Philip's formal challenge in her poetry as analogous to the historiographer's problem of how to represent legal non-persons.[47] As Philip fragments words into "non-sense," the words break "into sound, return to their initial and originary phonic sound—grunts, plosives, labials."[48] For Philip, "this language of grunt and groan, of moan and stutter,"[49] of "pure utterance,"[50] is a language that she *can* use to "not-tell" the story for which conventional telling is grossly inappropriate. "*Zong!* emphasizes the enfleshed voice," writes Dowling. Philip erases the intelligibility of the document until she arrives at a concept of poetic voice which "emphasizes corporeality rather than interiority [in part] because it refers to non-persons to whom such interiority was not considered applicable."[51]

We can also read Philip's erasures and breaks as her own attempts to speak outside the orders of New World language. Philip tries to dissociate her own authorial intention from the authoritative impulses of legal expression by erasing, breaking, crossing out, and murdering the bonds of association between lyric intelligibility and legal personhood. She writes, using terms borrowed from Philip Monk, of eventually "absolving [her]self of authorial intention":

I came to understand that I had … entirely absolved myself of "authorial intention," so much so that I asked the publishers to allow another name to accompany mine on the book. That generated some very interesting discussions regarding placement in libraries and whose name would be catalogued, the possibilities of confusion with more than one name and so on. They eventually went along with my request. Setaey Adamu Boateng is the other name on *Zong!* and represents the collective voice of the ancestors.[52]

For Philip, the desire to put one's name on a work is at direct odds with the aims of her conceptual collaboration with the ancestors. Philip endeavours to break into the silence created by the decision document to "hear" the voices silenced there. To do so would be impossible without the work of the Europeans whose names appear on the document and without the Africans whose deaths gave rise to the document and whose names were yet never recorded in the source text. The African names reappear in the footnotes of the poem: co-authors simultaneously resurfaced into memory by appearing on Philip's page, but still held in a space underneath (as though submerged by) the document's fragmented text.

THE CANADIAN CONTEXT OF ERASURE

There is nothing not-said.
—Vanessa Place

"Not-telling" is an apt metaphor, I think, for the logic of all four poets I have discussed so far. Both Rhodes's concept of "anti-poem" and Philip's concept of "not-telling" signal writing that is self-reflective about the socio-material conditions of literary production and defiant about assuming the privilege to "tell" within them. The documents with which these writers work suggest that rhetorical persuasiveness is effective only between mutually acknowledged agents of power. Consider the sound logic of the Kwakwaka'wakw elders in Morse's official correspondence; the mark of the unspeaking subject in Rhodes's Indian Act; the explanations of the Nisga'a informant when presented to Abel's Barbeau; or the protests of the African slaves in Philip's *Gregson v Gilbert*. Neither these bodies' rhetorical skills nor the defensibility of their moral positions can *mean* (i.e., be meaningfully heard, therefore be effectively persuasive or "mean" anything) in a context that simultaneously denies their ability to *tell* and constructs the legitimately "told" as an address to the centres of colonial state power. Still, these bodies, these subjects, leave traces on documents. For Morse, Rhodes, Abel, and Philip, erasure involves a literal repossession and deconstruction of the colonial order's texts. Erasure is a tool available for a guerilla *accounting* of voice, memory and identity outside the "grasp" of the English language, beyond the colonial, narrative structures of the tellable. These writers, who focus intently on the not-said, might take issue with Vanessa Place's statement.

"I white out and black out words (is there a difference?)," asks Philip.[53] Her question immediately forces us to consider the difference between language visibly obstructed and the *absence* of language from the page. The absent language of the erasure poem is legible as "absent" only to the degree that the reader has a contextual awareness of what is missing. Each of the four poets discussed chooses the technique of white-out/deletion. Each goes to pains not only to indicate their source texts, but to represent them, either as antecedent, background, or addendum to the poetry (save Morse, who is also the only poet who denies an explicit, political impulse to his work). Rhodes sets his text over the grey image of the application form; Abel cites Barbeau in lengthy passages before setting to work to white-out those passages; Philip reproduces *Gregson vs. Gilbert* in its entirety. Philip also uses grey print and overlapping print in "Ebora," the fifth movement of her book, to remind us visually that, for her, the source text (that is, the event and its traces, not the document) asserts a ghostly presence—not-dead, never entirely absent. The choices of these poets expose a potential ethics of citational, if not intellectual, transparency to be exercised at the heart of conceptual writing.

If blacking out words, as Travis MacDonald does in *O Mission Repo*, leaves, as it were, its alphabetic bodies under an undecipherable black bar on the page, thus focusing attention on the cover-up more than the victims of the crime, then whiting out words in a work to be reproduced in print or on a white, digital background effectively "disappears" them, even erasing the traces of their disappearance, creating absences visually undifferentiated from the rest of the page. In a black-out, the black bar is the scene of the crime; the white page is as stage or backdrop. In a white-out, the spaces haunted by the words now erased have no border around them; the white spaces of "absence" bleed into the space between lines and into the margin; the material page itself becomes a field of silent knowing, of non-speaking.

For these four poets, then, (who white-out, while conserving the memory of what has been erased), the white page is not mere backdrop. It is not an absolute, empty space which original language fills with knowledge, but a bounded zone; such poets activate our awareness of the page itself as a judicial space that legitimates the expressions that enter there. In the usual logic of the lyric poem, the material whiteness of the page has either not signified; has been imagined as the open, unraced, receptive mind of the reader; or has been theorized as the open field of energetic transfer. But in the erasures by Morse, Rhodes, Abel, and Philip, the white page also becomes visible as a discursive space in which relations of power play out. Their page is the page of visual poetry, where line-length, letter-shape and spatial orientation matter. But beyond that, for these poets, a white page is a "discursive forum" into which narratives, claims, attributions, and citations are either allowed or disallowed.

The difference between the white-out gesture and the black-out gesture on a source text is somewhat analogous to the marking and the non-marking of the racializing gaze on bodies. In white supremacist cultures, a gaze that "whites" a body makes its own gesture invisible; the gaze sees a body not as "Other" but as "not-Other."[54] In the same economy, "blacking" a body makes it hypervisible, "overbodied," and its blackness blocks the legibility of its subjective expression. To white-out a character is to assert the supremacy of page-space in allowing or disallowing expression; to black-out a character is to exploit the vulnerability of its embodied materiality, to see the character as nothing but black body, nothing but black ink.

American lawyer and poet Vanessa Place uses appropriative strategies that have been critiqued as operating from a sense of *un*accountability, one that is indifferent to the subject-positions of her various readers and that contrasts sharply with the sense of *accounting* that Abel, Philip, Morse, and Rhodes demonstrate. Nonetheless, when Place discusses American law as "a story-telling contest," invoking Derrida's concept of the author as "signatory of the text," she proposes a Conceptualist understanding of authorship, one that locates final power over reception with those who establish the context for reading a source text. She articulates a way of understanding the stance of the erasing author to the page and to the source text. She insists that "what matters depends on who makes matter matter,"[55] and this insistence remains surprisingly consistent with the relationality explored by Canadian and Indigenous writers pursuing decolonial writing strategies.

Place writes: "the signatory is not the source, for the signatory is the source of its reception.... The witness is the source, the law is the signatory."[56] In the adversarial court-space that she imagines, the locus of power does not reside with the testimony-giving, raw-material-providing witness, but resides with the recognized authority of the person who commits the testimony to the white paper and takes credit for it. Place says: "I am an author not by virtue of having written anything, but by virtue of th[e] law's recognition of me as signatory."[57]

The only difference between Place's approach to exposing the construction of authorial power and that of these poets who also exercise their powers of appropriation and redaction, is the angle from which they understand "poetry" and "the law" to be different contexts for their books. Place is a lawyer who brings a legal brief into the context of poetry so as to turn it into a "non-brief"; in one sense, she is moving a language of instrumentality into a particular space of aesthetics, one that stakes its claim on the value of absolute non-instrumentality. But if a writer does not differentiate so much between poetry and the law, and if a writer sees both poetic language and legal language as instrumental within the *colonial* context, then reframing a sourced text, or erasing a sourced text, does not generate conceptual energy only from turning an instrument of enforcement into an object of aesthetic reverberation. Morse, Rhodes, Abel, and Philip—and even Place—all see the language of poetry as potentially "enforcing," just like other disciplinary discourses. These poets create aesthetic objects by appropriating "outsider" texts into the disciplinary frame of poetry; but they *also* work as agents within the larger colonial context, by making transparent the ethical demands made on their own power positions, on the *ur*-poets who wield aesthetic, if not judicial, power.

Place and the aforementioned Canadian poets and Indigenous poets work not only as insiders to processes of lyric expressivity, going "outside" that discourse to make use of the found, but as insiders to the discursive space and norms of *colonialism*. Through acts of poetry, these poets perform roles as culture-makers, whistle-blowers, and law-watchdogs. Through these acts of poetry they position themselves "above the law"—not to make a point about art's moral non-investments in relation to the law, but as meta-legislators, witness to the law's language procedures.

The Flarf and Conceptualist movements, led in the US by Kenneth Goldsmith (and now Vanessa Place), advance a rhetoric of the found that takes, as a given, our access to masses of digital information. The contextual paradigm of Flarf and Conceptualism has emphasized the overwhelming ease with which volumes of text, volumes heretofore beyond the scale of the book or individual writer, can now be searched and "found," thanks to digital technologies. Erasure poetry in the American context has not rigorously critiqued the assumptions of technological literacy, access, and entitlement in this rhetoric.

But recently when Goldsmith publicly read, as his own found poem, an edited version of Michael Brown's autopsy report, the response of numerous critics indicated that Goldsmith had reached, indeed breached, the ethical limits of "uncreative" sourcing. "Conceptualism's relationship to 'found' text cannot be divorced from the colonial impulse to claim and maim," writes Joey de Jesus, in response to Goldsmith's performance. "Conceptualism creates yet another safe space for the ongoing appropriation, erasure and plagiarism of queer and/or non-white expression—in this case blackness."[58]

Perhaps now that critiques of the found strategies at the heart of Conceptualism (by American writers of colour like Joey de Jesus, Ken Chen, and Cathy Park Hong) have grabbed the spotlight, the American poetics of erasure might take up more explicit, vigorous interventions into the cultural politics of the found. For now, such discussions in the American context still involve a Black-White, post-slavery racial discourse that, at least in mainstream media and in critical discussion, eclipses discussions of American colonial relations with Indigenous peoples.

The Canadian context, by contrast, has in the past decade seen its race and identity politics shift away from a white-authored multiculturalism that congratulates itself for its embrace of the non-white "new immigrant," pivoting toward an unprecedented visibility of Indigenous people and their concerns in Canadian public discourse. Canadian mainstream media has been compelled to give sustained attention to the resistance movements of First Nations: disputes over proposed projects for pipelines of oil and gas in traditional territories, historic land-rights decisions on the West Coast, and the public findings of the Truth and Reconciliation Commission. In the aftermath of the deaths of Black Americans, like Eric Garner and Michael Brown, at the hands of police, critics went so far as to argue that Canada's analog for the charged Black-White racial tensions in the United States lies in our current climate of race relations between Aboriginals and non-Aboriginals.[59] Increasingly, and however begrudgingly, the Canadian popular consciousness has had to engage with voices that represent the Canadian police as state-sanctioned agents of violence against Indigenous people—voices that recount the founding of the Canadian state as a story of appropriation of land and resources.

Rhodes writes that recent works of Canadian found poetry are "much more interested in dissent" than earlier modernist, Canadian found poetry. Rhodes reads both Morse and Philip as thinkers "taken with post-colonial concerns," thinkers who expose "the ridiculousness and offensiveness of previous narrative structures" by deploying the same strategies of control and selection "against them."[60] These writers are also more interested in dissent than their American counterparts. Although Jordan Abel's work shows clear filiation with Goldsmith's *Gertrude Stein on Punctuation*, such work also forces us to face the legacy of cultural appropriation at work in modernist practice. Even Canadian poets who use erasure without openly engaging the colonial contexts of avant-garde practice are sensitive to the obvious commodification in the ethos of the motto: "steal like an artist." Gregory Betts's "plunderverse," for example, is a composition method involving erasure and recombining. Betts insists that plunderverse "is not a conventional 'theft' of another artist's work—it is an acknowledgement of the economy in which we artists work, signalling and acknowledging previous artists that have been influential and, yet, at the same time, participating in the creative economy."[61]

A SHARP WHITE BACKGROUND

"I feel most coloured when I am thrown against a sharp white background," reads an untitled 1990 painting by Glenn Ligon at the Whitney Museum. Ligon uses black oil-stick to stencil letters on a white wooden door, and stencils the same phrase over and over down the length of the door, in horizontal, wrapped lines that become increasingly blurred and illegible closer to the bottom of the painting. The phrase comes from Zora Neale Hurston's essay "How It Feels to Be Colored Me." An image of the painting is reproduced in Claudia Rankine's recent *Citizen: An American Lyric*. For many writers, as I've shown above, the literary page is a "sharp white background": a platform for the voice of privilege, an acquiescent backdrop that silently supports the performance of Eurocentric consciousness. Vanessa Place uses the language of another African-American painter, Kara Walker, when Place writes that she embodies "the perpetrator, historically and currently."[62] That is, Place cribs language from "A Proposition by Kara Walker" to describe "how it feels to be with her." Walker proposes: "The object of the painting is the subjugated Body. The Painter is the colonizing entity."[63]

Rhodes, Abel, and Philip also echo Walker's thinking when they each, in their own way, conceptualize the poet sitting like the colonizing, editorializing and legislating authority in relation to the material page. But in the essay that Place alludes to, Walker says: "The nigger is akin to the painter's canvas / an inert, ahistorical, expedient lie … Made to be a receptacle for Hubris.… The Painter creates the canvas over which ideals of dominance are drawn."[64] If, for Place, the Poet is analogous to Walker's painter, then her page, too, must also be analogous to Walker's Nigger: a receptacle for Hubris … a space over which ideals of dominance are written.

In readings of "White Out of Gone With The Wind by Vanessa Place," Place stands in silence, flipping the page, looking occasionally at the audience, and ends by reading the last, iconic line of the source text. Place calls the performance an erasure. "The silence, then, is ambiguous," writes Jacob Edmond. "It could mark Place's attack by deletion on *Gone with the Wind*'s racist ideology, or it could be a performance of that racist ideology's stifling of other voices."[65] What is unambiguous is that in such a performance Vanessa Place is the embodied orchestrator of that silence, staged within the spatio-temporal expectations of the poetry reading. By calling the piece a "white-out," she too associates "whiting" with the exercise of that silencing control.

When the discussed poets who write on the territories called Canada excise text in print, they bring their readers into the terrain of the visual, of the non-linguistic, doing so to demonstrate the stakes of silencing control. These Indigenous poets and Canadian poets also remind readers that a backdrop is not a neutral place, not an idealized silence upon which text sounds. The poets draw readers into an experience of the page as a subjugated white material upon which dominance plays itself out in language and documents its point of view. Place works with the same terrain: ostensibly reminding her listeners/readers that when she claims authorship, she takes charge of the silences as much as what is voiced. But Place could have whited out any text to assert this dominance, and she could have disseminated the intellectual property of any "notoriously litigious"[66] estate to try to provoke a lawsuit to raise questions about ownership of intellectual property. But Place seems to want to work with racist representations specifically. By choosing to re-voice the racism of a source text that she has chosen specifically *for* its racism, Place attempts to use avant-garde literary practices of framing and voicing to expose the racializing cruelty, indeed criminality, beyond the law—a cruelty regularly enacted *as silence* and that drives the power dynamics of American race relations. She calls her work a "necessary cruelty." But necessary for whom? Necessary *to* whom?

Sara Ahmed has written: "It has become commonplace for whiteness to be represented as invisible, as the unseen or the unmarked, as non-colour, the absent presence or hidden referent, against which all other colours are measured as forms of deviance."[67] "But to whom is whiteness invisible?" asks George Yancy. "Whiteness is invisible to those who inhabit it, to those who have come to see whiteness and what it means to be human as isomorphic."[68] Ahmed and Yancy suggest that we write and live in an economy of signification in which normalized white identity experiences itself only as *non-transparent*, as whitely coloured (rather than unmarked, transparent, universal) when examined alongside non-whiteness. Place's work can be understood, then, as white identity trying to make its own invisibility visible—to itself. As Aaron Kunin has noted, Place's ideas about white identity aren't so different from those of her detractors, but it seems Place is unaware that what she is saying isn't news.[69] Place's insistence on her cruelty as "necessary" makes sense only if one assumes this cruelty as an invisible or silenced part of one's own identity in the first place. Ironically, in order to experience the big reveal of Place's work as a significant unmasking, one has to be unaware of so much writing already out there. But as Crispin Sartwell writes, "One of the major strategies for preserving white invisibility to ourselves is the silencing, segregation, or delegitimation of voices that speak about whiteness from a non-white location."[70]

When Place argues that a white body "serves as both the defense against the State and as its emblem,"[71] she isn't saying anything that Morse, Rhodes, Abel, and Philip, haven't already explored with more aesthetic nuance in their own work. Place does not posit, as Kara Walker does, or as Jordan Abel does, that a person can consciously and critically take up a position of "authority over form, content, and interpretation" without having to presume that authority arises *only* out of one's racialized subject position. Philip is not sure that she can take up an authoritative position without assuming a privilege constructed on a history of cruelties, but unlike Place, Philip goes to great pains to try to "absolve" herself of authorial intention.

The erasurists writing in territories called Canada reproduce the cruel language of government officials, anthropologists, and lawyers without raising legitimate concerns about whether or not they are simply reiterating hate speech, because these erasurists build contexts of anti-oppression around their erasures. Morse's erasure is set within a polyvocal history of the Kwakwaka'wakw—a history that is a recognizable inheritor of Black Mountain aesthetics. Rhodes frames his work in X as "*The Heart of Whiteness* [that] terries in Indian territory,"[72] that specifically criticizes the aesthetics of a Canadian Confederation poet and the CanLit machinery that has idealized him. Abel uses Nisga'a pole-carving as the analogy for his stripping of citations down to graphic marks on the page before building new lyric poems upon their foundations. Philip adds a lengthy "Notanda" to her work so as to flag the conceptual conundrum that she negotiates when inhabiting the position of authorship while attempting to break apart racist language.

These poets effectively "activate" the reader's awareness of the white page as a silence that is a "receptacle for [a master's] Hubris … and [a space] over which ideals of dominance are written," but these poets also make clear that they do not presume to address predominantly white audiences, for whom it is "necessary" to be compelled into experiencing their own silence as complicit with systematic racism. These poets, who each come to their practice of erasure technique through poetics specific to each individual's relation to place and community, compel their readers to experience the page as a constructed silence subject to the whim of authors who embody, intersectionally, signatory power and racializing practice in the same writing hand. They address a diverse audience who may or may not already understand the presumption of objectivity and authority involved in the performance of whiteness. By practising erasure as a performance of representational power, these writers insist that all authors, always, are participating in the politics of what is represented and what is silenced.

NOTES

The epigraph for "The Canadian Context of Erasure" is from Vanessa Place, "The Case for Conceptualism," writing.upenn.edu/epc/authors/place/Place_Conceptual case1A.pdf.

1 Andrew David King, "Effaced Ballads: An Interview with Matthew Rohrer, Anthony McCann, and Joshua Beckman on Erasing the Romantics," *Kenyon Review* (30 November 2012).

2 Andrew David King, "The Weight of What's Left Out: Six Contemporary Erasurists on Their Craft," *Kenyon Review* (6 November 2012).

3 King, "The Weight."

4 King, "The Weight."

5 King, "The Weight."

6 King, "The Weight."

7 Andrew David King, "Theft as Art, Art as Theft: An Interview with Austin Kleon," *Kenyon Review* (26 August 2012).

8 King, "The Weight."

9 Lorraine Weir, "Discovery Passages," *Canadian Literature* 214 (Autumn 2012), 179.

10 Craig Dworkin, *Reading the Illegible* (Evanston: Northwestern University Press, 2003), 3.

11 Dworkin, *Reading*, 4–5.

12 Smaro Kamboureli, *On the Edge of Genre* (Toronto: University of Toronto Press, 1991), 102. The italics for *act* are added.

13 Ken Norris, "Ken Norris and Garry Thomas Morse Discuss *After Jack*," Talonbooks (23 July 2010).

14 Shane Rhodes, "Reuse and Recycle: Finding Poetry in Canada," *Arc Magazine* (1 May 2013).

15 Gary Thomas Morse, *Discovery Passages* (Vancouver: Talonbooks, 2011), 49.

16 Christopher Bracken, *The Potlatch Papers* (Chicago: University of Chicago Press, 1997), back cover.

17 Kevin Spenst, "Garry Thomas Morse," kevinspenst.com (24 June 2011).

18 Norris, "Ken Norris."

19 Spenst, "Garry."

20 Spenst, "Garry."

21 Shane Rhodes, "Shane Rhodes—*X: Poems and Anti-Poems* (An Interview)," *Toronto Quarterly* (19 September 2013).

22 Rhodes, "Shane Rhodes."

23 Shane Rhodes, *X: Poems and Anti-Poems* (Gibsons: Nightwood, 2013), 74.

24 Rhodes, *X*, 79.

25 Jordan Abel, *The Place of Scraps* (Vancouver: Talonbooks, 2013), 11.

26 Abel, *The Place of Scraps*, 97.

27 Abel, 105.

28 Abel, 139.

29 Abel, 105.

30 Abel, 179.

31 Abel, 25.

32 Abel, 163.

33 Abel, 173.

34 Abel, 47–55.

35 Ross Hair, *Ronald Johnson's Modernist Collage Poetry* (New York: Palgrave, 2010), 133.

36 Abel, *The Place*, 27.

37 King, "The Weight." The italics for *confronted* are added.

38 King, "The Weight."

39 M. NourbeSe Philip. *Zong!* (Middletown: Wesleyan University Press, 2008), 197.

40 Philip, *Zong!*, 189.

41 King, "The Weight."

42 King, "The Weight."

43 King, "The Weight."

44 Philip, *Zong!*, 189–91, 193–201, 204, 206–207.

45 Philip, 207.

46 Philip, 197.

47 Sarah Dowling, "Persons and Voices: Sounding Impossible Bodies in M. NourbeSe Philip's *Zong!*," *Canadian Literature* 210/211 (Autumn 2011): 44.

48 Philip, *Zong!,* 205.

49 Philip, 205

50 Philip, 207.

51 Dowling, "Persons and Voices," 54.

52 King, "The Weight."

53 Philip, *Zong!,* 193.

54 Rebecca Aanerud, "Fictions of Whiteness: Speaking the Names of Whiteness in US Literature," *Displacing Whiteness: Essays in Social and Cultural Criticism,* ed. Ruth Frankenberg (Durham: Duke University Press, 1997), 37.

55 Vanessa Place, "The Case for Conceptualism," Electronic Poetry Center, 7.

56 Place, "The Case," 8.

57 Place, 8.

58 Joey De Jesus, "Goldsmith, Conceptualism and the Half-baked Rationalization of White Idiocy," *Apogee* (18 March 2015).

59 "Michael Brown, Eric Garner Deaths 'Echo' Aboriginal Experience in Canada," cbc.ca (8 January 2015).

60 Rhodes, "Reuse."

61 Gregory Betts, "From Wit to Plunder in a Time of War," *The Poetic Front* 3 (2010).

62 Vanessa Place, "Artist's Statement: Gone With The Wind @Vanessa Place," genius.com (19 May 2015).

63 Kara Walker, "Manuscript for," *Rethinking Contemporary Art and Multicultural Education,* ed. Eungie Joo and Joseph Keehn II (New York: Routledge, 2011), 36.

64 Walker, "Manuscript," 38.

65 Jacob Edmond, "On Not Repeating 'Gone With the Wind': Iteration and Copyright," *Jacket2* (17 December 2012).

66 Place, "Artist's Statement."

67 Sara Ahmed, "Declarations of Whiteness: The Non-performativity of Antiracism," *Borderlands* 3.2 (2004).

68 George Yancy, *Look, A White! Philosophical Essays on Whiteness* (Philadelphia: Temple University Press, 2012), 7.

69 Aaron Kunin, "Would Vanessa Place Be a Better Poet If She Had Better Opinions?," nonsite.org (26 September 2015).

70 Crispin Sartwell, *Act Like You Know: African-American Autobiography and White Identity* (Chicago: University of Chicago Press, 1998), 9.

71 Place, "Artist's Statement."

72 Rhodes, *X,* 3.

LEANNE BETASAMOSAKE SIMPSON

caribou ghosts & untold stories

we are always almost drowning
we are the best trained troops
that refuse to fight

we are hyped up on aesthetics
and tripped up
by real life

we don't have time to feel these feelings
so we file that for
another day

we don't have to plan for the win
because we always lose
anyway

caribou ghosts & untold stories
bad timing
& smashed hearts

train tracks six pack riff raff
deadening regret
a collection of old parts

we get these little gifts
of tremendous, unclouded
by past dues

we get these tiny moments
but there's never
enough glue

we'll tie ourselves together
with bungee cords
and luck

bring the fish,
the fire,
& the new knife

catharsis is still elusive
so we'll save that
for another day

meet me at the underpass
rebellion is
on her way.

LEE MARACLE

Bobbi Lee, Indian Rebel

The PWM offices were on the second floor. They had a printing press and, off on a landing, a section for collating and stapling. A few PWM guys were there, along with about six NARP members. They were talking about Cuba and the Vietnamese revolution and as I looked around the place my eyes fell on a barrel of rifles standing in the comer. Wayne Thom was sitting there on top of them and I thought, "Christ! All this talk about revolution and here are all these rifles!" I was a bit scared but didn't know quite what to think of it. (About a week later I asked Ray about the guns and he said they belonged to the PWM and not NARP.) That first night I helped collate and staple their newsletter. People were talking and arguing all the time: about politics; about some guy who was coming over from Vancouver Island to speak, and a soccer game that was planned between the PWM and NARP on the weekend. There was a lot of teasing and joking going on, along with the work and beer drinking. It really wasn't much of a meeting; mainly a work session. When we'd finished they told me they were planning to sell the newsletter around town, especially at the Indian Centre dances. They also mentioned that they had this discussion group at the Centre in which NARP people participated. It was on Friday and they asked me to come along.

I went to the Andrew's place for the next meeting. We went downstairs and they were playing this tape by Stokely Carmichael. I noticed that everybody was drinking; in fact, Wayne Thom had already passed out. I thought it was pretty strange, but I didn't say anything. People drank and I didn't have anything against drinking.

The tape was about an hour and a half long and I listened to it carefully. Everyone laughed when Stokely was talking about Black people dyeing their hair, trying to straighten it, and girls putting on magnolia cream to look more white. It set me to thinking. I could remember when I was in school, how I always set my hair and wanted it to look curly—but it never lasted very long, the curls falling out in an hour or so. It always made me feel bad. And when I was sixteen I used to pluck my eyebrows to look more attractive by white standards. So I related to what Stokely had to say pretty well.

After the tape was over there was a discussion. Gordie did most of the talking; seemed he remembered everything on the tape and I thought he must have heard it several times before. He'd use some quote from Chairman Mao and relate it to a point Stokely made. At that time I knew nothing whatsoever about Mao Tse-tung and just sat there wondering what he was talking about. He kept talking about the "little red book" and repeating that "political power grows out of the barrel of a gun." That seemed to be his favourite saying. Gordie was a white guy, but because he was married to Gerri—who was an Indian like all the others—they allowed him to be a member of NARP. He was also very close to PWM, though I wasn't sure at that time whether he was a member or just a supporter.

Ray Thorn started arguing with him about how PWM people went around quoting Chairman Mao and doing very little else. "It's not good to keep on quoting and quoting! You can't learn Marxism by a mechanical process where you just go on quoting things till they stick." They talked and argued back and forth for about two hours and nobody else got to say anything, just sat and listened.

When it was over, people just went home. I stayed behind for a while talking to Gerri. She seemed a pretty sensible person and knowledgeable about different struggles going on. She talked about Vietnam and about how the Iroquois Confederacy had gone to the World Court to protest their people being drafted and sent to Vietnam against their will. They'd finally won their case. She also told me about some other people who were Red Power advocates: Larry Seymour, Duke Redbird—who was in some Saul Alinsky films—and Harold Cardinal. By the way she talked I felt that a lot was going on and that I was really out of it—behind the times. Finally, I said I had to go home and left. Stacy, who'd come to the discussion with me, drove me back to my mom's place.

I went to several NARP meetings after that. Most of the time I either talked to Gerri or listened to Ray and Gordie arguing. It almost seemed there was a personal thing between them. Once Gerri asked me if I wanted to go sell newspapers with her. NARP got the Panther paper and sold them up at Simon Fraser University (SFU) and the University of British Columbia (UBC). So I went up to SFU with her and was selling *The Black Panther* when a guy named Jamie Reed came up and started attacking us as being counter-revolutionaries and so forth. He was a member of the Internationalists, which later changed their name to the Communist Party of Canada, Marxist-Leninist (CPC-ML). I remember being taken aback because I didn't even know what a counter-revolutionary was—or that I was supposed to be a revolutionary in the first place. Finally I got mad. He was leaning against our table and screaming things in my face. "Just get out of here," I told him in a serious voice, "before I flatten you!" Gerri had been trying to reason with him but it was my experience with screamers that at some point or other they ended up taking a swing at you. Gerri was talking calmly about Black Power, what it was, and that NARP supported it. Then just as she was telling him he had no right to call her counter-revolutionary, some student came up and made some stupid comment about how proletarian poetry wasn't poetry at all. This diverted Jamie and, in the meantime, people started coming up and buying newspapers, curious to see what was going on. We sold out in a couple of hours and went home. On the way I asked Gerri who this guy Jamie was and she said, "Oh, they're all a bunch of crazies, these Internationalists. They go around quoting Mao and acting like a bunch of gangsters, beating up on people, just trying to intimidate everyone into agreeing with their line."

The next day we took some more papers out to the University of British Columbia and raised quite a stir. UBC was really a conservative school—still is—and there were a lot of anti-Panther people who came up and argued with us. One guy, a real racist, tried to intimidate us by saying things like, "Hell, what do you Indians know, anyway?" We just laughed at him, angry but thinking he was pretty stupid. This was my first experience with that type of political action—trying to engage in political discussion and so on. Actually, I didn't do much of the talking, but I listened a lot to Gerri and helped out where I could. She seemed to know what she was talking about and I respected her for it. On the way back I asked her how she came to know so much about the Panthers, Vietnam and so forth. She said she'd read quite a few books and things and gave me a reading list. I expressed some interest, but didn't really pick up on it right away.

ANNHARTE

cum cum how cum dat cums around even from behind

cum-fla-wid-me the skies choose symbiotic booze cruise wid me
transparent sway see thru gown shadow derrière sidewise flooze
cum-fla-wid-me the skies disguise our lives up size down prize
don drive dat car under influence go home alone let chauffeur
in slink white limo drive girl fla cruise fla low fla away ride way
lose exotic blues buzz pimp da hide pimp da pride height flight
just one commercial sets off fantasia an underclass entertainment
spree a black suited charlatan pours his alcohol beverage charm
invaded by his seductive chimerical stance transforms desire
croon da tune fla da moon mobility flair self fancy
fla da lady buzzard queen tiara envied by whirl
chancy girl shakes flamboyant headdress legacy
privileged plumes vary light stripe to dark rainbow
don't boast aloud or boast heart uppity comes round

manny booz ho cannot help notice wants her vanity to fly up his
ass his airline motto message to spread pleasure cum-fla-wid-me
crass for tricks sake he has to expose his prideful bum propel
brown cheeks stage a fatal attraction she cums slow circle wing
calculated to drop gently beside how beautiful dead he looks
delicious from behind rump saddle cause for celebration hold up
silver chalice to toast initiation of corpse composure such reeky
aroma from arsehole makes her look up close take quick peck
while her beak slides smoothly around the stink even still he does
not move but to semi relax sphincter extra calm porno pleasure

he's bit aroused she massages tiny little circles before her beak
inserts full tilt play and penetration so perverse shaman anus is
clued so cued sacred mischievous rite to suck absorb her entire
delicate head he must adjust her thrust inside surprise when bald
birdy wiggles free of snap shut buttock hold an all star wrestler
never that bold warn tease us to celebrate life responsible grasp
the turntable arm play record music humbly show off elegance

with minimal risk her crown us wrinkled anus like the one she
flew in to inspect without a cautious glance at expensive menu
stranger friction is how manny booz ho did not once let giggle
escape extent invasion caused her onset of baldness for
culture vultures he entraps infamous fembot domination

PART VII

COPYLEFT POETICS

KATIE L. PRICE

A ≠ A: The Potential for a Pataphysical Poetics in Dan Farrell's The Inkblot Record

The first A was perhaps congruent to the second, and we will therefore willingly write thus: A = A.

Pronounced quickly enough, until the letters become confounded, it is the idea of unity.

Pronounced slowly, it is the idea of duality, of echo, of distance, of symmetry, of greatness and duration, of the two principles of good and evil.
—Alfred Jarry, *Exploits and Opinions of Dr. Faustroll, Pataphysician*[1]

I am not suggesting switching from an uptight business suit into sincere jeans …
but rather acting out, in dialectical play, the insincerity of form as much as content.
—Charles Bernstein, "Comedy and the Politics of Poetic Form"[2]

The notion that we can be demystified, escape certain ideologies, or trade in certain ideologies for others—an uptight suit for sincere jeans—is itself a dangerous ideology that keeps us powerless. So what possibilities are left? Should poets simply give up and resign themselves to the status quo, regardless of their dissatisfaction? I contend that pataphysical texts like Dan Farrell's *The Inkblot Record* offer contemporary poetry a solution. Rather than attempt to alter the status quo or disrupt certain ideologies, pataphysical texts perform clinamatic swerves that show the arbitrariness and mutability of our understanding of the status quo. Rather than offering yet another alternative, ideological frame, they allow us to think about the logic of framing. This poetic work is vital to a contemporary poetry scene peppered with trends such as Flarf and New Formalism.[3] While making a larger claim for the importance of pataphysical practices for contemporary poetry, this paper takes *The Inkblot Record* as its main case study, because such a book exemplifies the political possibilities of a pataphysical poetics. Farrell's gesture of placing the language of psychology into the discourse of poetry enacts the paradox outlined by Alfred Jarry that A ≠ A. The politics of this move are small, but palpable. His poetics does not claim a "revolution of the word" or of the world, but rather performs an irreversible clinamatic swerve within them.

In 1898, *fin de siècle* French author, artist, and absurdist Jarry outlined his pseudoscience of 'pataphysics in *Exploits and Opinions of Dr. Faustroll, Pataphysician: A Neo-Scientific Novel*: "DEFINITION. Pataphysics is the science of imaginary solutions, which symbolically attributes the properties of objects, described by their virtuality, to their lineaments."[4] Even this complicated definition, however, is deceptively simple and does not adequately capture the complexities of 'pataphysics as outlined by Jarry. When Jarry initially decided to write more systematically about 'pataphysics, he planned to publish a treatise on the topic. Ultimately, however, he chose to stage his pseudoscientific philosophy as literature.[5] The decision to introduce his pseudoscience through a novel rather than through a treatise suggests that literature is the most appropriate venue in which to conduct 'pataphysical research (even research into how to define the term itself). The decision also reveals that, for Jarry, 'pataphysics could not be explained by critical, expository means alone; 'pataphysics had to be illustrated rather than described. *Exploits and Opinions*, which came out of Jarry's desire to write a treatise on 'pataphysics, must be viewed as his attempt not only to define the term, but to show 'pataphysics in (literary) action.

Jarry devotes an entire chapter of *Exploits and Opinions* to the "Definition" of 'pataphysics. Within this chapter, Jarry describes the science in conflicting ways, alternatively calling it "the science of that which is superinduced upon metaphysics," "the science of the particular," and that which "will examine the laws governing exceptions, and will explain the universe supplementary to this one."[6] The proliferating definitions speak to a key tenet of 'pataphysics: absolute facts, and therefore absolute definitions, do not exist. In this light, the official definition of the term is revealed to be a joke. And as if this were not enough, Jarry further complicates the definition by provocatively ending the chapter "upon the irreverence of the common herd whose instinct sums up the adepts of the science of 'pataphysics in the following phrase:".[7] Like the famous colon at the end of Ezra Pound's "Canto I," Jarry's colon acts as a frame for what follows, so that the rest of the book becomes, comically, "the phrase" that sums up 'pataphysics. Despite the individual differences among these definitions, the comic web of references woven by Jarry all work to support the initial purpose of 'pataphysics: to critique science's truth claims.

In *Alfred Jarry: A Critical and Biographical Study*,[8] Keith Beaumont outlines four specific critiques of science held by Jarry, providing a useful snapshot of these main concerns. First, Jarry challenges the idea that there are "laws" of science. In his opinion, they are only descriptive generalizations that attempt to link unique events and phenomena. Because all rules have exceptions, science deals with probabilities as opposed to actualities. Second, Jarry contends that explanations put forth by scientists are chosen arbitrarily, and these explanations are just some of the many possible solutions. In short, there are multiple ways of interpreting the same data. In *Exploits and Opinions*, Jarry gives the example of gravity:

> Instead of formulating the law of the fall of a body toward a center, how far more apposite would be the law of the ascension of a vacuum toward a periphery, a vacuum being considered a unit of non-density, a hypothesis far less arbitrary than the choice of a concrete unit of positive density such as water?[9]

Jarry asks why we assume that there is a force pulling us toward the earth when a theory that posits the opposite seems equally, or even more, viable.[10] Third, 'pataphysics questions the assumption that induction is a valid method for discovering truth. Lastly, 'pataphysics is skeptical of the use of sensory data as "evidence," since it always remains relative to a perceiver.[11] In sum, Jarry's "science" reacts to the explosion of a new faith in science— a faith that advocates for progress and the discovery of truth.[12] And while Beaumont is right to situate 'pataphysics within a critique of science, this critique alone has not made 'pataphysics influential for contemporary poets.

When I use the word "'pataphysical" in reference to contemporary poetry, I refer to that which, like 'pataphysics itself, wages critique through the tools used by Jarry: parody, mimicry, and exaggeration. Jarry is not sincerely proposing a new science—one that might get closer to the "real truth" than traditional science—instead, he offers an exaggerated, extreme, and eccentric version of scientific methods so as to expose their arbitrary nature. 'Pataphysics imagines a science that incorporates the exception, the accident, the slip, and the possible into our understanding of the repeatable, the expected, and the probable, thereby providing a project for avoiding generalities—a project best situated among the genres of satire, farce, and parody. In its purest form, then, 'pataphysics is more of a verb than a noun, perhaps explaining why, as Roger Shattuck argues, Jarry "never did much more than name it and sketch in its outlines."[13] To understand 'pataphysics, one must see it in action.

'Pataphysics was put to work in North America by the Toronto Research Group (TRG), formed in 1973 by Steve McCaffery and bpNichol. The TRG writes: "If 'pataphysics is 'the science of imaginary solutions' and the source of answers to questions never to be posed, then "pataphysics (the open quotation of a double elision) will be 'the literature of all imaginary sciences.'"[14] The move from the single elision to a double elision emphasizes the fact that contemporary 'pataphysical literature is involved in citation and quotation—open questioning of existing material—a move that becomes particularly important to Farrell's work. Although Farrell is not officially associated with the TRG or Canadian "Pataphysics, he is certainly influenced by their ideas and has remained in contact with others similarly influenced at the Kootenay School of Writing. In short, his work must be read with the "first amendment"[15] to Canadian "Pataphysics in mind.

The Inkblot Record collates one-sentence responses to the Rorschach test from six source texts, all published in New York between 1942 and 1989. These texts supply the content of the book; the form results from the simplest of all organized, linguistic procedures: alphabetization. The outcome is approximately 100 pages of block text (fully justified) with no paragraph breaks or any other indication of differentiation from one section to the next. Anaphora, however, heavily punctuates the text; repeated first words or phrases stand out because of the systematic organization:

Shape. Shape and appendages. Shape and head; climbing. Shape, black bear, no real body. Shape, coloring, white and gray stone. Shape inside a heart effect, a real heart. Shape, it has no head, part of tail, more nearly a moth with open wings, color has nothing to do with it. Shape of a pillow. Shape of urn, gray of wrought iron. Shape only. Shape, tail coming out. Shape with pendulum sticking out. Shaped like a heart. Shaped like that.[16]

Apart from the repetition and the alliteration, both of which occur by default in an alphabetized list, particularly in sentences that respond to a similar set of questions and visual stimuli,[17] the list draws out other striking parallels. These strange "shapes" become associated with altered bodies: "no real body," "no head," "part of tail," "tail coming out." Given the diversity of responses, and the even greater diversity of potential responses, repeated words in such a small section jar the reader. The sheer number of hearts, heads, and tails, as well as the two strange responses that invoke the notion of the "real," cause us to contemplate the connection between responses. In this form, the text showcases the highly individual nature of each response while accentuating the uncanny relationship between responses. Farrell's 'pataphysical gesture of transplanting raw, linguistic data from the realm of psychology into the discourse of poetry puts the language, as opposed to the patient, under the microscope.

Due to the book's alphabetical organization, it can be used as a kind of reference book, situating the poetic language in the discourse of information. This text's encyclopedic nature places it within a larger trend in contemporary poetry—a trend that Craig Dworkin has identified as "applied 'pataphysics," which engages in "the constructing of useless reference tools, the proposing of imaginary solutions, and the cataloguing of exceptions."[18] Farrell's text is a prime example of the kind of "useless reference tool" to which Dworkin alludes. In this form, the book grants us easy access to ridiculous facts: the only response given by a subject in these six source texts beginning with a "Q" is "Quite fat."[19] More subtly, Farrell resists commonplace assumptions about what makes a literary text cognizable by displacing himself as the authorial "I" and combining source material in a way that evacuates the text of any distinguishable subject.

Ironically, this move reclaims the Author that Roland Barthes pronounced dead. Farrell is not the author of *The Inkblot Record*, at least not in the traditional way that we think of the term "author." *The Inkblot Record* insists at every moment that Farrell's voice remains absent from the process of composition; the source texts are listed in the back of the book and the paratext includes a note that insists on Farrell's reluctance to tamper with the sentences in any way other than their organization: "Orthography in *The Inkblot Record* is consistent with [the source] texts."[20] Farrell's book literalizes Barthes's assertion that all texts consist of other texts. Barthes argues that a text is never an expression of inner feeling, but rather "a tissue of quotations drawn from the innumerable centres of culture."[21] Farrell takes literally Barthes's assertion that an author's "only power" comes from "mix[ing] writings."[22] Farrell responds to Barthes's cry that "the birth of the reader must be at the cost of the death of the Author."[23] Farrell calls authors to reclaim writing through reading. Farrell's position as "author" of this text is that of reader, disallowing critical readers to fall into the trap that Barthes describes, namely that the notion of authorship allows critics to close a text, to solve the puzzle sociologically, historically, or psychologically.[24] Asserting its status as a text that cannot be solved, *The Inkblot Record* is primed for a pataphysical parody of science's ideology.

The Inkblot Record is pataphysical in that it parodies the scientific method, systematically organizing the language used by clinical psychologists to diagnose patients and to analyze them, placing this language in a context where its aesthetic qualities can be examined. By putting the raw data into this new context, the text illustrates a pataphysical claim: that the solutions proposed by science, or any other discourse, are just one of many possible solutions, one out of many ways of looking at data. The notion that these sentences can be used to diagnose a human being is just one way of interpreting this data. When these sentences are stripped of their diagnostic potential and put into a literary context, can we come up with a different interpretation? Rather than generalize and extrapolate meanings from the sentences, *The Inkblot Record* attests to the particularity of every single response and showcases the exceptions to the rule. Farrell's text allows us to examine the bizarre, unexpected, and uncanny aspects of the responses—their rhythm, syntactical parallels, or simply their beauty: "Like a cockatoo, large, sharp beak, body, facing away,"[25] "Pair of eyeglasses. Pair of hands. Pair of pliers,"[26] "White dead bare branches."[27]

By cataloguing particulars in a pataphysical move that avoids generalizations, *The Inkblot Record* not only documents the expected responses to the Rorschach test—"a butterfly," "a cloud," "a flower"[28]—but also the anomalous responses. In fact, the cliché's main function in the text is to cast the anomalous responses into relief. "Pelvic bone. Pelvic bony structure. Penguin or seal, black. Penguin, white belly, feet. Penis. Penis there. People. People."— such a list accentuates the oddity of the responses located just a bit further down on the page: "Pistachio ice cream," "Pointed orange hats," "President Eisenhower."[29] The clichéd responses act as background to the figure of the particular. And since this is the product of systematic reading rather than authorial design, a reader cannot deny the reality of the peculiar responses.

In this form, the language becomes less about any individual subject than a searchable collection of linguistic oddities. Organized alphabetically and presented in bulk, the language attests to something beyond the psyche of any one subject. The language draws attention to other information, whether about the Rorschach test, the test subjects as a group, or the psychological industry during the second half of the twentieth century. But let us not get too optimistic. *The Inkblot Record*, like a good pataphysician, resists generalization at every moment; the truth of Farrell's book lies in the fact that it does not proffer any final claim. 'Pataphysics does not want to replace one system with another, but aims to highlight the absurdity of conflating truth with both systematicity and predictability.[30] *The Inkblot Record* enacts this pataphysical negation: it is neither/nor, and it is both/and. The negation exposes the disparate specificity of objects seen in a Rorschach image (which is neither one thing nor another), even as this negation exposes the cumulative ambiguity of objects seen in a Rorschach image (which is both this thing and another). These acts of negation with no value cannot, however, be taken as an argument for a nihilistic poetics. Indeed, Farrell's pataphysical practice is deeply rooted in politics.

Rather than propose an alternative, linguistic space that might be able to combat capitalism, for example, Farrell's text ends up describing, with 'pataphysical precision, the reactions of the subjects in the six source texts. In other words, rather than creating a language that attempts to disrupt its complicity in capitalism (as seen, for example, in Language poetry), Farrell's work shifts the focus to the materiality of existing language, already infused with exchange-value, but stripped of use-value. Silliman argues that "what happens when a language moves toward and passes into a capitalist stage of development is an anaesthetic transformation of the perceived tangibility of the word."[31] If we believe that "these developments are tied directly to the nature of reference in language, which under capitalism is transformed (deformed) into referentiality,"[32] then Farrell's book forces a new attention to the materiality of such capitalist language.[33]

One might argue that *The Inkblot Record*'s parody of psychology through an appeal to systematicity remains stunted by the fact that the Rorschach test has itself faced criticism for being a pseudoscience.[34] Examiners ask subjects to create imaginary solutions to the problem of the inkblot: "These slits here could be eyes too, like from a science fiction monster or something,"[35] "Well, you really have to use your imagination to see the tree,"[36] or "Well, if you really use your imagination you could make it a mushroom too."[37] The imaginary solutions that people conjure often verge on the hysterical:

> Two boys or young tough men with pug noses, wild green hair, probably Irish. Two bulls. Two cannibals over a brewing pot. Two chickens with their hands pushing away from each other. Two crabs and coral. Two crabs on either side. Two crickets sassing each other. Two crocodiles, looks like they're about to die. Two dancing ladies, each is missing a leg, an arm and a head.... Two frogs engaged in a rather profound discussion on the structure of the nervous system of which they have diagram right behind them.[38]

The test itself asks respondents to derive content from indeterminate forms, to make meaning out of strange, formless inkblots. The subjects admit that what they are offering is just one of many possible solutions, and the subjects often begin their responses with hesitation: "If I turn it this way ..."[39] and "This part could be...."[40] Despite the imagined nature of these responses, an anomalous response can still be diagnosed as a pathology.

The most controversial use of the Rorschach test occurred after World War II, when psychologists used it to note any common pathologies among captured Nazis. Although the psychologists could find no "specific inclination towards violence, aggression, or sadism," Eric A. Zillmer, in an interview with Sinja Najafi, noted that the test did reveal "an oversimplified problem-solving style," which he took to suggest that "they were not creative thinkers, were easily influenced by authority, were attracted to the rigid and quasi-military Nazi hierarchy, relied heavily on denial, and were lacking an 'internal moral compass.'"[41] Equating this lack of an "internal moral compass" with non-creativity (of the sort ironically practised by Farrell in his own book) is nothing if not an imaginary solution. If both the original responses to the Rorschach test and *The Inkblot Record* attest to their pataphysical nature, what does *The Inkblot Record* accomplish?

The text not only accentuates the materiality of language, but also highlights the status of language as linguistic data, allowing us to see how such linguistic data can be used to different ends.[42] Changing the frame shows that the language does not have to be interpreted psychologically. The language gets stripped of its use-value, while betraying its original context at every moment. Psychologist Bruno Klopfer notes:

> The distinguishing feature of *Psychodiagnostik*, as compared with previous attempts at using ink blots as psychological material, is the complete shift of emphasis from the more or less imaginative content of the subject's response to certain formal characteristics in the concept formations. In other words, the interest is not so much in what the subject sees as in his method of handling the stimulus material.[43]

In Farrell's presentation of inkblot responses, no given response can be attached to any one speaker, and the language is removed from the subject's "method of handling the stimulus material"; hence, the sentences are rendered invalid as diagnostic tools. As mentioned earlier, the text also resists the emergence of clear subjectivity. In the lengthy section of sentences that begin with "I," we sometimes hear intimate details about a person, but the notion that any knowable "I" can emerge from reading this text is soon disrupted by the proliferation of "I's":

> I always had a feeling he was a sneaky person, I remember him laying little traps for my mother, makes me feel he was a very alone person. I always wanted to play, but I worked since I was thirteen. I bet they have tartar. I can see the projectiles going. I can't look anymore, it's too frightening, it makes me feel crazy. I can't look or I'll go crazy again. I can't make anything out of all of it, but this lower part looks like a very exotic butterfly. I can't say what

else. I can't tell. I can't think of anything else. I couldn't see, that made it even more frightening.[44]

We may be prompted to think that we are learning something about a person—for example, the clause "I'm frightened" might suggest a particular respondent is easily afraid. However, given the juxtaposition of voices throughout this section, we might wonder whether or not we are learning more about the blots and the examiner, perhaps even the reader, than the so-called subject, since other respondents to the exam were similarly frightened.

The Inkblot Record asks its readers to perform a task similar to that of the patients undertaking a Rorschach test. Apart from the list of questions on the back cover and the list of sources printed at the back of the text, the paratext of *The Inkblot Record* does not indicate how Farrell produced the material by compiling responses to the Rorschach test. Even the cover is not the expected image of an inkblot, but rather a picture of the kind of rolling stool one might find in a doctor's office. In short, Coach House's paratextual decisions offer minimal guidance for a reader who wants to navigate the text, making the first reading a kind of test-case for the reader. Even after a reader becomes aware of the context, Dworkin argues that, if there is something to be diagnosed, it is the reader's projective habits: "Rather than ask what patients see in the form of blotted ink, [Farrell's] enjambed sentences prod us to perform the inverse function and imagine what image could have possibly provoked these texts."[45] The difference between Farrell's test and the Rorschach test is that Farrell will not be scoring us at the end. Through an appeal to the absurd, the amusing, and the artificial, a 'pataphysical text like *The Inkblot Record* highlights its contradictions and mocks any truth claim about what we might see within the Rorschach image of the text itself.

It would be impossible to catalogue all the possible responses to the Rorschach test, suggesting that *The Inkblot Record*, or any project like it, cannot give a complete account of the language used by Rorchach test subjects. But this fact is precisely our point: *The Inkblot Record* does not profess truth, but rather insists on its existence as a particular, isolated, discrete, and singular set of data. This data cannot be extrapolated from the sentences that comprise *The Inkblot Record*, since they do not add up to any generalization. But the data does allow us to notice facts about this language—facts previously indiscernible because of the context. Enlightenment may not be attainable; every insight has a blindness. And this is the lesson of 'pataphysics: everything is extremely particular, singular. Built into the definition of equivalency and identity is a potential for rupture, a fundamental difference. *The Inkblot Record*'s political power comes by enacting this phenomenon. The book demonstrates that no two solutions to the Rorschach test are the same and that each one is equally imaginary. Acknowledging the futility of such a complete reformation, pataphysical poets find promise in deformation.

The latter half of the twentieth century saw pataphysical experimentation and other anti-rational, anti-positivist discourses explode alongside a cultural shift characterized by a general distrust of truth claims, skepticism about the possibility of complete coherence, and a questioning of authority. This shift from absolutism to relativism manifested itself in a variety of artistic techniques from William Burroughs's "cut-ups," to Allan Kaprow's "happenings," on to Andy Warhol's "silkscreens." More recently, and at an exponential rate, poets have been turning to procedural techniques, like those found in *The Inkblot Record*.[46] These poets are not so much interested in "direct treatment of the thing" as "systematic treatment of the thing," using formulae, constricted vocabularies, and other experimental writing procedures.

Although pataphysics has undergone a general revival in many different contexts during the postwar era, this imaginary science has resurged dramatically in the scene of contemporary poetics. The last two decades have seen the expansion of Kenneth Goldsmith's UbuWeb,[47] a digital archive of all things avant-garde; Northwestern University Press published Christian Bök's *'Pataphysics: The Poetics of an Imaginary Science* as part of the series Avant-Garde and Modernism;[48] *Contemporary Literature* published Craig Dworkin's article "The Imaginary Solution";[49] Jerome McGann and Johanna Drucker launched a lab dedicated to Applied Research in Patacriticism;[50] and *Open Letter* published a special issue on Canadian "Pataphysics.[51] Some of the main concepts taken up by poetic avant-gardes from 'pataphysics are the notion of equivalence, the idea of the clinamen, and a belief in absurdity. Equivalence has come to represent the idea that one "solution" is not more correct than any other; they are all equally imaginary.[52] The clinamen, a term that Jarry appropriates from

Lucretius, is the small swerve or deviation that any atom might make spontaneously in its movement, suggesting that no action is perfectly repeatable and that all actions can happen by accident.[53] Lastly, contemporary poets latch on to the absurdity of 'pataphysics: they engage in exaggeration, parody, and mockery, all of which they employ to showcase the arbitrariness of thought. In short, beginning with what Beaumont has called a "Jarry revival,"[54] North American poets have been participating in pataphysical practices (as seen, for example, in such cases as these: the use of aleatoric procedures in the work of Jackson Mac Low and John Cage; the use of scientific precision in the work of Ron Silliman and Christian Bök; the attention to the combinatory possibilities of the alphabet in Steve McCaffery and bpNichol; or the exploration of virtual, textual spaces by Brian Kim Stefans and Nick Montfort).[55]

This postwar flowering of such pataphysical enterprises might be no surprise given their affinity with postmodernist sensibilities.[56] Despite the small amount of critical work on 'pataphysics, the similarities in the thinking of Jarry, Derrida, and even the Nietzsche of *The Gay Science*, have been outlined.[57] I argue, however, that Jarry might more appropriately be seen as a literary forerunner to Paul Feyerabend, who has argued against adhering to any specific method or theory, whether that be a "gay science" or deconstruction. In Feyerabend's last letter, he writes:

> It is very important not to let this suspicion *deteriorate into a truth*, or a theory, for example into a theory with the principle: things are never what they seem to be. Reality, or Being, or God, or whatever it is that sustains us cannot be captured that easily. The problem is not why we are so often confused; the problem is why we seem to possess useful and enlightening knowledge.[58]

"Deteriorate into a truth" gets at the heart of Feyerabend's critique: all truth claims are false—even this one—and to assume their truth is to deteriorate. We might summarize this view with the help of a popular sign at political rallies: "If your beliefs fit on a sign, think harder." The irony of the sign—that the statement itself fits on the sign—captures a 'pataphysical sentiment that is not simply a performative contradiction. When considering 'pataphysics, we must always remember Jarry's clinamen, which acts as a constant disturbance behind the "sign" of his science.

Rather than arguing over whether or not it is possible for poetry either to establish new linguistic orders or to avoid any political valence whatsoever, 'pataphysical texts use various formal tactics to re-imagine the biases, ideologies, and predilections of existing discourses. 'Pataphysical texts do not attempt to escape ideology or to disrupt ideology, but rather they attempt to expose the political, if not the aesthetic, aspects of language—aspects that close readings show are always intertwined. Instead of using language in a non-normative way that disrupts its complicity with capitalism, or any other "ism," 'pataphysical poetry participates in the kind of enterprise described by Michel Foucault, who notes that "[ideology] always stands in virtual opposition to something else which is supposed to count as truth," but "the problem does not consist in drawing the line between that in a discourse which falls under the category of scientificity or truth, and that which comes under some other category, but in seeing historically how effects of truth are produced within discourses which in themselves are neither true nor false."[59]

Even if the relationship between Jarry's 'pataphysics and Farrell's cataloguing is imaginary, reading the text as if this relationship were real allows us to situate the text within both the current moment and the literary past. Understanding the history and afterlives of 'pataphysics (including Canadian 'Pataphysics) can help critics to account for the political importance of a poetry that neither exerts its power by attempting to instigate social change directly nor exerts its power by asserting its imaginary status beyond politics. Farrell's poetics does not even claim a "revolution of the word," let alone a revolution of the world. Rather, Farrell's text performs an irreversible, clinamatic swerve within the world of words. Just as the sentences that comprise *The Inkblot Record* can never be completely severed from their original context, so also can these same sentences, once published in this book, never again be seen outside of their requoted context. By showing that the same linguistic data can be used to very different ends, the book reveals both the arbitrariness and the mutability in our view of any data. *The Inkblot Record* not only "lays bare the device," but playfully enacts the art of (re)devising.

NOTES

1 Alfred Jarry, *Exploits and Opinions of Dr. Faustroll, Pataphysician: A Neo-Scientific Novel*, trans. Simon Watson Taylor (Boston: Exact Change, 1996), 75.

2 Charles Bernstein, "Comedy and the Poetics of Political Form," *The Politics of Poetics Form* (New York: Roof Books, 1990), 235–244.

3 Flarf began as a listserv for the Flarfist collective in 2001. Initial members included Nada Gordon, K. Silem Mohammad, and Gary Sullivan. Flarfists used the Internet as a source of text, entering strange combinations of terms into search engines so as to garner unusual, and often inappropriate, if not offensive, outcomes. For a brief introduction, see John Tranter, ed., "Jacket Flarf Feature," *Jacket* 30, http://jacketmagazine.com/30/index.shtml. See also Kenneth Goldsmith, "Introduction to Flarf vs. Conceptual Writing," for the Whitney Museum of American Art (17 Apr. 2009), http://writing.upenn.edu/epc/authors/goldsmith/whitney-intro.html. For an excellent critique of Flarfist techniques, see Dan Hoy, "The Virtual Dependency of the Post-Avant and the Problematics of Flarf: What Happens When Poets Spend Too Much Time Fucking Around on the Internet," *Jacket* 29, http://jacketmagazine.com/29/hoy-flarf.html. New Formalism began in the 1980s with writers who called for a return to older forms that emphasized rhyme and metre. See Monroe K. Spear, "The Poetics of the New Formalism," *Hudson Review* 43.4 (1991): 549–562. In my mind, Flarf and New Formalism represent two reactions to the problem of form in contemporary poetics. Flarfists take the "form" of the Internet and evacuate it of all meaning—turning it into a game and using it as a venue for low jokes. New Formalism has reacted in the opposite way, arguing that the only way to reclaim poetic form is to return to older understandings of form.

4 Jarry, *Exploits*, 22. Although *Exploits and Opinions* was written in 1898, it was not published until 1911, fulfilling Jarry's postscript: "This book will not be published integrally until the author has acquired sufficient experience to savor all its beauties in full" (136).

5 Jarry, xi.

6 Jarry, 21.

7 Jarry, 24.

8 See Keith Beaumont, *Alfred Jarry: A Critical and Biographical Study* (New York: St. Martin's Press, 1984).

9 Jarry, *Exploits*, 22.

10 N. Katherine Hayles uses a similar example in *The Cosmic Web: Scientific Field Models and Literary Strategies in the Twentieth Century* (Ithaca: Cornell University Press, 1984), 19. She explains the current scientific moment: "Imagine, for example, that we are sitting in a diner, waiting for a hamburger. In the ordinary view the plate, knife, and fork, and ketchup bottle are 'real,' while the pattern they form is a transitory artifact of their relative positions. But suppose that we were to shift our perspective so that we regarded the pattern as 'real,' and the ketchup bottle, plate, knife, and fork as merely temporary manifestations of that particular pattern."

She argues that this shift in world view resembles the change in perspective caused when Copernicus proves that the Earth does not occupy the centre of the universe. Such a shift, which leads ultimately to recents trends in science, like quantum mechanics, provides evidence for the world becoming more 'pataphysically minded.

11 Beaumont, *Alfred Jarry*, 191–193.

12 Beaumont, 190–191. Jarry was part of an anti-positivist reaction to science around the turn of the twentieth century—a reaction that Beaumont says had three main critiques: "Firstly, the movement questioned the methods of science, pointing out (a) that science deals not in certitudes but merely in useful hypotheses containing a greater or lesser degree of 'probability'; and (b) that science deals not in literal descriptions but in 'working models' or 'symbols' of reality. Secondly, it questioned the equation of 'reality' with the merely scientifically observable and measurable, arguing that it is only a part of total reality which is accessible to such observation and measurement. Thirdly, it questioned the doctrine of epistemological realism (or 'naive realism')—the view accepted, at least implicitly, by the great majority of scientifically-minded thinkers in the third quarter of the nineteenth century, that through our senses we perceive the world exactly as it is."

13 Roger Shattuck, *The Banquet Years: The Arts in France, 1885–1918* (London: Jonathan Cape, 1969), 188.

14 Steve McCaffery and bpNichol, *Rational Geomancy: The Kids of the Book-Machine; The Collected Research Reports of the Toronto Research Group 1973–1982* (Vancouver: Talonbooks, 1992), 7.

15 McCaffery and bpNichol, *Rational Geomancy*, 301.

16 Dan Farrell, *The Inkblot Record* (Toronto: Coach House Books, 2000), 61.

17 Although the way that the Rorschach test has been administered has changed over time, those who administer the test typically ask any number of stock questions and use the same ten stock inkblots. *The Inkblot Record*'s paratext frames the book around the systematic questioning of an imagined examiner. The back cover reads, "What do you see? Why? What would it be? What was the difference? What might that reflect in your life? What made you think of that? What kind of an animal is it? What in the card gave the impression of mice? What about this part? What's the connection? What gave you that impression? What do you mean by that? What do you mean? What do they remind you of? What does that make you think of? What does that call to mind? What does it remind you of? Was this part of it? Shape too? Only shape? Nothing else? Is the sex organ male or female? Is there anything else about them? Is it big or small? Is it a face? How much of the face do you see? How do you see it? For example? Do you see more than the profile in any of these? Do you have any special reason for calling them bears? Do they seem alive? Do they have anything to do with each other? Does it look like it's moving? Could you tell what gives that feeling? Anything else?"

18 Craig Dworkin, "The Imaginary Solution," *Contemporary Literature* 48.1 (2007): 29–60. 32. Some exemplary poets that Dworkin addresses in his essay are Kenneth Goldsmith, Douglas Huebler, Darren Wershler, Christian Bök, and Judith Goldman.

19 Dan Farrell, *The Inkblot Record*, 56.

20 Farrell, 111.

21 Roland Barthes, "The Death of the Author," *Image Music Text*, trans. Stephen Heath (New York: Noonday, 1977), 142–148. 146.

22 Barthes, "The Death," 146.

23 Barthes, 148.

24 Barthes, 147.

25 Barthes, 44.

26 Barthes, 55.

27 Barthes, 102.

28 Barthes, 5.

29 Barthes, 56.

30 Beaumont writes, "To read ['pataphysics] as a 'serious' attempt to affirm 'beliefs,' new or old, would be a total misunderstanding of Jarry's purpose" (199).

Although here Beaumont is specifically referring to the last chapter of Faustroll, he makes the same argument for the book (and 'pataphysics) in general.

31 Ron Silliman, "Disappearance of the Word, Appearance of the World," *The L=A=N=G=U=A=G=E Book* (Carbondale: Southern Illinois University Press, 1984), 121–132. 125.

32 Silliman, "Disappearance," 125.

33 See Dworkin, "The Imaginary Solution," 42. He notes: "Part of Farrell's larger project has been to chart the psychological matrix of capitalism, and the ways in which even the most scientific discourses, with all of their cultural authority and supposed objectivity, are of course socially constructed and implicated."

34 The validity and usefulness of the Rorschach test has been widely debated. See James M. Wood, M. Teresa Nezworski, and William J. Stejskal, "The Comprehensive System for the Rorschach: A Critical Examination," *Psychological Science* 7.1 (1996): 3–10.

35 Farrell, *The Inkblot Record*, 73.

36 Farrell, 101.

37 Farrell, 90.

38 Farrell, 84–85.

39 Farrell, 107.

40 Farrell, 81.

41 Sina Najafi, "Bats and Dancing Bears: An Interview with Eric A. Zillmer," *Cabinet* 5 (Winter 2001/2002), http://www.cabinetmagazine.org/issues/5/najafi.php.

42 For another example of this phenomenon, see Kenneth Goldsmith, *Day* (Great Barrington: The Figures, 2003).

43 Bruno Klopfer, *Rorschach Technique: A Manual for a Projective Method of Personality Diagnosis* (New York: World Book Co., 1942), 4.

44 Farrell, *The Inkblot Record*, 24–25.

45 Dworkin, "The Imaginary Solution," 42.

46 See Marjorie Perloff, *Unoriginal Genius: Poetry by Other Means in the New Century* (Chicago: University of Chicago Press, 2010). Perloff deals specifically with texts that rely heavily on citation.

47 The "Ubu" of UbuWeb is a direct reference to Alfred Jarry's most famous character, the star of three plays: *Ubu Rex*; *Ubu Cuckolded*; and *Ubu Enchained*.

48 Christian Bök, *'Pataphysics: The Poetics of an Imaginary Science* (Evanston: Northwestern University Press, 2002).

49 Craig Dworkin, "The Imaginary Solution," 29–60.

50 See http://www.patacriticism.org. As of December 2010, the website is currently unavailable.

51 Toronto Research Group, ed., "Introduction," *Canadian "Pataphysics: Open Letter* 4.6–7 (1980–81): 7–8. Canadian poets have had the most sustained, intimate engagement with 'pataphysics, and their influence cannot be overestimated. For more on Canadian "Pataphysics and the TRG, see Steve McCaffery and bpNichol, *Rational Geomancy*. For a critical view on the subject, see Peter Jaeger, *ABC of Reading TRG* (Vancouver: Talonbooks, 1999).

52 The rationalization for the title of *Rational Geomancy* is telling of this idea's influence: "We mean by Rational Geomancy the acceptance of a multiplicity of means and ways to reorganize those energy patterns we perceive in literature. There can be no absolute interpretation (i.e., system of alignment) for the geomantic view of literature sees interpretation as any system of alignment, any organization and/or reorganization of those energy patterns. As we shall see later interpretation of this kind is equivalent to both a reading and a writing upon the ground of all literature." *Rational Geomancy*, 153.

53 For a more extensive discussion of the clinamen, see Christian Bök, *'Pataphysics*, 43–45. See also Warren F. Motte Jr., "Clinamen Redux" in *Comparative Literature Studies* 23.4 (1986): 263–281. "Clinamen" has become a central term for several poets, most notably Steve McCaffery and Joan Retallack.

54 "The Jarry Revival" is the title for the introduction to *Alfred Jarry: A Critical and Biographical Study* by Keith Beaumont.

55 For examples of poets who might be classified more loosely as 'pataphysical, see Charles Bernstein, "Poetry Ordinary and Extraordinary: The Pataque(e)rics of Everyday Life" (Syllabus, Princeton University, Fall 2011), http://www.writing.upenn.edu/bernstein/syllabi/Princeton-F11.html. See also Charles Bernstein, "Unsettling the Word: Attack of the Difficult Poems" (Syllabus, University of Pennsylvania, Spring 2011), http://www.writing.upenn.edu/bernstein/syllabi/unsettling.html. Bernstein introduced his recent coinage, "pataqueerical," at Columbia University in 2010 for the conference Rethinking Poetics.

56 Although the difference (or not) between modernism and postmodernism undergoes constant dispute, Jarry's pseudoscience falls more in line with the popular understanding of postmodernism as a questioning of "grand narratives."

57 See Stephen Barker, "Canon-fodder: Nietzsche, Jarry, Derrida (The Play of Discourse and the Discourse of Play)," *Journal of Dramatic Theory and Criticism* 69 (1989): 69–83.

58 Paul Feyerabend, *Against Method: Outline of an Anarchistic Theory of Knowledge*, 4th ed. (London: Verso, 2010), xvi.

59 Michel Foucault, "Truth and Power," *The Foucault Reader* (New York Pantheon, 1984), 51–75. 60.

DARREN WERSHLER

Everyday Practice Before and After Conceptual Writing

It is only possible to be ambivalent about conceptual writing,[1] and always has been. The reason for my ambivalence has a lot to do with the relationship between conceptual writing and the notion of literary genius, both in terms of what it obscures, and what it has become.

THE TROUBLE WITH GENIUS

Precisely in order to describe the author-function of conceptual writing, Marjorie Perloff dialectically refines the notion of the modern genius to make it useful in the contemporary moment. She accomplishes this by unburdening the genius of the criteria of originality.

> Once we grant that current art practices have their own particular momentum and *inventio*, we can dissociate the word *original* from its partner *genius*. If conceptual poetry makes no claim to originality—at least not originality in the usual sense—this is not to say that *genius* isn't in play. It just takes different forms.[2]

What I want to discuss is the importance of the negative complement to Perloff's own dialectic: the ground which the brilliance of genius (even the uncreative kind) obscures. This ground is the condition for the appearance and continued existence of unoriginal genius in a literary context.

As Gilles Deleuze and Félix Guattari describe in *A Thousand Plateaus*, modern methods for creating openness and multiplicity in the fragmented work of art might succeed on the level of literary innovation, but totaliza-tion reaffirms itself at the level of the author. The genius of the experimental modernist author is that such an author can produce a fragmented mas-terpiece more realistic than realism: "The world has become chaos, but the book remains the image of the world.... A strange mystification: a book all the more total for being fragmented."[3] The unity of the author as subject remains more or less intact, which is convenient for critics, because it reifies traditional literary values and allows for the production of literary inter-pretations to proceed. The cost for that totalization is a series of systemic exclusions to which contemporary literary studies remains oblivious.

We could call this the "Wives of Geniuses I Have Sat With" problem. In *The Autobiography of Alice B. Toklas*, Stein, in the guise of Alice, writes:

> Before I decided to write this book my twenty-five years with Gertrude Stein, I had often said that I would write, The wives of geniuses I have sat with. I have sat with so many. I have sat with wives who were not wives, of geniuses who were real geniuses. I have sat with real wives of geniuses who were not real geniuses. I have sat with wives of geniuses, of near geniuses, of would be geniuses, in short I have sat very often and very long with many wives and wives of many geniuses.[4]

The wives of geniuses are supposed to serve as the ground against which the figures of the geniuses stand out. Stein makes the ridiculous and arbi-tary structure of this relationship visible by first occupying the position of the male genius herself, then occupying the position of Alice to comment on it. As Barbara Will describes, "the result is a massive send-up of con-ventional norms of gender, identity, and discursivity within which genial male authority or wifely passivity can be articulated."[5] Here's the difficulty: Stein could point to this structure, but it was politically and aesthetically important for her to occupy the ambivalent space of the modern genius in order to do so. As Deleuze and Guattari argue, the result is that the struc-ture of the genius author remains intact, despite the way in which Stein's experimental text makes its support-structure suddenly and embarrass-ingly evident.

Genius and avant-gardism aren't going to go away as cultural catego-ries, but I don't think they're where the production of cultural difference is actually located. Ostensibly countercultural groups like poets are very much a part of contemporary cultural machinery. They have established roles, practices, modes of production and circulation, and their own criteria for success. Change occurs elsewhere.

So, what is the ground of unoriginal genius?

There are several ways to answer that question, and none of them are flattering. A growing number of poets and critics have pointed out, and continue to elaborate on, the predominance of white, cis-gendered upper-middle-class males in conceptual writing, and the ideological formations that have made that positioning possible (see especially Julia Spahr and Stephanie Young's "Foulipo"[6] and recently, Fred Moten's "On Marjorie Perloff").[7] My response to such critiques is simply, yes. I'm not interested in attempting to refute them, and I'm not the person to articulate them further. But they are not the subject of this essay, which concerns the nature of my own longstanding, well-documented ambivalences about conceptual writing as a practice from before it had its name or its current notoriety, and extending into the uncertainties of the present.

Conceptual writing had a potential for a particular critique of literary studies in general and the culture of poetry in particular, but that potential remained embryonic because of the manner in which events unfolded over the last two decades.

What I was hoping for, at minimum, was that conceptual writing would be the occasion to recognize the richness and sophistication of everyday cultural practice in a networked digital milieu, and that the vehicle for that recognition would be conceptual writing's engagement with the media, formats, and genres of digital information. In a best-case scenario, such a recognition would have been accompanied by a serious interrogation of the objects and methods of literary criticism, of the author-function of the poet, and of the deeply parochial nature of poetic culture.

Instead, conceptual writing became conceptual poetry: that is, yet another way to write more poems. The machinery of literary production (let alone the machinery of culture at large) remained untouched by the entire process. Subsequently, contemporary celebrity culture discovered that it could use an unlikely mixture of everyday conceptualism and conceptual poetry as a tool to enhance its own power. Ironically, this occurs when celebrities use conceptual practice as a tactic for asserting that they too are "just folks."

In what could be called poetic justice, unoriginal genius becomes the ground for celebrity conceptualism.

EVERYDAY AMBIVALENCE

There are a set of contemporary everyday practices and cultural techniques that precede, exist coterminously with, and have survived the demise of conceptual writing. To varying degrees, interest in these practices appears in Flarf, conceptual writing, and electronic literature. For want of a better term, I call these practices "everyday conceptualism."

Both "everyday" and "conceptualism" have complex intellectual histories that extend back decades (and, by some accounts,[8] by centuries). For an introduction to theories of the everyday, Stephen Johnstone's anthology *The Everyday* is helpful.[9] For conceptual art proper, *Conceptual Art: A Critical Anthology* by Alexander Alberro and Blake Stimson is a good starting point.[10] Michael Sheringham's *Everyday Life: Theories and Practices from Surrealism to the Present* is particularly useful, because it emphasizes the imbrication of the two terms: "Since the 1960s, artistic practice has often consisted in doing away with the artwork and devising ways of focusing the viewer's attention on 'mere real things.'"[11] But this is not, and has never been, a simple process that invariably produces successful results, because its object is far from simple.

As Henri Lefebvre, the major theorist of everyday life in "modernity," has noted, the salient feature of the everyday is its ambivalence. The everyday is "[a] mixture of nature and culture, the historical and the lived, the individual and the social, the real and the unreal, a place of transitions, of meetings, interactions and conflicts."[12] It is the site of the mundane and the tedious grinding processes that characterize human existence, but also of the events that escape them. Everyday life contains the possibility for critique and thus for its own transformation. Even before yoking the everyday to any form of conceptual art practice, then, it's necessary to be thinking about how to conceive of the everyday while holding these aspects in tension.

In "Everyday Speech," Maurice Blanchot concurs:

> Always the two sides meet: the daily with its tedious side, painful and sordid (the amorphous, the stagnant), and the inexhaustible, irrecusable, always unfinished daily that always escapes forms or structures (particularly those

of political society: bureaucracy, the wheels of government, parties). And that there may be a certain relation of identity between these two opposites is shown by the slight displacement of emphasis that permits passage from one to the other; as when the spontaneous, the informal—that is, what escapes forms—becomes the amorphous and when, perhaps, the stagnant merges with the current of life, which is also the very movement of society.[13]

Blanchot's point, which he reiterates thoughout the piece, is the slipperiness of the concept: the everyday constantly eludes our ability to easily categorize it. It takes on different flavours and textures at different levels of society, as people perform their everyday practices in myriad ways.

One of the complex things about the everyday is its relationship to the creative process. Lefebvre insists that the everyday exists in productive tension with creativity rather than serving as its opposite: "it is in everyday life and starting from everyday life that genuine creations are achieved, those creations which produce the human and which men produce as part of the process of becoming human: works of creativity."[14] For Lefebvre, the creative and the mechanical aspects of the everyday form "a permanently reactivated circuit."[15] Mike Featherstone elaborates: as forms of specialized theoretical knowledge like the arts and sciences develop, they separate from the ground of the everyday, until the knowledge they produce feeds back in order to "rationalize, colonize and homogenize everyday life."[16] Everyday life is what authenticates creative acts, but these acts in turn interrogate our sense of what is possible within everyday practice.[17]

Johnstone jokes that "most artists don't read Henri Lefebvre or Michel de Certeau in order to discover the ordinary,"[18] but few people in general read or view the work of the artists who spent the last century "discovering the ordinary." Even when non-artists do encounter art that concerns the everyday, as Johnson observes in reference to the range of perspectives in his anthology, "the question of what actually happens to quotidian phenomena when they are recoded into art is still a thorny issue for many critics."[19]

I think that what everyday conceptualism investigates isn't the individual writing subject so much as it is "the linguistic and cultural community in which that self is a participant."[20] The writing subjects engaging in such practices are often unaware of or completely indifferent to the long history of experimental aesthetic strategies, though their entire culture is steeped in them. They don't always identify as poets or artists. Some aren't even human. They don't call what they produce art or literature, nor do they circulate it through the machinery of literary or artistic production. But because the people who encounter everyday conceptualism don't think of it as art or literature, nor do they imagine its creators as literary authors or artists, it remains largely invisible to scholars, theorists, and critics.

As Michel de Certeau, Fredric Jameson, and Carl Lovitt note in "The Oppositional Practices of Everyday Life," the inability of scholarship to comprehend everyday practice is not a new problem:

> [Research institutions tend] to retain from such practices and activities the merest physical or linguistic *objects*, which are then labelled according to their thematics and their places of origin, placed under glass, offered up for exegesis, and asked to disguise ... the legitimation of an order which its custodians consider to be immemorial and "natural." In other cases, from the *languages* of such social operations, they extract tools and products to be ranged in exhibits of technical gadgets, spread out inertly along the borders of an untroubled system.[21]

The artifacts (textual or otherwise) that any given practice produces are not the same as the practice. The institutions and disciplines that extract and circulate objects from such practices do so for their own purposes, which are often inimical to those of the practitioners. The ongoing controversy over Dominic Gagnon's film *Of the North* is a case in point. The film is a 74-minute mashup whose director says "he drew from around 500 hours of footage of the circumpolar region and stitched it together at his computer in Montreal. The soundtrack is made up of Inuit musicians—also taken from web clips—and sound design by the filmmaker himself."[22] The film description on the website for Dokufest, The International Documentary and Short Film Festival, situates *Of the North* in the history of revolutionary critique: "[Gagnon] creates an anti-exotic Vertovian 'Kino-Eye,' which reveals trashy and unbridled acculturation and takes apart the existing clichés about the Inuit, too often confined to the borders of the contemporary world."[23] That many people, including, but not limited to, Inuit artists and filmmakers, continue to argue that the film perpetuates the very stereotypes which it claims to criticize, demonstrates the range and gravity of the problem.

In the specific case of literary studies, scholars still have not developed a vocabulary to talk about the aesthetic aspects of daily practice in general without claiming them for literature, or insisting that poets have some sort of special status as a result of doing what many others are also doing. Engaging with these practices could have taught us how to interpret them—and, by extension, it might have made us realize that the materiality, production, circulation, transfiguration, and consumption of media-forms should matter more to literary studies than they do. It might even have led to an interrogation of what matters to literary studies, and of the kinds of claims that we make for literature's power.

Perloff's question is "how has the digital dissemination of new poetry and poetics ... affected the writing of poetry itself?"[24] Mine is different. Has thinking about daily cultural practice in a networked digital world sufficiently affected how we think about aesthetic categories like poetry or the author-function of the poet?

EVERYDAY CONCEPTUALISM

In order to make sense of this question, we first need to ask another. What does everyday conceptualism look like? Some examples follow. I have years of accumulated folders of such things, but these four will do for now.

1 *Pepys' Diary.*[25] On 26 December 2002, Phil Gyford launched the blog *Pepys' Diary*, on which he posted a new entry every day from the voluminous diary of seventeenth-century British Parliamentarian and businessman Samuel Pepys. Gyford completed the project for the first time on 31 May 2012, then rolled it back to the start and began again. Gyford comes from the world of strategic design, so this is not a literary project, but, as Russell Davies wrote, part of "the non-commercial, hobbyist web that destroyed so many business models back then and which no one talks about any more."[26] On one hand, then, the *Diary* is close to the notion of everyday practice as a kind of popular "rip-off" tactic,[27] but it's also complicit with the functioning of the neoliberal "creative" economy. In terms of its prescience, duration, scope, and execution, *Pepys' Diary* vaults over the head of any number of conceptualist literary book-reblogging projects, but makes no claims for the refined sensibilities of its creator or for its own aesthetic

merit. It's a vital bit of context for many examples of digital conceptual writing practice, but I've never heard a literary critic even mention it.

2 **Every Death in The Game of Thrones Series, Tabbed.**[28] This is the title of a Reddit post from 2013 that received 2,493 points (91 percent upvoted) and garnered 1,019 comments. It is still popular enough that it occasionally drifts back on to the Reddit front page and has been circulating on Twitter as well. This example is much humbler in scale and aspiration than my first. It resembles any number of aesthetic, treated-book projects, but it moves through different channels of circulation. Because it's associated with a Reddit username ("force-duse" https://www.reddit.com/user/forceduse, it has a very different author-function than a poet or an artist. What's important here is not just the ostensible contents of the image that appeared on Reddit—a snapshot of the five published volumes of the *Game of Thrones* series in a stack on a table, with coloured Post-it tabs protruding from the top end, each marking the death of a character in the book. What matters is the documentation of this object as a digital snapshot, its posting on social media, the rituals of commenting, upvoting and downvoting, subsequent reposting on other networks (with and without attribution), the algorithmic oversight and metadata gathering associated with all of these activities, and the business models of companies like Reddit that position its users as their product. *This* is the material and political economy of contemporary textual production, literature included, and it needs to figure in critical interpretation (not just literary criticism, which sorely needs such analysis) far more than it does.

3 *The Leila Texts.*[29] From 2007 to 2012, writer Leila Sales saved and blogged the messages that were sent to her (on average, five times a day), all of which should have gone to other Leilas on the Verizon network. What's of interest is not just the mildly humorous content of the texts. This "side project" is exemplary of the casual projects of collection and curation elsewhere online, and, for that matter, in poetry and art, but this project would be excluded from consideration by many critics because its author writes young adult fiction. I've written elsewhere about the formal resemblance between conceptual writing and fanfiction,[30] so I won't go into detail here. Back on the subject of

political economy, I'd suggest that we need to address more than the way that affect and syntax shift to accomodate the formal and medial contraints of cellphone screens and SMS protocols. The circumstances of its production and appearance in the context of the largest US provider of wireless communication services, and the vertical integration of hardware platforms, software and carriers, is worth considering, as is the fact that this is the sort of thing that can result in bestselling books (like the Tumblr feed *Texts from Dog*)[31] or bestselling books *and* a television contract for a situation comedy, starring William Shatner (as in the case of the Twitter feed *Shit My Dad Says*).[32]

4 *The Nanex Crop Circle of the Day*.[33] Given that somewhere between 49 percent and 61 percent of Internet traffic is now robotic, depending on whose numbers you believe,[34] it's worth mentioning nonhuman aesthetics at this point. Procedural and algorithmic writing have been around for a long time, but humans have been minority producers and consumers of text for years (somewhere, Friedrich Kittler is grimly satisfied). In 2010, a stock monitoring company called Nanex began posting examples of visualizations of bizarre patterns produced by robotic price-cycling, which was occurring hundreds of times a day, even when robots were minor contributors to online stock-trading activity. On the *Harriet* blog, Christian Bök has described these patterns as "unique, visual poem[s]."[35] But seeing these visualizations as poems is part of *human* aesthetics. We also need to think about what nonhumans write, and how they read (each other and us), if we're going to understand twenty-first-century textual economies.

There are multitudes of other things I could have cited here. These examples skew toward the "successful" end of the spectrum, at least in terms of finding an audience of some sort, for some period of time, which is not always the desired outcome for everyday conceptualism.

In the early days of Twitter, for example, I noticed that I was being followed by a Japanese account that followed only people named Darren. There were maybe seventeen Darrens at most on the "Following" list, and the account never posted a thing. People making pixelated murals in office windows out of Post-it Notes have an audience of their co-workers and random passersby, but only for as long as they can maintain the goodwill of management and the custodial staff. They are also engaging in everyday conceptualism. And so are the throngs of people making and posting the "fanboy supercuts" first described by Andy Baio in 2008.[36] Or the funny and clever Amazon reviews, Craigslist ads, and eBay auctions that each constitute new literary forms. The top positive and top critical reviews for "BiC for Her Medium Ballpoint Pen—Black, Box of 12," on Amazon.co.uk, for example, demonstrate how a form like the online consumer review, a genre whose ostensible purpose is conveying consumer information, becomes a vehicle for social satire:

Top positive review
See all 342 positive reviews›
2,837 of 2,897 people found this helpful
5.0 out of 5 stars Great product!
By A keen skier on 3 September 2012

My husband has never allowed me to write, as he doesn't want me touching men's pens. However when I saw this product, I decided to buy it (using my pocket money) and so far it has been fabulous! Once I had learnt to write, the feminine colour and the grip size (which was more suited to my delicate little hands) has enabled me to vent thoughts about new recipe ideas, sewing and gardening. My husband is less pleased with this product as he believes it will lead to more independence and he hates the feminine tingling sensation (along with the visions of fairies and rainbows) he gets whenever he picks it up.

Top critical review
6,460 of 6,538 people found the following review helpful
1.0 out of 5 stars Insufficient, 28 Aug. 2012

By Mr. J. Stevens
Normally I only use pens designed and created for real men, in colours appropriate to such instruments of masculinity—black like my chest hair or blue like the steely glint of my eyes, or the metallic paintwork of my convertible Mustang sportscar. Imagine then the situation I found myself in when, upon taking delivery of another shipment of motorbike parts and footballs, I reached for and grasped not my normal BIC pen, but a "BIC for Her

Amber Medium Ballpoint Pen" (evidently ordered by my well-meaning, but ill-informed girlfriend whilst my back was turned). I knew something was wrong when I had to physically restrain my hands, gnarled and worn from a lifetime of rock-climbing and shark-wrestling, from crushing the fragile implement like a Fabergé egg. Things only went downhill from there.

Normally my hand writing is defined and strong, as if chiselled in granite by the Greek gods themselves, however upon signing my name I noticed that my signature was uncharacteristically meandering and looping. More worryingly the dots above the I's manifested themselves as hearts, and I found myself finishing off the signature with a smiley face and kisses. Obviously I had no choice but to challenge the delivery man to a gun fight on the rim of an erupting volcano in order to reassert my dominance. Had I not won this honourable duel this particular mistake might have resulted in a situation that no amount of expensive single malt whiskey and Cuban cigars could banish. I leave this review here as a warning to all men about the dangers of using this particular device, and suffice-it-to-say will return to signing my name with a nail gun as normal.[37]

Such personal practices interest me even more than the examples that I've listed above, but they are more difficult to document.

Everyday conceptualism includes a wide range of author-functions, formats, and genres, all of which lie well outside the ambit of poetry, and arguably of literature itself. It occurs on the level of the everyday, and tends to manifest itself in the forms that John Guillory refers to as "information genres."

INFORMATION GENRES AND THE POET AS ANTENNA

I've been trying to find a way to write about this sort of phenomena since the late 1990s. Reading John Guillory's article "The Memo and Modernity" in 2004 gave me a language to do so.[38] Before there was a clear consensus about what it was or what it was going to be called, what conceptual writing did was to draw attention to the rhetorical aspects of mundane forms of writing that canonical literature usually neglects: weather reports, legal transcripts, social media feeds, stock quotes, Usenet posts, and so on. These texts make up the bulk of everything that's written, but we pretend that they don't matter in any capacity other than the moment. Guillory describes such texts as belonging to what he calls "information genres."

In order to use these genres to convey that peculiar modern invention we call "information," we have to pretend that they have no rhetorical value of their own that might taint it.[39] By repackaging great swaths of information in media and formats other than the ones in which it initially appeared, conceptual writing drew attention to the fact that all writing is poetic in that it always says more than we intend, and we assign value to it in keeping with large sets of external factors that sometimes have little to do with the ostensible content.

What everyday conceptualism demonstrates is that poets are far from the only ones who engage in such practices, and that they're not necessarily the best at them when they do. Further, the framing of such practices as literary or artistic might draw attention to them in a limited capacity, among literary critics, but it also turns them into something else—a style that can be mobilized elsewhere, to very different effect. What I wanted to have followed on the heels of conceptual writing was a general interrogation of literariness, poeticity and the author-function in the contemporary moment, but what happened instead in both theory and practice was a redoubled emphasis on the figure of the poet-celebrity as an exemplary conduit for emergent media practice.

The "artist as antennae" has been one of the command metaphors behind the discourse of poetry and technology for about a century.[40] In 1922, Ezra Pound declaimed that "Artists are the antennae of the race."[41] Marshall McLuhan expanded the metaphor in 1964, writing that "Art as radar acts as an "early alarm system."[42] Christopher Dewdney's "Parasite Maintenance" updated the technology in McLuhan's metaphor for the late twentieth century, imagining the poet as a satellite dish: "The radio telescope becomes a model of the bi-conscious interface between 'the mind' and signals from the 'outside' which the poet receives."[43] What these models have in common is that they imagine communication in terms of a more or less linear transmission whose success hinges on the refined sensibilities of the artist. As James Carey pointed out, the transmission model of communication is always wrapped up in "complementary models of power and anxiety."[44] But poets don't lead, and it's time to get over our anxiety about that.

Moreover, the model of poet-as-*bricoleur* (or, to use the metaphors of the moment, "curator" or "DJ") reifies the notion of genius in the form of the person with an especially refined sense of taste (with all of the class implications that that implies left intact). For want of space and time, I'll recommend "Post-Postmodernism?"—Owen Hatherley's critique of Nicolas Bourriaud on this subject.[45]

So, I'm not impressed by projects like 89Plus and Hans Ulrich Obrist's "Poetry Will Be Made by All!" because it entirely misses the point.[46] When everybody makes poetry, the residual cultural privilege that clings to the position of the poet should disappear. In 2014, poetry sales in Canada hovered around 0.17 percent of all book sales,[47] and they haven't changed much from that figure over the last half decade. At such a time, gathering "1000 Books by 1000 Poets" is much less interesting to me than what everyone other than self-identified poets do in other contexts. What we have overlooked for too long are the messy, contingent ways in which media, formats, and genres overlap each other. Rather than origins or influences, it might be more productive to consider, as Foucault suggests, institutionalizations, transformations, affiliations, and relationships.[48]

The cycling between everyday and aesthetic conceptualism isn't an either-or proposition, "art = good; everyday = bad" or "everyday = good; art = bad." Nor is it simply a matter of maintaining a kind of homeostasis, because the dialectic can take genuinely surprising turns—and such turns can be antithetical to anything resembling critique. The most recent ambivalent, dialectical transformation in the long series of pairings of the everyday and the exceptional is the development of celebrity conceptualism.

CELEBRITY CONCEPTUALISM

For at least half a century, critics and artists have been trying without cease to use art and daily life to correct each others' perceived shortcomings. As Featherstone notes, the process of "de-differentiation" that I imagined would result after conceptual writing has happened before, in other contexts. This struggle can take (and has taken) a number of forms, one of which is the critique of the artist as heroic or special in some way:

[T[his can also be manifest in the critique of the heroic image of the cultural specialist, the scientist, artist or intellectual as hero, in favour of an emphasis upon everyday mundane practices which are regarded as equally capable of producing what some want to regard as extraordinary or elevated insights or objectifications.[49]

Featherstone's larger point is that the value of everyday life relates to the value of its counter-concept. When artists are culturally important, everyday life is downplayed. When the cultural capital of art drops, populism prevails. So what happens in the contemporary moment, which is dominated by a discourse of celebrity?

Celebrity studies is a large and growing field with a substantial critical literature, and it is of increasing relevance to all aspects of cultural studies, including literary studies, where authors at all levels are now arguably celebrities first and producers of texts second. If the everyday and the aesthetic have long mainted themselves in a sort of dialectical impasse, the discourse of celebrity derives much of its power by subsuming both categories in what P. David Marshall calls a "contradictory discourse of both value and valuelessness." Celebrity is at once a way of becoming visible on the world stage, while at the same time admitting that it's entirely possible to achieve such visibility without having achieved anything of cultural significance.[50] For Marshall, celebrity is the antithesis of earlier notions of cultural heroism, where the hero's actions matter precisely because they emerge from, and make a contribution back to, everyday life.

Several conceptual writers have achieved some degree of fame, or, at least, notoriety. They are, however, still poets, and thus most likely to serve as vanishing mediators in a process that is currently allowing actual celebrities to bolster their fame by making incursions into the everyday via avant-garde artistic strategies from the previous century.

The next logical step after the period of cycling between the aestheticization of the everyday and the corresponding secularization of the aesthetic is yet another dialectical elaboration, which subsumes the whole process: celebrity conceptualism. This practice allows a celebrity to demonstrate simultaneously that they have a more refined aesthetic sensibility than other celebrities *and* that they are "just folks" messing around with social media in the same goofy ways as the rest of us, without any tedious mucking about with the world of small-press poetry and university professors.

Celebrity conceptualism is an identifiable part of the shift in the cultural logic of celebrity that Marshall has described as a move from a regime of representation (where celebrities provide a point of identification for a mass audience in an era of broadcast media) to one of presentation (where they ostensibly open their private world for public consumption in an era of networked digital media).[51] This is not an entirely new phenomenon, and it probably has its relative beginnings in the 1980s. By the end of the 1990s, Brian Joseph Davis was lampooning it in *Portable Altamont*.[52] But as a result of smartphones, tablets, and other forms of mobile media, it has increased in its frequency and visibility.

What does celebrity conceptualism look like? Here are some examples (and again, there are many, many others):

1 *Richard Dreyfuss Reads the iTunes EULA*.[53] On 8 June 2011, tech journalists at *C|Net* posted a dramatic reading by actor Richard Dreyfuss of the Apple iTunes End User License Agreement (EULA). These documents are notoriously long and incomprehensible to anyone other than contract lawyers—in other words, they are a textbook example of an information genre. There was already considerable public discourse about Apple's EULAS in particular, because two months earlier (27 April 2011), *South Park* first screened its infamous episode, "HUMANCENTiPAD,"[54] detailing the horrible things that befall those who do not read the fine print. By popular demand, *C|Net* subsequently made audio files of the performance available for remixing, indicating not only popular demand to do so, but the long-established deskilling of digital remixing into something that is now an established part of everyday practice. As for Dreyfuss, who had been out of the spotlight for many years at this point, he had more to gain from participating in this exercise than not.

2 *Cindy Crawford Photographed Reading Uncreative Writing*.[55] In the year 2011, celebrity conceptualism broke. In November, the Poetry Foundation's blog *Harriet* posted a photo by New York paparazzo and book enthusiast Lawrence Schwartzwald, who photographed supermodel Cindy Crawford reading Kenneth Goldsmith's *Uncreative Writing*. Schwartzwald specializes in photographs of celebrities, poets at launches and other events, New Yorkers reading, and, occasionally, New York celebrities reading poetry. The Crawford photo is thus part of a well-developed aesthetic practice. In Schwarzwald's body of work, there is at least one similar example (also from 2011), capturing Katie Couric in the act of reading Charles Bernstein's *Attack of the Difficult Poems*,[56] another work of avant-garde poetics

by one of the few members of the preceding avant-gardes to receive conceptual writing with an open mind. What these examples point to is that celebrity conceptualism is not an individual process that stems directly from celebrities, geniuses, or other special individuals, but the culmination of complex assemblages of agents. Entire communities of individuals figure into this production, including writers, editors, and celebrities (in this case, supermodels and news commentators), artists from other fields, as well as people on the street, all willing to be staged, photographed, and viewed. The publishing schedules of institutions like established literary journals are involved, as are technologies like database-driven weblogs, RSS feeds, social media, and print books. Techniques like candid photography, blogging, reading series, book launches, and social media posting, all play a role. Celebrity conceptualism did not just *happen*, nor did it *happen to* poetry in some regrettable predatory fashion. The poetry community played an active and willing role in producing it.

3 *Jennifer Garner Reads Go the Fuck to Sleep for Vanity Fair.*[57] The commissioned, celebrity stunt is now not only part of the production of the conceptualist celebrity; it is also an established journalistic genre. That it appears in *Vanity Fair* means that it serves the double duty of performing not just for a general audience, but for other celebrities. The prose of Joanna Robinson, author of the piece, draws on the cadences and tropes of a voiceover advertising a new situation comedy: "Samuel L. Jackson recorded the audiobook in classic deadpan, while Werner Herzog put an accented spin on his version. But what those and other celebrity readings lacked was the chipper-but-frazzled delivery of a mother on the verge."[57] The everyday travails of a divorced mother of three are inseparable from both the archness of an established aesthetic sophistication and a lifestyle of nearly unimaginable wealth and privilege. Incidentally, *Go the Fuck to Sleep* was published in 2011.

4 *Shia LaBeouf.* There was nothing bizarre about LaBeouf's behaviour in 2014–2015. A generous reading would be that his behaviour was perfectly continuous with more than a century of avant-garde practice, from Dada onward (and for the non-generous reading, substitute "art-school boy" for "avant-garde" in the previous sentence). Moreover, his

behaviour was also typical of the mode of "parallel publicity" that Marshall described in 2006 as part of the celebrity regime of presentation:

> We are seeing an acceleration of scandal not between acting assignments for major stars but during the release of films to generate parallel publicity. The film star's aura of distance and distinction is breaking down as the film commodity's capacity to generate unique cultural capital dissolves. For actors, this is a new level of publicizing to strengthen their own presence and capital—but it betrays a decline in overall significance of the industry and their stars. It also underlines the dispersal of information about celebrities as it proliferates via the Web and its blogs, via fan websites and through the new mediascape more rapidly and with less possibility for industry control.[58]

Another entire essay could be written about the manner in which LaBeouf imbricated conceptual writing into his stunts during this period—and how conceptual writing aided and abetted the publicity process. (I pointed out LaBeouf's plagiarism of *Uncreative Writing* to Goldsmith in an email on 2 January 2014, and he began speaking to the press about it shortly after.) But again what interests me is the way that everyday conceptualism rather than conceptual writing established the conditions for this phase of LaBeouf's career two years earlier. The posting of the song "Shia LaBeouf" to SoundCloud by the musician Rob Cantor in 2012, followed by its subsequent spread through Facebook, Reddit, Tumblr, and the open web, with a revival in 2014 after the video release of a melodramatic operetta online,[59] all demonstrate a collective desire to imagine, if not a collective striving to produce, LaBeouf as someone more interesting than the earlier, blander phases of his career might suggest. Becoming a celebrity conceptualist was the most predictable thing that LaBeouf could have done.

BASTA

By way of conclusion, I'd like to return to the thesis that conceptual writing will serve as the vanishing mediator between everyday conceptualism and celebrity conceptualism. It's worth noting that one of the major organs of digital, popular memory has neatly excised conceptual writing from its recounting of this period of LaBeouf's career, although it's easy to find in journalism all over the web. Kenneth Goldsmith appears twice in all of

Know Your Meme, but as of this writing, not in any of the entries on Shia LaBeouf's conceptualist phase.[60] And, if conceptual writing and unoriginality was briefly contrary to popular desires and practices, it is no longer so. As Ian Bogost notes, "The truth is: nobody wants new experiences. Not many of them anyway. And that's fine. Nobody wants new genre fiction, either. Small shifts."[61] We are in a deeply unoriginal cultural moment, and conceptual practice is a daily occurrence.

The most radical thing that we white, cis-, upper-middle-class poets could do, for the moment, would be to embrace that vanishing to give up the Modernist author-function of poet-genius. That is, to accept the demands of the moment, and to evacuate the role in favour of something else: a sustained attention to everyday, creative practice, which now, for better or worse, also includes celebrity conceptualism. As Sheringham notes, to pay attention to the everyday is to focus not upon "the niceties of individual psychology," but upon "a commonality of experience that is endlessly forming and reforming in human activities and encounters."[62] Sometimes being an agent of history is about knowing when to shut the fuck up.

NOTES

1 "Conceptual writing" is an umbrella term for a heterogeneous set of early-twenty-first-century writing practices that respond to the implications of a networked digital milieu for the creative process, for the social function of authorship, and for the economy of publishing. Conceptual writing makes frequent (though not exclusive) use of compositional constraints (for example, alphabetization, organization by syllabic length), which act as a means for organizing their source material—often appropriated at length from discourses that have been neglected by canonical literature (for example, weather reports, legal transcripts, Usenet posts). Conceptual writing eschews the syntactic opacity that has characterized L=A=N=G=U=A=G=E poetry, even though the former draws inspiration from many of the latter's texts. See Darren Wershler, "Conceptual Writing," *The Johns Hopkins Guide to Digital Media*, ed. Marie-Laure Ryan, Lori Emerson, and Benjamin J. Robertson (Baltimore: Johns Hopkins University Press, 2014).

2 Marjorie Perloff, "Unoriginal Genius: Walter Benjamin's Arcades as Paradigm for the New Poetics," *Études Anglaises* 2.61 (2008). See also Marjorie Perloff,

Unoriginal Genius: Poetry by Other Means in the New Century (Chicago: University of Chicago Press, 2010), 229–252.

3 Gilles Deleuze and Félix Guattari, *A Thousand Plateaus: Capitalism and Schizophrenia*, trans. Brian Massumi (Minneapolis: University of Minnesota Press, 1987), 6.

4 Gertrude Stein, *The Autobiography of Alice B. Toklas*, ed. Carl Van Vechten (New York: Vintage Books, 1962), 13.

5 Barbara Will, *Gertrude Stein, Modernism, and the Problem of "Genius,"* (Edinburgh: Edinburgh University Press, 2000), 143.

6 Juliana Spahr and Stephanie Young, "Foulipo (Talk for CalArts Noulipo Conference, Fall 2005)," *Drunken Boat* 8 (2006), http://www.drunkenboat.com/db8/.

7 Fred Moten, "On Marjorie Perloff," *Entropy* (28 December 2015), entropymag.org/on-marjorie-perloff/.

8 See especially Mike Featherstone, "The Heroic Life and Everyday Life," *Theory, Culture and Society* 9 (1992): 159–182.

9 Stephen Johnstone, ed., *The Everyday* (Documents of Contemporary Art series) (London: Whitechapel/MIT Press, 2008).

10 Alexander Alberro and Blake Stimson, eds., *Conceptual Art: A Critical Anthology* (Cambridge: MIT Press, 1999).

11 Michael Sheringham, *Everyday Life: Theories and Practices from Surrealism to the Present* (Oxford: Oxford University Press, 2006), 79–80.

12 Henri Lefebvre, *Critique of Everyday Life, Volume 2: Foundations for a Sociology of the Everyday*, trans. John Moore (London: Verso, 2002), 11.

13 Maurice Blanchot, "Everyday Speech," trans. Susan Hanson, *Yale French Studies* 73 (1987): 12–20, 13–14.

14 Lefebvre, *Critique*, 44.

15 Lefebvre, 45.

16 Featherstone, "The Heroic," 159–182, 162–163.

17 Lefevbre, *Critique*, 45.

18 Johnstone, *The Everyday*, 16.

19 Johnstone, 10.

20 Sheringham, *Everyday*, 253.

21 Michel de Certeau, Fredric Jameson, and Carl Lovitt, "On the Oppositional Practices of Everyday Life," *Social Text* 3 (1980): 3–43, 4.

22 Simon Nakonechny, "Tanya Tagaq Threatens Legal Action Against 'Racist' Quebec Film 'Of the North,'" CBC News Montreal (25 November 2015), http://www.cbc.ca/news/canada/montreal/tanya-tagaq-of-the-north-1.3336733.

23 Dokufest, "Of the North," Edition XV (2015). http://dokufest.com/2015/movie/of-the-north/.

24 Perloff, *Unoriginal*, 232.

25 Samuel Pepys, *Pepys' Diary*, Phil Gyford (2002), http://www.gyford.com/phil/writing/pepys_diary/.

26 Russell Davies, "History Will Remember Samuel Pepys' Blog," *Wired UK*, Ideas Bank (11 April 2012), http://www.wired.co.uk/magazine/archive/2012/05/ideas-bank/history-will-remember-samuel-pepys-blog.

27 De Certeau, Jameson, and Lovitt, 3–4.

28 Forceduse, "Every Death in The Game of Thrones Series, Tabbed," 20 Nov 2013. https://www.reddit.com/r/pics/comments/1r175h/every_death_in_the_game_of_thrones_series_tabbed.

29 Leila Sales, *The Leila Texts* (13 August 2007), http://theleilatexts.blogspot.ca/.

30 Darren Wershler, "Conceptual Writing as Fanfiction," *Fic: Why Fanfiction Is Taking Over the World*, ed. Anne Jamison (Dallas: Smartpop, 2013), 363–371.

31 Joe Butcher, *Texts from Dog* (5 April 2012), http://textfromdog.tumblr.com. See also Benedicte Page, "Headline to Publish Texts from Dog," *The Bookseller* (23 July 2012), http://www.thebookseller.com/news/headline-publish-texts-dog.

32 Justin Halpern, *Shit My Dad Says* (3 August 2009), https://twitter.com/shitmydadsays?lang=en. See also *New York Times* Best Sellers: Hardcover Nonfiction (20 June 2010), www.nytimes.com/best-sellers-books/2010-06-20/hardcover-nonfiction/list.html; Hugh Hart, "Shit My Dad Says: Twitter Got Me a Sitcom Deal," *Wired* (10 November 2009), www.wired.com/2009/11/shit-my-dad-says.

33 Nanex. "Crop Circle of the Day—Quote Stuffing and Strange Sequences" (12 July 2010), http://www.nanex.net/FlashCrash/CCircleDay.html.

34 Google. "2015 Percentage of Robot Traffic Online," https://www.google.ca/search?q=2015+percentage+of+robot+traffic+online&ie=utf-8&oe=utf-8&gws_rd=cr&ei=xWeNVt6sC8yke87yvpAD.

35 Christian Bök, "Conceptual Literature in the Wild," *Harriet* (10 April 2012), http://www.poetryfoundation.org/harriet/2012/04/conceptual-literature-in-the-wild.

36 Andy Baio, "Fanboy Supercuts, Obsessive Video Montages," *Waxy* (11 April 2008), http://waxy.org/2008/04/fanboy_supercuts_obsessive_video_montages.

37 "BiC for Her Medium Ballpoint Pen—Black, Box of 12: Customer Reviews," Amazon.co.uk (6 March 2016), http://www.amazon.co.uk/BiC-For-Her -Medium-Ballpoint/product-reviews/B004FTGJUW.

38 John Guillory, "The Memo and Modernity," *Critical Inquiry* 31 (2004): 108–132.

39 Guillory, "The Memo," 111–112.

40 This passage on the metaphor of the poet as antenna comes from a forthcoming piece that I wrote on conceptual writing to accompany the exhibition *Postscript: Writing after Conceptual Art* (first staged at the Museum of Contemporary Art in Denver, from 12 October 2012 to 3 February 2013), http://mcadenver.org/ postscript.php). The piece is, ironically, called "Best Before Date." The text is on my website: http://www.alienated.net/poetics/best-before-date.

41 Ezra Pound, "Paris Letter: December 1921," *Dial* LXXII.1 (1922): 73.

42 Marshall McLuhan, *Understanding Media: The Extensions of Man* (New York: New American Library, 1964), xi.

43 Christopher Dewdney, *Alter Sublime* (Toronto: Coach House Press, 1980), 77.

44 James W. Carey, *Communication as Culture: Essays on Media and Society*, Rev. ed. (London: Routledge, 2009), 27.

45 Owen Hatherley, "Post-Postmodernism?" *New Left Review* 59 (September– October 2009), https://newleftreview.org/II/59/owen-hatherley-post -postmodernism.

46 "89plus and the LUMA Foundation Announce First 89plus Exhibition," Press release (14 January 2014), http://www.89plus.com/luma-foundation-announce -89plus-exhibition.

47 BNC Research, *The Canadian Book Market 2014*, BookNet Canada, http://www .booknetcanada.ca/canadian-book-market.

48 Michel Foucault, *Foucault Live: Interviews, 1961–84*, trans. John Johnson, ed. Sylvère Lotringer, Foreign Agents Series (New York: Semiotext(e), 1996), 46.

49 Featherstone, "The Heroic," 163.

50 P. David Marshall, "The Genealogy of Celebrity: Introduction," *A Companion to Celebrity*, ed. P. David Marshall and Sean Redmond (Hoboken: John Wiley & Sons, 2015), 16.

51 P. David Marshall, "New Media—New Self: The Changing Power of Celebrity," *The Celebrity Culture Reader*, ed. P. David Marshall (London: Routledge, 2006), 634–644, 642.

52 Brian Joseph Davis, *Portable Altamont* (Toronto: Coach House Books, 2005).

53 Rafe Needleman, "Richard Dreyfuss Reads the iTunes EULA," *C|Net* (8 June 2011), http://www.cnet.com/news/richard-dreyfuss-reads-the-itunes-eula/.

54 Trey Parker (dir.), "HUMANCENTiPAD," in *South Park* (27 April 2011), http://www.imdb.com/title/tt1884035.

55 Harriet Staff, "Cindy Crawford Reads Kenny Goldsmith's *Uncreative Writing*," Photograph by Lawrence Schwartzwald, *Harriet* (4 November 2011), http://www.poetryfoundation.org/harriet/2011/11/cindy-crawford-reads-kenny-goldsmiths-uncreative-writing/.

56 Charles Bernstein, "Book Party for 'Attack of the Difficult Poems,'" in *Jacket2* (27 May 2011), http://jacket2.org/commentary/book-party-attack-difficult-poems.

57 Joanna Robinson, "Watch Jennifer Garner Read an Expletive-Laden Bedtime Story," *Vanity Fair* (1 March 2016), http://www.vanityfair.com/hollywood/2016/02/jennifer-garner-go-the-fuck-to-sleep.

58 Marshall, "New Media," 643.

59 digipen70 et al., "Actual Cannibal Shia LaBeouf," *Know Your Meme* (1 May 2012), http://knowyourmeme.com/memes/actual-cannibal-shia-labeouf.

60 Moran Horan, "Shia LaBeouf," *Know Your Meme* (27 June 2014): http://knowyourmeme.com/memes/people/shia-labeouf. See also "Related Sub-Entries" (9 March 2016), http://knowyourmeme.com/memes/shia-labeouf/children.

61 Ian Bogost, "The Truth Is," Twitter.com. (7:51 AM—16 Mar 2016), https://twitter.com/ibogost/status/710070890948526080.

62 Sheringham, *Everyday*, 398.

DEREK BEAULIEU

Prose of the TransCanada

MOEZ SURANI

1988

Bandit

Hooper

Catch and Kill / Sadhbhavna [Goodwill]

Danto

Flavius

Golden Pheasant

Packer

Zafar 7 [Victory 7]

Trishul [Trident]

विराट [Giant]

Ramadan Mubarak [Blessed Ramadan]

ه†اللى†اعل†ان ل†توك†[In God we Trust]

Praying Mantis

Displace

Prone

Black Thunder II

Red Bean

Linger

Agree

Checkmate

Mount Hope III

غ†ارچ†لچ†[Forty Stars]

Katzen
Forough Javidan [Eternal Light]
Mersad [Ambush]
Vuiswys
Cornerstone
Cactus
Marion

DANI SPINOSA

Anxious Influence: Reading John Cage Theoretically

Introduction: Rhizome
Joyce's & cyclic & just & concept & just & crystallize. & jumping & cat; & Jacob & cells & Jean & command & just & canal-rhizome & just & concepts, & jostle & coexist, & just & cat & just & conjunction &

1914: One or Several Wolves?
jeopardizes, & counted & just & castrater & joins & color & just & certainly & Jean & camphorated & Jung & certain & jaws? & crowd & jerseys, & clan & Jaw & cry & *just* & child, & jaw & Castration, & just & castration. & join & can & journey & course & just & character; & "Jackals & can & jackals & castration & jackals & camel: & jackals & castration & just & criticizing &

1874: Three Novellas, or "What Happened?"
just & colonel & just & completely & just & coincide & just & could & James & clear-cut & just & counts & James's & cannot & just & could & James. & changed & jumps & catastrophe & jailbreak & contrasts & just & crossing & Joyce's & continued. & judged & contours, & jerks." & cutting & justice, & caused & Julien & children & jumps & claps & Jackson & creates & joy, & coming & judge & Chekhov & judgments & cherish &

1837: Of the Refrain
jumps & chaos & join & cosmic & join & customary & "jumps & cross & jumped & chaos & Jakob & components & just & course, & just & can &

joy & carries & joy & counterpoint, & joy & character & just & constituted & just & can & Jerusalems & cases & just & consolidations & James, & consistent & just & cut & Just & closure & jure & creator: & juxtaposition, & conceptions & judgment: & cosmic, & judgment; & Cosmos & jumble & cosmic & just & crystal & *Joke* & concentrated & jambe & Childhood & just & cosmic & just & chromaticism &

Conclusion: Concrete Rules and Abstract Machines

Judgment & Classical & just & code & jump & carry & just & considered &

PART VIII

EPILOGUE

ANDRÉ ALEXIS

On Amanda PL's Cancelled Exhibit

To begin with, a recent situation: Visions Gallery in Toronto cancelled an exhibit by an artist who calls herself Amanda PL. The problem, it seems, is that Amanda PL has used elements in her painting that resemble elements in the work of Norval Morrisseau and the Woodland School of Indigenous artists. After receiving complaints that PL's work is an act of cultural appropriation, the gallery cancels her solo exhibit.

And then another situation: Hal Niedzviecki, after telling us that he doesn't believe in cultural appropriation and informing us about how Indigenous writers work—hint: they don't write "what they know"—proposes a so-called Appropriation Prize for best work of appropriation—that is, fiction written from the perspective of a culture or race to which the author does not belong. This is an idea so bewilderingly silly that you can't help wondering if Niedzviecki is dull or, like the Jonathan Swift of "A Modest Proposal," beyond measure in his brilliance.

If only because the Amanda PL incident has more nuances, we begin there....

I'm not an expert on the matter, but it seems that "cultural appropriation" means, in this situation, that Morrisseau's work, being that of an Indigenous artist, has a context and content that PL—who is not Indigenous—does not understand. She has, therefore, no right to take these elements out of their context and use them without regard to their meaning in Indigenous culture.

There are levels of irony at play in all this. To begin with, Norval Morrisseau was himself criticized for using Indigenous sacred symbols in his work. He was accused of debasing them. There is a consistency here, but how strange that some of the condemnation of PL would necessarily be a condemnation of Morrisseau, too. Morrisseau defended his work on the grounds that his painting was an agent of change. And, showing the sacred in a different context as it did, his work gave renewed power to the sacred by allowing another vantage on it, by restoring its strangeness. The images and symbols are not important in themselves. Their power fades or even dies. The renewal of their power is one of the byproducts of Art. Morrisseau himself used Christian symbols with Indigenous ones. In so doing, he could point to what both traditions venerate: the things beyond words and signs.

That's not to say that it's impossible to misuse sacred symbols. It clearly *is* possible. The wanton display of sacred objects—or the display of an "Eskimo" skeleton in a museum—is despicable because it refuses to acknowledge that things from other cultures can have deep meaning in the way that things in our culture do, that things in other cultures can be sacred, that they are more than curios, and that human remains are not just worthy of dignity but deserving of it. This will seem obvious to most people, I imagine. As it will seem obvious that none who truly thought of Qisuk as human—as opposed to a "specimen"—would have countenanced a display of his skeleton in the American Museum of Natural History.

The problem with cultural appropriation resides in the use of humans or human artifacts as if they were instruments, there to say what we choose to have them say. But, to my mind, some of the recent talk about Morrisseau's work also has the feel of a reduction. What's most unsettling about the veneration of Norval Morrisseau is that it does not allow the work of an artist (Morrisseau) to be fully part of the common stream (visual art). It reduces Morrisseau's work to one of its aspects: the use of sacred symbols, the illustration of sacred narratives. But Morrisseau and the other members of the Woodland School were *artists*. It isn't the Woodland Church or the Woodland Cult. They were influenced by European work. The abstract paintings of Benjamin Chee Chee, for instance, are the work of a painter working in a medium that he knows intimately. To deny this aspect of Morrisseau or Chee Chee is to make them servants of the sacred rather than renewers of it. Priests, in other words. Which they were not. It sometimes feels as if the words "cultural appropriation" have been used to create a straitjacket for Indigenous artists: a straitjacket similar to the ones for which "black artists" or "gay artists"—name your minority—are fitted.

It's not difficult to understand the impulse to preserve for Indigenous use signs and symbols that have Indigenous origins and specific meanings within Indigenous spirituality. But if Indigenous spirituality is valuable to humans—as opposed to valuable only to a specific and small group of humans—what's served by this hiving off, this making unavailable? *Cui bono*, as the Latin has it: who benefits from this exclusivity?

I'm not suggesting that there's no good answer to that question. On the other hand, some of the reactions to Amanda PL's work—and the justifications of those reactions—have been bizarre. The idea, for instance, that a white artist (Amanda PL) influenced by an Indigenous artist (Norval Morrisseau) is effecting some sort of "cultural genocide"—words actually used—is not just over the top. It's contrary to common sense. The most influential and *living* spiritual doctrines that we know are precisely those that are widely disseminated and interpreted in the widest variety of ways. To imagine Indigenous spirituality as common is not to imagine it dead. It's to imagine it as vivid as Christianity or Buddhism. The same can be said of "culture." Films and music from the United States—all of which disseminate American values—have massive influence not because they are kept from other cultures but because they have been ruthlessly exported and exploited—exploited by Americans, yes, but also by those who take American music and film in unique directions.

This is, I guess, as good a place to talk about Hal Niedzviecki as any. In Spring 2017, Niedzviecki wrote an editorial in which he suggested that there is no such thing as cultural appropriation. To me, the piece seemed, first of all, arrogant. It wasn't arrogant because it suggested that cultural appropriation does not exist. It was arrogant because it lumped all Indigenous writing together and then asserted that many Indigenous writers do not write "what they know" but, rather, "what they don't know." The assertion that, say, Eden Robinson, Thomas King, and Tomson Highway—to choose three interesting writers at random—are at all similar in their procedures is a flagrant display of the reductionism that I spoke of earlier.

Niedzviecki's editorial drew exactly the kind of response you'd imagine. People were outraged. There then followed the usual pattern. Niedzviecki resigned his editorial post and wrote an apology for his words. He thus became the usual kind of martyr for "free speech" aficionados: those who believe not so much in free speech but in speech without consequences. And now an "Appropriation Prize" is being funded in Niedzviecki's honour. The amusing thing—if you find any of this even remotely amusing—is that if you take the idea behind an "appropriation prize" seriously, a prize jury would regularly have to enact the arrogance that Niedzviecki showed in the first place. Who, for instance, gets to judge if a white writer's black character is "faithful"? Who gets to judge if a black writer's Caucasian character is faithful to "real Caucasians"?

All of these ideas—those brought on by PL's exhibit and Niedzviecki's resignation—feel more urgent, to me, lately, because I have been wrestling with some of them in my own work. I'm a writer of fiction who is obsessed with the idea of place. In the novel that I'm currently writing, I have tried to give voice to the Canadian forest—well, Ontario scrub, anyway. Naturally, I wondered if I had the right to use the names of Indigenous gods in my work. It seemed to me that the land I love had been travelled—it's mysteries named—hundreds of years before me, that at some point an Indigenous artist had looked on a (cleaner, less cemented) version of our landscape and listened for its voice. Why should I have to refer to Judeo-Christian gods or Greek gods—gods who are strange to my land—when speaking of the holy? Do I have the right to speak the sacred names of those whose names are part of the language that I speak? (Toronto, Ottawa, Saskatchewan—our most beautiful names come from those who've been here longest.)

I decided not to use the names and gods because, in the end, I wasn't at ease with them. Certainly, I was less familiar with them than I am with the Greek pantheon, say. The culture of the people who first named the land isn't taught to me. I don't know their religions. I wish I did know them. I wish I had been taught them. And, in fact, I feel at times as if I have been excluded—by white culture, not Indigenous culture—from a birthright. Or is it my birthright? To what extent do I have common cause with the people of the nations, whose ancestors walked the land before me, those who were the first to walk the land?

I don't know the answers to these questions, of course. I ask them respectfully and with a proper place cleared within to *hold* the answers. I can't help feeling, though, that as some of us celebrate (and others ruefully acknowledge) Canada's 150th "birthday," we have devised a transgression—"cultural appropriation"—that, if indiscriminately punished, runs the risk of *hiding* Indigenous Canadian culture, not preserving it. We risk effecting, through kindness, the kind of exclusion that the first Europeans effected through violence.

JORDAN ABEL

A Line Can Be Drawn: An Interview

EDs: Your three books *The Place of Scraps, Un/inhabited,* and *Injun,* all render, or mis/treat, or mine politically problematic found text. Where does your interest in appropriation stem from? What happens when a text, especially an unloved text, is treated as raw matter?

JA: I've been thinking about this a lot lately. Especially in the wake of a few of the recent conversations about cultural appropriation. For me, you can't really talk about the kind of conceptual/literary appropriation that's in my work without also talking about cultural appropriation, colonial appropriation, and ultimately colonialism.

So when Hal Niedzviecki writes in the editorial introduction to *Write* magazine that he doesn't "believe in cultural appropriation," I have to wonder if he even knows what cultural appropriation is and/or if he knows how appropriation (both in a historic and contemporary sense) has functioned as a mechanism of colonialism. Unfortunately, Niedzviecki isn't alone. There are a lot of people that don't understand this stuff. Or choose not to understand. That's more or less why I write about appropriation.

Likewise, as you note, my writing is also built out of appropriated texts. For example, in *The Place of Scraps,* the narrative revolves around Marius Barbeau (an early-twentieth-century salvage anthropologist who stole and removed totem poles from struggling communities). Each piece begins with a section of text pulled directly from Marius Barbeau's book

Totem Poles. The subsequent pages are then formed by way of erasure out of Barbeau's work. So, the book goes back and forth between Barbeau's writing and erasures of Barbeau's writing. To me, the erasures of Barbeau's words are moments where Indigenous presences are articulated. Likewise, these are also moments where resistance is articulated. Conceptual/literary appropriation, in this context, allows me to comment not only on the destructive mechanisms and outcomes of appropriation, but also allows me to begin to explore pathways back through/out of appropriation. The damage that Barbeau (and the whole era of salvage anthropology) did to Indigenous communities is real. Some of it seemingly irreparable. But we are still here. Indigenous peoples are still here. We didn't disappear. And we can find ways to respond.

EDs: *The Place of Scraps* is a beautiful textual/paper carving of Barbeau's text, so elegantly framed by the story of your own family connection to wood carving and, of course, the Nisga'a tradition of totem carving. You manage a remarkable intersection of decolonial resurgent writing with contemporary avant-garde techniques of re-situating found text in new contexts. What led you to that intersection, and (if you will permit us extending the metaphor) do you see those roads of avant-garde and decolonial writing as running perpendicular or parallel to one another?

JA: When I was first writing *The Place of Scraps*, I often found that I would begin unintentionally with a moment of frustration. I would read Marius Barbeau's words and immediately want to erase, disrupt, and intervene. I've really had only a few conversations with my dad about Nisga'a carving, but from what I understand, he liked to carve until a pattern or an image revealed itself. If there's any similarity to the erasures in *The Place of Scraps* and traditional carving techniques, I would say that might be it.

You know, there are a few writers out there that I do seem to share that intersection with. I'm thinking of a few of Shane Rhodes's books, like *X* and *Dead White Men*. Also Rachel Zolf's *Janey's Arcadia* and Joshua Whitehead's *Full-Metal Indigiqueer*.

The thing is that we may have all arrived there by different pathways. When I think about my creative practice, I tend not to think about my work as either being decolonial or avant-garde. I think of it mostly as Indigenous writing. Or perhaps Nisga'a writing. Except that I don't tend to write poetry that is formed by Nisga'a knowledge, Nisga'a world views, or Nisga'a understandings. Actually, I often find myself writing about being disconnected from my home community by way of colonial violence.

Perhaps it's not so much of an intersection for me. I would suggest instead that I'm using some of the tools/methods of avant-garde writing in an attempt to capture my lived experienced as an urban Indigenous person and an intergenerational survivor of residential schools.

EDs: Yes, there is something productive in the fragmentation, disruption, and even frustration built into many of those techniques that connect to (and contest) the violence of colonization. Your writing seems to explore the limit cases of such expressibility, testing the colonial conditions of a self in text. Do you ever worry about your voice being overrun by the settler texts that you use? Or, how have you managed to find a balance between expression and representation versus contestation and disruption?

JA: Just thinking about my second book *Un/inhabited*—which attends to sentences extracted from a corpus of western novels that deal with the issues of land, ownership, and territory—there's a way in which my disruptions of found text function as my artistic voice. The settler texts are there, yes. But I am *un*settling them. So, if anything, my voice is probably overrunning the settler texts.

I guess that's really the balance. Which authorial voices are audible in my writing? The settler voices? My voice? And if it's my voice, is that an Indigenous voice? When does the writing cease to be settler writing? When does it become Indigenous writing? And what defines Indigenous writing anyway?

EDs: People are talking about a resurgence of Indigenous culture, or even a renaissance of traditional practices and world view. Has the broader movement of Indigenous writing in Canada, and the "decolonial turn," been helpful for your own writing, or are you suspicious of some of its (especially state-led) manifestations?

JA: Resurgence as a movement is really interesting to me. I think that the advocates of Indigenous nationalism and resurgence are really on to something when they argue for moving towards Indigenous knowledges, Indigenous world views, and Indigenous languages. Likewise, I do think that there is something really generative to be gained from moving away from purely decolonial frameworks.

That being said, as both as an urban Indigenous person and as an intergenerational survivor of residential schools, I have to say that Indigenous resurgence isn't accessible to all Indigenous people. Just thinking about my own personal experience, I've had a very difficult time embracing Indigenous resurgence because of the way that colonialism has severed and fractured my connection to my Indigenous family and community. What resurgent frameworks often ignore is that access to community is not equal for every Indigenous person. Again, though, resurgence is perhaps the best pathway forward for Indigenous peoples if we can overcome these hurdles.

In terms of a broader movement of Indigenous writing, I am deeply grateful for all of the Indigenous writers that have paved the way. It wasn't that long ago that we weren't even allowed to tell our own stories. If we wanted to say something, to write something, it had to be filtered through an established non-Indigenous writer. So if there is a renaissance, it's one with momentum. We have been slowly working towards this. There's a historical trajectory here.

EDs: The city becomes an interesting problem in such a renaissance, at once perhaps more open to disruptive narratives (cities are perpetually remaking themselves), but also all mixed up in the world in every possible sense of the term. You've spoken about being an urban Indigenous author, and how that has affected your sense of identity and writing. You've also spoken about the importance of the Indigenous momentum that is fuelling so much of the arts dialogue right now in Canada. I wonder, now, about the urban dimension of your work. Specifically, how the context of Vancouver shapes your practice. I can well imagine connections to the materialist praxis of the KSW, for instance, including their comfort with fragmented language and the politicization of work. Have the legacies of that place, with its own particular poetic (or other artistic) traditions, been productive influences for you?

JA: Vancouver has definitely shaped my artistic practices. When I think back to *The Place of Scraps*, so many of the later sections of that book looked specifically to how Vancouver, as a city, utilized and strategically deployed Indigenous art. But the significance of Vancouver to my artistic practice is about more than just how Indigenous art is positioned within the city (and/ or about how Indigenous art circulates throughout the city). Vancouver is also important to me because it's the place where I was born. It's the place where my parents lived and worked and created art. I don't think that I could have written *The Place of Scraps* in any other city.

You know, I probably should have a stronger connection to the KSW than I actually do. I keep wondering if I'm in, if I'm not in. Did my invitation get lost in the mail somewhere? Was I supposed to fill out an application form? Am I supposed to go to meetings? Are we disbanded? I'm in the Kootenays right now. Where is everybody? To be honest, I'm probably closer to the Hootenanny School of Writing, and I'm not even sure what they do.

EDs: Vancouver also has a rich history of visual poetry, thinking back to bill bissett, Judith Copithorne, and even bpNichol, who got his start in the city. We've talked about the carving element of your work, including the collages in *The Place of Scraps*, but not its participation in the school of visual (or even concrete) poetics. The ink-faded maps of *Un/inhabited* reminded me of Steve McCaffery's large-scale concrete poems, including the riotous space of *Carnival*. Even *Injun* has some exploded text that foregrounds the material presence of the letters over their expression. How do you see your use of space and ink in your works in relation to what McCaffery and Nichol used to call the "language revolution" of concrete poetry? There seems to be an obviously different, but insistently similar, spirit of hope that increased consciousness of words and letters can shift the body politic in some way.

JA: Vancouver absolutely has a rich history of visual poetry. bissett was definitely an influence, especially for the *The Place of Scraps*. I remember looking at some of his concrete photographic poems before I wrote my first book, and I just fell in love with his style. But there were other Vancouver poets too that have been deeply influential. I'm thinking about writers like Jen Currin, Donato Mancini, Stephen Collis, Jordan Scott, Billeh Nickerson, Elizabeth Bachinsky, Sachiko Murakami, Wayde Compton, and Lisa Robertson. It's not just the visual poets who influenced and inspired me, but instead it was a whole community of writers.

In terms of aligning my work with the likes of McCaffery and Nichol, I would say that there are definitely moments when a line can be drawn, connecting our work. I'm cool with that. As a reader of poetry, I love what they do. As a writer, I would say that I'm very interested in the materiality and aesthetics of language, but also the content. In many ways, I'm interested in focusing on the surfaces of language and text as way to address depths otherwise unaddressable. Perhaps a line can be drawn there, too.

EDs: Looking forward, what do you hope for of the avant-garde in Canada, and what needs to happen in order to pull off your vision or hope for writing in the future?

JA: In terms of CanLit, I think we can learn a lot from the #Honouring-IndigenousWriters movement. I don't think that it's so much about what comes next or how we shape whatever that is. I think that it's more about what we do now. For me, that movement really focuses in on reading, celebrating, and ultimately honouring Indigenous writers and artists. Those are moves that can be made in the here and now. We can choose to pay attention to the amazing work that has already been accomplished. And we can choose to build on that work. I'm sure that doing so would have some kind of impact on what follows. Although who knows what that will be.

PART IX

AFTER MATTER

Notes and Acknowledgements

This book stems from the rich network of conversations and presentations that took place at the conference *Avant Canada: Artists, Prophets, Revolutionaries* at Brock University from 5 to 7 November 2014. Our gratitude extends to the organizers, facilitators, chairs, volunteers, and hosts of that event, alongside the over 100 presenters who made it such a vital gathering. We owe a special note of gratitude to Karis Shearer, from the Conference Organizing Committee, who was instrumental in the transition from event to text. Our gratitude goes to all the contributors in this book: Lisa Robertson, Liz Howard, Kristine Smitka, Stephen Cain, Julia Polyck-O'Neill, Mike Borkent, Eric Schmaltz, Kelly Mark, Kaie Kellough, Michael Roberson, Kit Dobson, Dorothy Trujillo Lusk, Erín Moure, Donato Mancini, Myra Bloom, Sonnet L'Abbé, Leanne Betasamosake Simpson, Lee Maracle, Annharte, Katie L. Price, Darren Wershler, Derek Beaulieu, Dani Spinosa, Moez Surani, André Alexis, and Jordan Abel. We are grateful to Eleanor Nichol for offering the help and support of the Estate of bpNichol, and for permission to reproduce the works in this book. We are grateful to Siobhan McMenemy, our indefatigable editor, who steered this book to publication with much grace and aplomb. We also thank Erín Moure for editorial insights. Finally, for support, mentoring, and general good-will, we give warm thanks to Lisa Quinn, Clare Hitchens, Dean Irvine, Neta Gordon, Laura Moss, Helen Hajnoczky, Erin Wunker, Jay MillAr, Rolf Maurer, Christine Stewart, Julia Bloch, Kenna O'Rourke, Arnold McBay, and Neil Hennessy.

Notes on the Text

"The Collective": A version of this text was originally delivered as a keynote address at the conference The Concept of Vancouver, as part of the series Two Days of Canada, at Brock University on 14 October 2016; the text later appeared on *Harriet: A Poetry Blog*. A part of this work was also published by *Canadian Art* (Winter 2017).

"Against Assimilation I Rose into Poetry": A version of this paper was presented at "Emergent Insurgencies: Social Justice and Contemporary Form Symposium" for the TIA House at University of Calgary on 4 March 2016.

"The Sublation of Obduracy": A version of this text was presented at the conference Avant Canada: Poets, Prophets, Revolutionaries, as part of the series Two Days of Canada, at Brock University on 5 November 2014.

"A Vision in the UofT Stacks": A version of this text was presented at the conference Avant Canada: Poets, Prophets, Revolutionaries, as part of the series Two Days of Canada, at Brock University on 7 November 2014.

"Words With(out) Syntax": A version of this text was presented at the conference Avant Canada: Poets, Prophets, Revolutionaries, as part of the series Two Days of Canada, at Brock University on 5 November 2014.

"Avant Comics": A version of this text was presented at the conference Avant Canada: Poets, Prophets, Revolutionaries, as part of the series Two Days of Canada, at Brock University on 7 November 2014. The author would like to thank the Estate of bpNichol and Steve McCaffery for their kind permission to reprint the comics found in this chapter.

"A Field Guide": This visual poem is from a larger project called A *Field Guide to North Concrete*. The author would like to thank angela rawlings, Derek Beaulieu, and Kaie Kellough for their permission to use their signatures in this work.

"National" and "Time": These visual poems consist of Letraset on archival matte board, 24 x 24 in., 2015. [Photo credit: Toni Hafkenscheid.]

"Continents": A version of these texts was previously published in *Matrix Magazine* (Issue 100, Winter 2015). These imprints are excerpts from a series that explores the loss, acquisition, and migration of languages (be they dialects, créoles, pidgins, and vernaculars) throughout the African diaspora. The series is dedicated to Clarence Roger London.

"Transformation or Resistance": A version of this text was presented at the conference Avant Canada: Poets, Prophets, Revolutionaries, as part of the series Two Days of Canada, at Brock University on 5 November 2014.

"A Poetics of Neoliberalism": A version of this text was presented at the conference Avant Canada: Poets, Prophets, Revolutionaries, as part of the series Two Days of Canada, at Brock University on 5 November 2014.

"Sleek Vinyl Drill": This poem was originally published in *Ogress Oblige* (San Francisco: Krupskaya, 2001).

"Pillage 12 ('Anaximenes')": This version of the poem was originally published in *Pillage Laud* (Toronto: BookThug, 2011).

"If Violence (Hey You)": This poem is a selection from the poem of the same name originally published in *Buffet World* (Vancouver: New Star, 2011).

"Messy Confessions": This text is previously unpublished.

"Erasures Written on Territories Called Canada": This text is previously unpublished.

"caribou ghosts & untold stories": This poem is dedicated, out of respect, to the intelligence and commitment of Black Lives Matter Toronto for halting the Pride Parade in 2016. This poem was original published in *The Accident of Being Lost* by Leanne Betasamosake Simpson (Toronto: House of Anansi Press, 2017). Reprinted by permission of House of Anansi Press Inc., Toronto. www.house ofanansi.com.

"Bobbi Lee, Indian Rebel": This excerpt is taken from the novel *Bobbi Lee, Indian Rebel* (Toronto: Women's Press, 1990). PWM refers to the Progressive Workers Movement, a Vancouver-based political party that ran candidates in the federal election for 1965. NARP refers to the Native Alliance of Red Power, a Maoist and Troskyist advocacy group, founded in 1967 for off-reserve Indigenous people.

"cum cum how cum dat cums around even from behind": This poem was originally published in *Indigena Awry* (Vancouver: New Star Books, 2012).

"A ≠ A": An earlier version of this article appeared in *Canadian Literature* 210/211 (Autumn 2011): 27–41.

"Everyday Practice Before and After Conceptual Writing": A version of this text was presented at the conference Avant Canada: Poets, Prophets, Revolutionaries, as part of the series Two Days of Canada, at Brock University on 6 November 2014.

"Prose of the TransCanada": This text includes details from a work originally published as "Moments Café #8: Prose of the TransCanada" (Toronto: Book-Thug, 2014). The complete work was projected onto the Calgary Tower on 28–29 April 2014.

"1988": This text is a chapter from عملية Operación Opération Operation 行动 Операция, a book-length poetic inventory of all military operations conducted by UN-member Nations since the organization's inception in 1945. The text was chosen, in part, because the date refers to the year in which bpNichol died.

"Anxious Influence: Reading John Cage Theoretically": This text reads through a selection of chapters from *A Thousand Plateaus: Capitalism and Schizophrenia* by Gilles Deleuze and Félix Guattari, recording the set of alternating occurrences of words whose inital letter is either J or C (the monogram of John Cage).

"On Amanda PL's Cancelled Exhibit": A previous version of this essay appeared in *The Globe and Mail* on 12 May 2017, under the title "The Complex Issues within Cultural Appropriation and Art."

"A Line Can Be Drawn": This interview was conducted by email between March 2017 and July 2017.

About the Authors

JORDAN ABEL is the author of three books of poetry, including *Injun* (which has won the Griffin Poetry Prize). Abel is a doctoral graduate in the Department of English at Simon Fraser University, where he specializes in the study of Indigenous literature.

ANDRÉ ALEXIS has published ten books of fiction, including *Fifteen Dogs* (for which he has won the Scotiabank Giller Prize). Among the many other awards earned by him, he has also won the Windham-Campbell Literature Prize in recognition for the merits of his career.

ANNHARTE is a performative, storytelling author with several volumes of poetry, including (among others) *Indigena Awry* and *Coyote Columbus Café*. Baker has co-founded the Regina Aboriginal Writers Group and the Aboriginal Writers Collective of Manitoba.

DEREK BEAULIEU is a globally renowned maker of visual poetry. Beaulieu has published more than a dozen books, including *Kern, Flatland,* and *How to Write*. He has served as the Poet Laureate of Calgary, and he has published hundreds of chapbooks through his micropresses.

GREGORY BETTS is the author of the scholarly treatise *Avant-Garde Canadian Literature*, and he has published several volumes of poetry, including (among others) *If Language* and *The Others Raisd in Me*. Betts is an alumnus of York University, and he teaches at Brock University and University College Dublin.

MYRA BLOOM holds a Ph.D. in Comparative Literature from the University of Toronto. Bloom specializes in the study of identity politics in the literature of both Canada and Quebec. She is the reviews editor at *The Puritan* literary magazine, and she teaches in the English department at Concordia University.

CHRISTIAN BÖK is the author of *Eunoia* (a bestseller that has won the Griffin Poetry Prize). Bök is working on *The Xenotext* (a poem, encoded into the genome of a deathless bacterium). A Fellow in the Royal Society of Canada, he now teaches at Charles Darwin University.

MIKE BORKENT holds a Ph.D. in English Literature from the University of British Columbia, and he specializes in the study of visual poetry, comics, and cognitive poetics. He has published in such journals as *Visible Language*, *Cognitive Linguistics*, *Canadian Literature*, and *Literature & Translation*.

STEPHEN CAIN is the co-author of *Encyclopedia of Fictional and Fantastic Languages*, and he has published several volumes of poetry, including (among others) *Dyslexicon* and *False Friends*. Cain is an alumnus of York University, where he now teaches Canadian literature.

KIT DOBSON is the author of the scholarly treatise *Transnational Canadas*, and (with Smaro Kamboureli) he has co-edited a volume of interviews entitled *Producing Canadian Literature*. Dobson serves on the Board for NeWest Press, and he teaches at Mount Royal University.

LIZ HOWARD is the author of *Infinite Citizen of the Shaking Tent* (for which she has won the Griffin Poetry Prize). Howard holds an M.F.A. in Creative Writing from the University of Guelph. She has published her poetry in such venues as *The Puritan* and *The Capilano Review*.

KAIE KELLOUGH is the author of *Accordéon* (which has been nominated for the Amazon.ca First Novel Award). He is a masterful performer of sound poems, and his collection of poetry, entitled *Magnetic Equator*, is forthcoming from McClelland & Stewart.

SONNET L'ABBÉ is the author of two books of poetry: *A Strange Relief* and *Killarnoe*. Her chapbook, *Anima Canadensis*, has won the 2017 bpNichol Chapbook Award. She teaches at Vancouver Island University.

DOROTHY TRUJILLO LUSK is an alumna of the Kootenay School of Writing. Lusk has published several volumes of poetry, including *Redactive* and *Ogress Oblige*. Her chapbooks include *Oral Tragedy* and *Volume Delays*. She has studied printmaking at the Vancouver School of Art.

DONATO MANCINI is an alumnus of the Kootenay School of Writing. Mancini is the author of several volumes of poetry, including (among others) *Ligatures, Aethel*, and *Buffet World*. He is also the author of a scholarly treatise entitled *You Must Work Harder to Write Poetry of Excellence*.

LEE MARACLE is the author of several volumes of fiction (including *Will's Garden* and *Celia's Song*). Maracle has received a Queen's Diamond Jubilee Medal for her mentorship of Aboriginals, and she has also received the Premier's Award for Excellence in the Arts.

KELLY MARK is a conceptual artist, who holds a B.A. in Fine Art from the Nova Scotia College of Art and Design. Mark has exhibited her artworks at many global venues, including (among others) The Power Plant in Toronto and the IKON Gallery in Birmingham.

ERÍN MOURE is the author of more than nineteen books of poetry, including *Furious* (which has won the Governor General's Award). Moure has translated more than sixteen books of poetry into English, and she has been shortlisted three times for the Griffin Poetry Prize.

JULIA POLYCK-O'NEILL is a doctoral graduate in the program of Interdisciplianary Humanities at Brock University, where she specializes in the study of avant-garde movements in Vancouver. She is also a doctoral fellow for Editing Modernism in Canada (EMiC).

KATIE L. PRICE holds a Ph.D. in English from the University of Pennsylvania. Price has co-edited the website for *Avant Canada* at Jacket2—a website that commemorates the conference Avant Canada: Poets, Prophets, Revolutionaries, at Brock University on 4–6 November 2014.

MICHAEL ROBERSON holds a Ph.D. in English Literature from the University of Calgary. Roberson specializes in the study of contemporary, experimental literature in North America. Examples of his scholarship have appeared in *Mosaic* and *Open Letter.*

LISA ROBERTSON is an alumna of the Kootenay School of Writing. Robertson is the author of more than a dozen books of poetry, including (among others), *3 Summers, The Men,* and *The Weather*. She has received an Honorary Doctorate of Letters from Emily Carr University.

ERIC SCHMALTZ is a SSHRC Postdoctoral Fellow at the University of Pennsylvania, where he specializes in the study of Canadian literature with an emphasis on interdisciplinary poetries. He is the author of *Surfaces.*

LEANNE BETASAMOSAKE SIMPSON is the author of not only *Islands of Decolonial Love* (an album of poems and music), but several volumes of nonfiction (including *The Accident of Being Lost*). An activist in the protests for Idle No More, she has taught at campuses across Canada.

KRISTINE SMITKA teaches English Literature at the University of Alberta. Smitka has co-edited the anthology of essays, entitled *Counterblasting Canada* (about the academic coteries of Marshall McLuhan). She is also the English reviews editor for *Papers of the Bibliographical Society of Canada.*

DANI SPINOSA is a poet who has authored not only a literary chapbook entitled *Glosas for Tired Eyes*, but also an academic treatise, entitled *Anarchists in the Academy*. She is also one of the two founding editors of Gap Riot Press.

MOEZ SURANI is the author of three books of poetry, including *Operations.* Surani has won a variety of prizes for his work, including the Great Blue Heron Poetry Prize from *The Antigonish Review*. He has won a Chalmers Arts Fellowship for the merits of his writing.

DARREN WERSHLER is the author of *The Iron Whim* (a treatise about type-writing), and he has published works of poetry (including *The Tapeworm Foundry*). A founder of Conceptualism, he occupies the Research Chair in Media and Contemporary Literature at Concordia University.

Bibliography

"8 Things You Need to Know about Bill C-51." BCCLA.org. 11 March 2015. https://bccla.org/2015/03/8-things-you-need-to-know-about-bill-c-51/.

"89plus and the LUMA Foundation Announce First 89plus Exhibition." 89plus.com. 14 January 2014. http://www.89plus.com/luma-foundation-announce-89plus-exhibition/.

"2013 CWILA Count." CWILA.com. http://cwila.com/2013-cwila-count-infographic/.

"2015 Percentage of Robot Traffic Online." Google.ca. https://www.google.ca/search?q=2015+percentage+of+robot+traffic+online&ie=utf-8&oe=utf-8&gws_rd=cr&ei=xWeNVt6sC8yke87yvpAD.

Aanerud, Rebecca. "Fictions of Whiteness: Speaking the Names of Whiteness in US Literature." In *Displacing Whiteness: Essays in Social and Cultural Criticism*, edited by Ruth Frankenberg, 35–59. Durham: Duke University Press, 1997.

Abel, Jordan. *The Place of Scraps*. Vancouver: Talonbooks, 2013.

"About KSW." KSWnet.org. 5 July 2011. http://www.kswnet.org/index.html.

Adams, James. "Margaux Williamson: Meet the Artist Whose Life Has Been the Stuff of Fiction." *The Globe and Mail*, 24 May 2014. http://m.theglobeandmail.com/arts/art-and-architecture/margaux-williamson-a-postmodern-moment-for-an-artist-whose-life-has-been-the-stuff-of-fiction/article18829644/?service=mobile&page=all.

Ahmed, Sara. "Declarations of Whiteness: The Non-performativity of Antiracism." *Borderlands* 3.2 (2004). http://www.borderlands.net.au/vol3no2_2004/.

Alberro, Alexander, and Blake Stimson, eds. *Conceptual Art: A Critical Anthology*. Cambridge: MIT Press, 1999.

Altman, Anna. "Two Versions, One Heti." *The Paris Review*. 27 July 2012. http://www.theparisreview.org/blog/2012/07/27/two-versions-one-heti/.

Andrews, Bruce. *Paradise and Method: Poetics and Praxis*. Evanston: Northwestern University Press, 1996.

Annharte. *Exercises in Lip Pointing*. Vancouver: New Star Books, 2003.

Antin, David. *What It Means to Be Avant-garde*. Toronto: Emergency Response Unit, 2010.

Antliff, Mark. *Avant-Garde Fascism: The Mobilization of Myth, Art, and Culture in France, 1909–1939*. Durham: Duke University Press, 2007.

Armand, Louis (Baron de Lahontan). *Mémoires de l'Amerique Septentrionale*. Amsterdam: Chez François L'Honoré & Co., 1703.

Artaud, Antonin. "Shit to the Spirit." In *Antonin Artaud Anthology*, edited by Jack Hirschman, 105–112. San Francisco: City Lights Books, 1965.

Avison, Margaret. "Interview with Sally Ito: The Quiet Centre Inside." In *I Am Here and Not There: An Autobiography* by Margaret Avison, 310–325. Erin: Porcupine's Quill, 2009.

———. *Sliverick*. Toronto: Ganglia, [1969].

Baio, Andy. "Fanboy Supercuts, Obsessive Video Montages." Waxy.org. 17 November 2011. http://waxy.org/2008/04/fanboy_supercuts_obsessive_video_montages/.

Bakhtin, Mikhail. *The Dialogic Imagination: Four Essays*. Edited by Michael Holquist. Translated by Caryl Emerson and Michael Holquist. Austin: University of Texas Press, 2011.

Balkind, Alvin. "Acknowledgements." In *Concrete Poetry: An Exhibition in Four Parts*, edited by Ray Johnson and Michael Morris. Vancouver: University of British Columbia Fine Arts Gallery, 1969.

Barber, John. "How Should a Novel Be? Don't Ask Sheila Heti." *The Globe and Mail*. 13 April 2013. http://www.theglobeandmail.com/arts/books-and-media/book-reviews/how-should-a-novel-be-dont-ask-sheila-heti/article11134050/?page=all#dashboard/follows/.

Barker, Stephen. "Canon-fodder: Nietzsche, Jarry, Derrida (The Play of Discourse and the Discourse of Play)." *Journal of Dramatic Theory and Criticism* 69 (1989): 69–83.

Barnholden, Michael, and Andrew Klobucar, eds. *Writing Class: The Kootenay School of Writing Anthology.* Vancouver: New Star, 1999.

Barthes, Roland. "The Death of the Author." In *Image Music Text,* translated by Stephen Heath, 142–148. New York: Noonday, 1977.

Bataille, Georges. "The Solar Anus." In *Visions of Excess: Selected Writings, 1927–1939,* translated by Alan Stoekl, with Carl L. Lovitt and Donald M. Leslie, 5–9. Minneapolis: University of Minnesota Press, 1985.

Bayard, Caroline. *The New Poetics in Canada and Quebec: From Concretism to Post-modernism.* Toronto: University of Toronto Press, 1989.

Beaulieu, Derek. *Kern.* Los Angeles: Les Figues, 2014.

———. *Prose of the TransCanada.* Toronto: BookThug, 2011.

Beaumont, Kenneth. *Alfred Jarry: A Critical and Biographical Study.* New York: St. Martin's Press, 1984.

"*Beautiful Losers* Praised and Condemned." Hosted by Adrienne Clarkson and Paul Soles. *Take 30.* CBC.ca. 23 May 1966. http://www.cbc.ca/archives/entry/beautiful-losers-praised-and-condemned.

"Bechdel Test Movie List." Bechdeltest.com. http://bechdeltest.com/statistics/.

Bell, John. *Invaders from the North: How Canada Conquered the Comic Book Universe.* Toronto: Dundurn Press, 2006.

Bernstein, Charles. *A Poetics.* Cambridge: Harvard University Press, 1992.

———. "Book Party for 'Attack of the Difficult Poems.'" *Jacket2.* 27 May 2011. http://jacket2.org/commentary/book-party-attack-difficult-poems.

———. "Comedy and the Poetics of Political Form." In *The Politics of Poetics Form: Poetry and Public Policy,* edited by Charles Bernstein, 235–244. New York: Roof Books, 1989.

———. *Content's Dream: Essays, 1975–1984.* Evanston: Northwestern University Press, 2001.

———. "Poetry Ordinary and Extraordinary: The Pataque(e)rics of Everyday Life." Syllabus. Princeton University, Fall 2011. http://www.writing.upenn.edu/bernstein/syllabi/Princeton-F11.html.

———. "Unsettling the Word: Attack of the Difficult Poems." Syllabus. University of Pennsylvania, Spring 2011. http://www.writing.upenn.edu/bernstein/syllabi/unsettling.html.

Betts, Gregory. *Avant-Garde Canadian Literature: The Early Manifestations.* Toronto: University of Toronto Press, 2013.

———. "From Wit to Plunder in a Time of War." *The Poetic Front* 3 (2010). http:// journals.sfu.ca/poeticfront/index.php/pf/article/viewFile/36/35.

———. "Postmodern Decadence in Canadian Sound and Visual Poetry." In *Re: Reading the Postmodern: Canadian Literature and Criticism after Modernism*, edited by Robert David Stacey, 151–179. Ottawa: University of Ottawa Press, 2010.

———. "We Stopped at Nothing: Finding Nothing in the Avant-Garde Archive." *Amodern* 4 (March 2015). http://amodern.net/article/nothing/.

"BiC for Her Medium Ballpoint Pen—Black, Box of 12: Customer Reviews." Amazon.co.uk. 6 March 2016. http://www.amazon.co.uk/BiC-For-Her-Medium -Ballpoint/product-reviews/B004FTGJUW.

Biggs, Joanna. "It Could Be Me." *London Review of Books* 35.2 (January 2013): 31–32. http://www.lrb.co.uk/v35/n02/joanna-biggs/it-could-be-me.

Billingham, Susan E. *Language and the Sacred in Canadian Poet bpNichol's* The Martyrology. Queenston: Edwin Mellen, 2000.

Bissett, Bill. "! ! ! ! !." *Alphabet* 13 (June 1967): 94–95.

Blackburn, Robert H. *Evolution of the Heart: A History of the University of Toronto Library up to 1981*. Toronto: University of Toronto Press, 1989.

Blanchot, Maurice. "Everyday Speech." Translated by Susan Hanson. *Yale French Studies* 73 (1987): 12–20.

Bogost, Ian. "The Truth Is." Twitter.com. 16 March 2016. https://twitter.com/ ibogost/status/710070890948526080.

Bök, Christian. "Conceptual Literature in the Wild." *Harriet*. 10 April 2012. http:// www.poetryfoundation.org/harriet/2012/04/conceptual-literature-in-the -wild/.

———. *Crystallography*. Toronto: Coach House Press, 1994.

———. "Getting Ready to Have Been Postmodern." In *Re: Reading the Postmodern: Canadian Literature and Criticism after Modernism*, edited by Robert Stacey, 87–101. Ottawa: University of Ottawa Press, 2010.

———. "Nickel Linoleum." *Open Letter* 10.4 (1998): 62–74.

———. '*Pataphysics: The Poetics of an Imaginary Science*. Evanston: Northwestern University Press, 2002.

———. "TISH and Koot." *Open Letter* 12.8 (2006): 97–104.

Bonin, Vincent, and Grant Arnold. "Conceptual Art in Canada 1965–1980: An Annotated Chronology." In *Traffic: Conceptual Art in Canada 1965–1980*, edited by Grant Arnold and Karen Henry, 123–149. Vancouver: Douglas & McIntyre, 2012.

Borges, Jorge Luis. "The Library of Babel." In *Labyrinths: Selected Stories and Other Writings*, edited by Donald A. Yates and James E. Irby, translated by William Gibson, 51–58. New York: New Directions, 1964.

Bowering, George. "Vancouver as Postmodern Poetry." In *Vancouver: Representing the Postmodern City*, edited by Paul Delany, 21–43. Vancouver: Arsenal Pulp, 1994.

Bracken, Christopher. *The Potlatch Papers*. Chicago: University of Chicago Press, 1997.

Brittain, Donald, dir. *Ladies and Gentlemen, Mr. Leonard Cohen*. Performed by Leonard Cohen. Ottawa: National Film Board of Canada, 1965.

Brooker, Bertram. *Think of the Earth*. Toronto: Brown Bear Press, 2000.

———. "When We Awake! A General Introduction." In *Yearbook of the Arts in Canada 1928–1929*, edited by Bertram Brooker, 1–19. Toronto: Macmillan Company, 1929.

Brown, Wendy. *Walled States, Waning Sovereignty*. New York: Zone Books, 2010.

Buñuel, Luis, dir. *Un Chien Andalou*. Paris: Les Grand Films Classiques, 1929.

Bürger, Peter. "Avant-Garde and Neo-Avant-Garde: An Attempt to Answer Certain Critics of *Theory of the Avant-Garde*." *New Literary History* 4 (2010): 659–715.

———. *Theory of the Avant-Garde*. Translated by Michael Shaw. Minneapolis: University of Minnesota Press, 1984.

Burnett, David. *Town*. Toronto: McClelland & Stewart, 1986.

Butcher, Joe. *Text from Dog*. 5 April 2012. http://textfromdog.tumblr.com/.

Butling, Pauline, and Susan Rudy, eds. *Writing in Our Time: Canada's Radical Poetries in English (1957–2003)*. Waterloo: Wilfrid Laurier University Press, 2005.

Cain, Stephen. "Introduction." In *bp: beginnings*, edited by Stephen Cain, 7–28. Toronto: BookThug, 2014.

Călinescu, Matei. *Five Faces of Modernity: Modernism, Avant-Garde, Decadence, Kitsch, Postmodernism*. Durham: Duke University Press, 1987.

"The Canadian Book Market 2014." Booknetanada.ca. http://www.booknetcanada.ca/canadian-book-market/.

Carey, James W. *Communication as Culture: Essays on Media and Society*. Rev. ed. New York: Routledge, 2009.

Chandler, John Noel. "Incoherent Thoughts on Concrete Poetry." *Artscanada* 26 (1969): 11–13.

Chen, Ken. "Authenticity Obsession, or Conceptualism as Minstrel Show." AAWW. org. 11 June 2015. http://aaww.org/authenticity-obsession/.

Chute, Hillary. "Graphic Narrative." In *The Routledge Companion to Experimental Literature,* edited by Joe Bray, Alison Gibbons, and Brian McHale, 407–419. New York: Routledge, 2012.

"Cindy Crawford Reads Kenny Goldsmith's *Uncreative Writing.*" Photographed by Lawrence Schwartzwald. *Harriet.* 4 November 2011. http://www.poetry foundation.org/harriet/2011/11/cindy-crawford-reads-kenny-goldsmiths -uncreative-writing/.

Cohen, Leonard. *Beautiful Losers.* Toronto: McClelland & Stewart, 1991.

Coleman, Daniel. "From Contented Civility to Contending Civilities: Alternatives to Canadian White Civility." *International Journal of Canadian Studies* 38 (2008): 221–242.

Collis, Stephen. "The Call to Be Disobedient: On Michael Nardone." *Jacket2.* Special Feature on "Avant Canada" (2016). http://jacket2.org/article/call-be -disobedient.

Connolly, William. *The Fragility of Things: Self-Organizing Processes, Neoliberal Fantasies, and Democratic Activism.* Durham: Duke University Press, 2013.

"Cops Ban 'Lewd' Drawings." *This Hour Has Seven Days.* CBC.ca. 6 February 1966. http://www.cbc.ca/player/play/1704547774.

"Crop Circle of the Day—Quote Stuffing and Strange Sequences." Nanex.net. 12 July 2010. http://www.nanex.net/FlashCrash/CCircleDay.html.

Danto, Arthur Coleman. "Correspondance School Art." *The Nation* (1999): 30.

Davey, Frank. *Aka bpNichol: A Preliminary Biography.* Toronto: ECW, 2012.

———. "Introduction." *The Writing Life: Historical and Critical Views of the TISH Movement,* edited by C. H. Gervais, 15–26. Coatsworth: Black Moss, 1976.

———, ed. *TISH: No. 1–19.* Vancouver: Talonbooks, 1975.

David, Jack. "Introduction." In *As Elected: Selected Writing 1962–1979,* edited by bpNichol and Jack David, 9–31. Vancouver: Talonbooks, 1980.

———, and Caroline Bayard. *Out-posts/Avant-posts.* Erin: Press Porcépic, 1978.

Davies, Russell. "History Will Remember Samuel Pepys' Blog." *Wired UK.* 11 April 2012. http://www.wired.co.uk/magazine/archive/2012/05/ideas-bank/ history-will-remember-samuel-pepys-blog.

Davis, Brian Joseph. *Portable Altamont.* Toronto: Coach House Books, 2005.

Dawson, David. "A Poem Is an Expanding Structure of Thought." In *TISH: No. 1–19,* edited by Frank Davey, 26. Vancouver: Talonbooks, 1975.

Dean, Michelle. "Listening to Women: Why Smart, Serious Men Have Misunderstood Sheila Heti's New Book." *The Slate Book Review*. 29 June 2012. http://www.slate.com/articles/arts/books/2012/06/sheila_heti_s_how_should_a_person_be_reviewed_.html.

de Certeau, Michel. *The Practice of Everyday Life*. Translated by Steven Rendall. Berkeley: University of California Press, 1984.

———, Fredric Jameson, and Carl Lovitt. "On the Oppositional Practices of Everyday Life." *Social Text* 3 (1980): 3–43.

Deerchild, Rosanna. *Calling Down the Sky*. Markham: BookLand Press, 2015.

De Jesus, Joey. "Goldsmith, Conceptualism and the Half-baked Rationalization of White Idiocy." *Apogee*. 18 March 2015. http://www.apogeejournal.org/2015/03/goldsmith-conceptualism-the-half-baked-rationalization-of-white-idiocy.

Delany, Paul, ed. *Vancouver: Representing the Postmodern City*. Vancouver: Arsenal Pulp, 1994.

Deleuze, Gilles, and Félix Guattari. *A Thousand Plateaus: Capitalism and Schizophrenia*. Translated by Brian Massumi. Minneapolis: University of Minnesota Press, 1987.

Derksen, Jeff. *Annihilated Time: Poetry and Other Politics*. Vancouver: Talonbooks, 2009.

———. *The Vestiges*. Vancouver: Talonbooks, 2013.

———, Lisa Robertson, Nancy Shaw, and Catriona Strang. "Coasting." In *A Poetics of Criticism*, edited by Juliana Spahr, Mark Wallace, Kristin Prevallet, and Pam Rehm, 301–304. Buffalo: Leave, 1994.

Dewdney, Christopher. *Alter Sublime*. Toronto: Coach House Press, 1980.

Digipen70 et al. "Actual Cannibal Shia LaBeouf." *Know Your Meme*. 1 May 2012. http://knowyourmeme.com/memes/actual-cannibal-shia-labeouf.

Donnelly, Elisabeth. "Why Does Women's Confessional Writing Get People So Riled Up?" *Flavorwire*. 8 July 2014. http://flavorwire.com/466230/why-does-womens-confessional-writing-get-people-so-riled-up.

Dowling, Sarah. "Persons and Voices: Sounding Impossible Bodies in M. NourbeSe Philip's *Zong!*" *Canadian Literature* 210/211 (Autumn 2011): 43–58.

Doyle, Sady. "Vulnerability: The New Girl Power." *In These Times*. 14 August 2012. http://inthesetimes.com/article/13638/vulnerability_the_new_girl_power.

Dragland, Stan. "Afterword." In *Beautiful Losers* by Leonard Cohen. Toronto: McClelland & Stewart, 1991.

Druick, Zoë. *Projecting Canada: Government Policy and Documentary Film at the National Film Board*. Kingston: McGill-Queen's University Press, 2007.

Duffy, Dennis. "Beautiful Beginners." *The Tamarack Review* 40 (Summer 1966): 75–79.

DuPlessis, Rachel Blau. "Pater-Daughter: Male Modernists and Female Readers." In *The Pink Guitar: Writing as Feminist Practice*, 41–67. New York: Routledge, 1990.

Dutton, Paul. "bpNichol: Drawing the Poetic Line." In *St. Art: The Visual Poetry of bpNichol*, curated by Gil McElroy, 31–45. Charlottetown: Confederation Centre Art Gallery and Museum, 2000.

Dworkin, Craig. "The Imaginary Solution." *Contemporary Literature* 48.1 (2007): 29–60.

———. *Reading the Illegible*. Evanston: Northwestern University Press, 2003.

———, and Kenneth Goldsmith. *Against Expression: An Anthology of Conceptual Writing*. Evanston: Northwestern University Press, 2011.

Edmond, Jacob. "On Not Repeating 'Gone With the Wind': Iteration and Copyright." *Jacket2*. 17 December 2012. http://jacket2.org/commentary/not-repeating -gone-wind.

Edwards, Stassa. "Enough 'Oversharing': It's Time to Retire One of the Media's Favorite Words." *Salon*. 17 July 2014. http://www.salon.com/2014/07/17/ enough_oversharing_its_time_to_retire_one_of_medias_favorite_words/.

Elder, Alan C. *A Modern Life: Art and Design in British Columbia, 1945–1960*. Vancouver: Vancouver Art Gallery/Arsenal Pulp, 2004.

El Refaie, Elisabeth. "Multiliteracies: How Readers Interpret Political Cartoons." *Visual Communication* 8.2 (2009): 181–205.

Eichhorn, Kate, and Heather Milne, eds. *Prismatic Publics: Innovative Canadian Women's Poetry and Poetics*. Toronto: Coach House Books, 2009.

Fanon, Frantz. *The Wretched of the Earth*. New York: Grove Press, 2004.

Farrell, Dan. *The Inkblot Record*. Toronto: Coach House Books, 2000.

Featherstone, Mike. "The Heroic Life and Everyday Life." *Theory, Culture and Society* 9 (1992): 159–182.

Felski, Rita. *Beyond Feminist Aesthetics*. Cambridge: Harvard University Press, 1989.

Feuer, Menachem. "Personal Accounts of the Schlemiel (Take 1)—Schlemiel, the Son of Schlemiel." *The Home of Schlemiel Theory*. 18 February 2013. http:// schlemielintheory.com/2013/02/18/personal-accounts-of-the-schlemiel-take-1 -schlemiel-the-son-of-schlemiel/.

———. "The Postmodern Chelm, or The Artistic Community in Sheila Heti's 'How Should a Person Be?' – Part I." *The Home of Schlemiel Theory.* 11 June 2014. http://schlemielintheory.com/2014/06/11/the-postmodern-chelm-or-the -artistic-community-in-sheila-hetis-how-should-a-person-be-part-i/.

Feyerabend, Paul. *Against Method: Outline of an Anarchistic Theory of Knowledge.* 4th ed. London: Verso Books, 2010.

Flood, Alison. "Men Still Dominate Books, World Study Shows." *The Guardian.* 6 March 2013. http://www.theguardian.com/books/2013/mar/06/men -dominate-books-world-study-vida.

Florida, Richard. *The Rise of the Creative Class.* New York: Basic Books, 2002.

Flusser, Vilém. *Does Writing Have a Future?* Minneapolis: University of Minnesota Press, 2011.

Forceduse. "Every Death in The Game of Thrones Series, Tabbed." Reddit.com. 20 November 2013. https://www.reddit.com/r/pics/comments/1r175h/every_ death_in_the_game_of_thrones_series_tabbed/.

Foucault, Michel. *The Birth of Biopolitics: Lectures at the Collège de France, 1978–1979.* Edited by Michel Senellart. Translated by Graham Burchell. New York: Picador, 2008.

———. *Foucault Live: Interviews, 1961–84.* Edited by Sylvère Lotringer. Translated by John Johnson. New York: Semiotext(e), 1996.

Friskney, Janet. *New Canadian Library: The Ross–McClelland Years, 1952–1978.* Toronto: University of Toronto Press, 2007.

Frye, Northrop. "Canada and Its Poetry." In *The Collected Works of Northrop Frye,* vol. 12, edited by Jean O'Grady and David Staines, 26–38. Toronto: University of Toronto Press, 2003.

Fukuyama, Francis. *The End of History and the Last Man.* New York: Avon Books, 1992.

Fulford, Robert. "Leonard Cohen's Nightmare Novel." *Toronto Daily Star*, 26 April 1966.

Gabilliet, Jean-Paul. "Comic Art and *Bande Dessinée*: From the Funnies to Graphic Novels." In *The Cambridge History of Canadian Literature*, edited by Coral Ann Howells and Eva-Marie Kröller, 460–477. New York: Cambridge University Press, 2009.

Galloway, Alexander R. "The Game of War: An Overview." *Cabinet* 29 (2008): 67–71.

Gammel, Irene. "Introduction." In *Confessional Politics,* edited by Irene Gammel, 1–10. Carbondale: Southern Illinois University Press, 1999.

Gibson, James J. *The Ecological Approach to Visual Perception.* Boston: Houghton Mifflin, 1979.

Gill, Jo. "Introduction." In *Modern Confessional Writing: New Critical Essays,* edited by Jo Gill, 1–10. New York: Routledge, 2009.

Gillis, Stacy, Gillian Howie, and Rebecca Munford, eds. *Third Wave Feminism: A Critical Exploration.* New York: Palgrave Macmillan, 2004.

Gilmore, Leigh. *Autobiographics.* Ithaca: Cornell University Press, 1994.

"Glenn Ligon: Audio Guide Stop for Glenn Ligon, *Untitled (I Feel Most Colored When I Am Thrown Against a Sharp White Background),* 1990." Whitney Museum of American Art. http://whitney.org/WatchAndListen/720.

Godard, Barbara. "Ex-centriques, Eccentric, Avant-Garde: Women and Modernism in the Literatures of Canada." *Room of One's Own* 8.4 (1984): 57–75.

———. "Notes from the Cultural Field: Canadian Literature from Identity to Hybridity." *Essays on Canadian Writing* 72 (Winter 2000): 209–247.

Goldsmith, Kenneth. "Introduction to Flarf vs. Conceptual Writing." Whitney Museum of American Art. 17 April 2009. http://writing.upenn.edu/epc/authors/goldsmith/whitney-intro.html.

———. *Soliloquy.* New York: Granary Books, 2001.

Greenspan, Alan. "I Was Wrong about the Economy. Sort of." *The Guardian.* 24 October 2008. http://www.theguardian.com/business/2008/oct/24/economics-creditcrunch-federal-reserve-greenspan.

Groensteen, Thierry. *The System of Comics.* Translated by Bart Beaty and Nick Nguyen. Jackson: University Press of Mississippi, 2009.

Guenther, Leah. "Bridget Jones's Diary: Confessing Post-feminism." In *Modern Confessional Writing: New Critical Essays,* edited by Jo Gill, 84–99. New York: Routledge, 2009.

Guilbaut, Serge. *How New York Stole the Idea of Modern Art: Abstract Expressionism, Freedom, and the Cold War.* Translated by Arthur Goldhammer. Chicago: University of Chicago Press, 1983.

Guillory, John. "The Memo and Modernity." *Critical Inquiry* 31 (2004): 108–132.

Gyford, Phil. *The Diary of Samuel Pepys.* http://www.pepysdiary.com/.

Hair, Ross. *Ronald Johnson's Modernist Collage Poetry.* New York: Palgrave, 2010.

Halpern, Justin. *Shit My Dad Says.* 3 August 2009. https://twitter.com/shitmydadsays?lang=en.

Harrison, Keith. "*Ladies and Gentlemen … Mr. Leonard Cohen:* The Performance of Self, Forty Years On." In *Image Technologies in Canadian Literature: Narrative,*

Film, and Photography, edited by Carmen Concilio and Richard J. Lane, 65–80. Brussels: PIE Peter Lang, 2009.

Hart, Hugh. "Shit My Dad Says: Twitter Got Me a Sitcom Deal." *Wired*. 10 November 2009. www.wired.com/2009/11/shit-my-dad-says/.

Harvey, David. *A Brief History of Neoliberalism*. Oxford: Oxford University Press, 2005.

———. *Seventeen Contradictions and the End of Capitalism*. Oxford: Oxford University Press, 2014.

———. *Spaces of Hope*. Berkeley: University of California Press, 2000.

Hatfield, Charles. *Alternative Comics: An Emerging Literature*. Jackson: University Press of Mississippi, 2005.

Hatherley, Owen. "Post-Postmodernism?" *New Left Review* 59 (September–October 2009). https://newleftreview.org/II/59/owen-hatherley-post-postmodernism.

Hayles, N. Katherine. *The Cosmic Web: Scientific Field Models and Literary Strategies in the Twentieth Century*. Ithaca: Cornell University Press, 1984.

Heti, Sheila. *How Should a Person Be?* Henry Holt and Company, 2012.

———. "I Hadn't Even Seen the Alhambra." *London Review of Books* 34.16 (August 2012): 31–32. http://www.lrb.co.uk/v34/n16/sheila-heti/i-hadnt-even-seen-the-alhambra.

Heywood, Leslie and Jennifer Drake. "Introduction." In *Third Wave Agenda: Being Feminist, Doing Feminisms,* edited by Leslie Heywood and Jennifer Drake, 1–20. Minneapolis: University of Minnesota Press, 1997.

———. "'It's All about the Benjamins': Economic Determinants of Third Wave Feminism in the United States.'" In *Third Wave Feminism: A Critical Exploration,* edited by Stacy Gillis, Gillian Howie, and Rebecca Munford, 13–23. New York: Palgrave Macmillan, 2004.

———. "We Learn America Like a Script: Activism in the Third Wave; or, Enough Phantoms of Nothing." In *Third Wave Agenda: Being Feminist, Doing Feminisms,* edited by Leslie Heywood and Jennifer Drake, 40–54. Minneapolis: University of Minnesota Press, 1997.

Hilder, Jamie. "Concrete Poetry and Conceptual Art: A Misunderstanding." *Contemporary Literature* 54.3 (2013): 578–614.

Holbrook, Susan. "FL, KAKA, and the Value of Lesbian Paragrams." *Tessera* 30 (2001): 41–52.

Holmes, Anna. "The Age of Girlfriends." *The New Yorker*. 6 July 2012. http://www.newyorker.com/books/page-turner/the-age-of-girlfriends.

Horan, Molly. "Shia LaBeouf." *Know Your Meme.* 27 June 2014. http://knowyour meme.com/memes/people/shia-labeouf.

Hoy, Dan. "The Virtual Dependency of the Post-Avant and the Problematics of Flarf: What Happens When Poets Spend Too Much Time Fucking Around on the Internet." *Jacket* 29. http://jacketmagazine.com/29/hoy-flarf.html.

Huebener, Paul. *Timing Canada: The Shifting Politics of Time in Canadian Literary Culture.* Montreal: McGill-Queen's University Press, 2015.

Hutcheon, Linda. "*Beautiful Losers*: All the Polarities." *Canadian Literature* 59 (1974): 42–56.

———. *The Canadian Postmodern.* Toronto: Oxford University Press, 1988.

———. "The Glories of Hindsight: What We Know Now." In *Re: Reading the Postmodern: Canadian Literature and Criticism after Modernism,* edited by Robert David Stacey, 39–53. Ottawa: University of Ottawa Press, 2010.

———. *A Poetics of Postmodernism: History, Theory, Fiction.* London: Routledge, 1988.

———. *The Politics of Postmodernism.* London: Routledge, 2002.

———. *A Theory of Parody: The Teachings of Twentieth-Century Art Forms.* New York: Methuen, 1985.

Jaeger, Peter. ABC of Reading TRG. Vancouver: Talonbooks, 1999.

———. "An Interview with Steve McCaffery on the TRG." *Open Letter* 10.4 (1998): 77–96.

Jaffe, Aaron. *Modernism and the Culture of Celebrity.* New York: Cambridge University Press, 2005.

Jameson, Fredric. *Postmodernism, or, The Cultural Logic of Late Capitalism.* Durham: Duke University Press, 1991.

Jarry, Alfred. *Exploits and Opinions of Dr. Faustroll, Pataphysician: A Neo-Scientific Novel.* Translated by Simon Watson Taylor. Boston: Exact Change, 1996.

Jelinek, Estelle C. "Introduction: Women's Autobiography and the Male Tradition." In *Women's Autobiography: Essays in Criticism,* edited by Estelle C. Jelinek, 1–20. Bloomington: Indiana University Press, 1980.

Johnson, Mark. *The Meaning of the Body: Aesthetics of Human Understanding.* Chicago: University of Chicago Press, 2007.

Johnson, Ray, and Michael Morris, eds. *Concrete Poetry: An Exhibition in Four Parts.* Vancouver: University of British Columbia Fine Arts Gallery, 1969.

Johnstone, Stephen, ed. *The Everyday.* London: Whitechapel/MIT Press, 2008.

Kamboureli, Smaro. *On the Edge of Genre.* Toronto: University of Toronto Press, 1991.

"Ken Norris and Garry Thomas Morse Discuss *After Jack*." Talonbooks.com. 23 July 2010. http://talonbooks.com/meta-talon/ken-norris-and-garry-thomas-morse -discuss-after-jack.

King, Andrew David. "Effaced Ballads: An Interview with Matthew Rohrer, Anthony McCann, and Joshua Beckman on Erasing the Romantics." *The Kenyon Review*. 30 November 2012. http://www.kenyonreview.org/2012/11/effaced -ballads-an-interview-with-matthew-rohrer-anthony-mccann-and-joshua -beckman-on-erasing-the-romantics/.

———. "Politics, Erasure, and a 'Sometimes Genuine Music.'" *The Kenyon Review*. 25 October 2012. http://www.kenyonreview.org/2012/10/politics-erasure-and -a-sometimes-genuine-music.

———. "Theft as Art, Art as Theft: An Interview with Austin Kleon." *The Kenyon Review*. 26 August 2012. http://www.kenyonreview.org/2012/08/austin-kleon -interview/.

———. "The Weight of What's Left Out: Six Contemporary Erasurists on Their Craft." *The Kenyon Review*. 6 November 2012. http://www.kenyonreview.org/ 2012/11/erasure-collaborative-interview/.

King, James. *Jack: A Life with Writers: The Story of Jack McClelland*. Toronto: Alfred A. Knopf, 1999.

Klein, Naomi. *This Changes Everything: Capitalism vs. the Environment*. Toronto: Alfred A. Knopf, 2014.

Klopfer, Bruno. *Rorschach Technique: A Manual for a Projective Method of Personality Diagnosis*. New York: World Book Co., 1942.

Knausgård, Karl Ove. *My Struggle, Books 1–5*. Translated by Don Bartlett. New York: Archipelago, 2012–2015.

Kraus, Chris. "What Women Say to One Another: Sheila Heti's *How Should a Person Be?*" LA *Review of Books*. 18 June 2012. http://lareviewofbooks.org/ review/what-women-say-to-one-another-sheila-hetis-how-should-a -person-be#.

Krishtalka, Sholem. "Me and You and Her and Us and Them: A Conversation on Using and Being Used." *C Magazine* 109 (2011): 4–13.

Kunin, Aaron. "Would Vanessa Place Be a Better Poet If She Had Better Opinions?" Nonsite.org. 26 September 2015. http://nonsite.org/article/would-vanessa -place-be-a-better-poet-if-she-had-better-opinions.

Laclau, Ernesto, and Chantal Mouffe. *Hegemony and Socialist Strategy*. 2nd ed. London: Verso Books, 2001.

La Force, Thessaly. "Sheila Heti on *How Should a Person Be?*" *The Paris Review.* 18
    June 2012. http://www.theparisreview.org/blog/2012/06/18/sheila-heti-on-how
    -should-a-person-be/.

Le Heup, Jason. "Skateboards and Sucker Fish: An Introduction." *The Capilano
    Review* 2.33 (2001): v–vii.

Lefebvre, Henri. *Critique of Everyday Life. Vol. 2 of Foundations for a Sociology of the
    Everyday,* translated by John Moore. London: Verso Books, 2002.

Leigh, Brandi. "An Introduction to the Group of Seven." Arthistoryarchive.com.
    2008. http://www.arthistoryarchive.com/arthistory/canadian/The-Group-of
    -Seven.html.

Lejeune, Philippe. *On Autobiography.* Edited by Paul John Eakin. Translated by
    Katherine Leary. Minneapolis: University of Minnesota Press, 1989.

Lerner, Ben. *Leaving the Atocha Station.* Minneapolis: Coffee House Press, 2011.

Lorde, Audre. "Age, Race, Class, and Sex: Women Redefining Difference." In *Sister
    Outsider: Essays and Speeches,* 114–123. Berkeley: Crossing Press. 2007.

———. "The Master's Tools Will Never Dismantle the Master's House." In *Sister
    Outsider: Essays and Speeches,* 110–113. Berkeley: Crossing Press, 2007.

MacSkimming, Roy. *The Perilous Trade: Book Publishing in Canada, 1946–2006.*
    Toronto: McClelland & Stewart, 2007.

Mann, Ron, dir. *Comic Book Confidential.* Toronto: Sphinx Productions, 1988.

Maracle, Lee. "Decolonization and the Avant-Garde." Keynote Address for the con-
    ference, "Avant Canada: Artists, Prophets, Revolutionaries" at Brock University
    in St. Catharines. 5 November 2014.

———. *Memory Serves: Oratories.* Edmonton: NeWest Press, 2015.

Marshall, P. David. "The Genealogy of Celebrity: Introduction." In *A Companion
    to Celebrity,* edited by P. David Marshall and Sean Redmond, 15–20. Hoboken:
    John Wiley & Sons, 2015.

———. "New Media—New Self: The Changing Power of Celebrity." In *The Celebrity
    Culture Reader,* edited by P. David Marshall, 634–644. London: Routledge, 2006.

McCaffery, Steve. "The Death of the Subject: The Implications of Counter-Commu-
    nication in Recent Language-Centered Writing." *Open Letter* 3.7 (1977): 61–77.

———. "*The Martyrology* as Paragram." *Open Letter* 6.5–6 (1986): 191–206.

———. *North of Intention: Critical Writings, 1973–1986.* New York: Roof Books, 1986.

———. "The Politics of the Referent." *Open Letter* 3.7 (1977): 60.

———, and bpNichol. *Rational Geomancy: The Kids of the Book Machine.* Vancou-
    ver: Talonbooks, 1992.

McClelland & Stewart Fonds. William Ready Division of Archives and Research Collections, McMaster University.

McCloud, Scott. *Understanding Comics: The Invisible Art.* New York: HarperCollins, 1994.

McGill, Robert. "A Necessary Collaboration: Biographical Desire and Elizabeth Smart." *English Studies in Canada* 33.3 (September 2007): 67–88.

McLeod, Neal. "Introduction." In *Indigenous Poetics in Canada*, edited by Neal McLeod, 1–16. Waterloo: Wilfrid Laurier University Press, 2014.

McLuhan, Marshall. *Understanding Media: The Extensions of Man.* Toronto: McGraw-Hill, 1964.

Meskin, Aaron. "Comics as Literature?" *British Journal of Aesthetics* 49.3 (2009): 219–239.

Mesure, Susie. "Rise and Rise of the Woman-child." *The Independent.* 7 January 2015. http://www.independent.co.uk/news/people/news/rise-and-rise-of-the-womanchild-8165992.html.

"Michael Brown, Eric Garner Deaths 'Echo' Aboriginal Experience in Canada." CBC.ca. 8 January 2015. http://www.cbc.ca/news/canada/british-columbia/michael-brown-eric-garner-deaths-echo-aboriginal-experience-in-canada-1.2892903.

Moran, Joe. *Star Authors: Literary Celebrity in America.* Sterling: Pluto Press, 2000.

Morris, Simon, dir. *Sucking on Words: A Documentary about Kenneth Goldsmith.* Leeds: Information as Material, 2007.

Morse, Gary Thomas. *Discovery Passages.* Vancouver: Talonbooks, 2011.

Moten, Fred. "On Marjorie Perloff." *Entropy*, 28 December 2015. entropymag.org/on-marjorie-perloff/.

Motte, Jr., Warren F. "Clinamen Redux." *Comparative Literature Studies* 23.4 (1986): 263–281.

Munford, Rebecca. "'Wake Up and Smell the Lipgloss': Gender, Generation and the (A)politics of Girl Power." In *Third Wave Feminism: A Critical Exploration,* edited by Stacy Gillis, Gillian Howie, and Rebecca Munford, 142–153. New York: Palgrave Macmillan, 2004.

Murakami, Sachiko. *Rebuild.* Vancouver: Talonbooks, 2011.

Nadel, Ira Bruce. *Various Positions: A Life of Leonard Cohen.* Toronto: Random House, 1996.

Najafi, Sina. "Bats and Dancing Bears: An Interview with Eric A. Zillmer." *Cabinet* 5 (Winter 2001/2002). http://www.cabinetmagazine.org/issues/5/najafi.php.

Nakonechny, Simon. "Tanya Tagaq Threatens Legal Action Against 'Racist' Quebec Film 'Of the North.'" CBC.ca. 25 November 2015. http://www.cbc.ca/news/canada/montreal/tanya-tagaq-of-the-north-1.3336733.

Needleman, Rafe. "Richard Dreyfuss Reads the iTunes EULA." C|Net. 8 June 2011. http://www.cnet.com/news/richard-dreyfuss-reads-the-itunes-eula/.

Nichol, bp. "Another Disgustingly Sentimental Editorial." Ganglia 2.1 (1969).

———. bp: beginnings. Edited by Stephen Cain. Toronto: BookThug, 2014.

———, ed. The Cosmic Chef: An Evening of Concrete. Ottawa: Oberon, 1970.

———. Craft Dinner. Toronto: Aya Press, 1978.

———. Ganglia Press Index 1964 to 1983. Toronto: Ganglia [grOnk ZAP 3], 1983.

———. Grease Ball Comics. Toronto: CURVD H&Z #195, 1983.

———. Konfessions of an Elizabethan Fan Dancer. Edited by Nelson Ball. Toronto: Coach House Books, 2004.

———. "Last Wall and Test a Minute." Notebook 1968. Simon Fraser University Special Collections and Rare Books. Ms.C. 1223.

———. The Martryology Book 6. Toronto: Coach House Press, 1987.

———. Meanwhile: The Critical Writings of bpNichol. Edited by Roy Miki. Vancouver: Talonbooks, 2002.

———. "THIS IS A POME ABOUT WHERE I WORK." Ganglia 1.1 (1964).

———. A Vision in the UofT Stacks. Toronto: TONTO or, 1966.

Nichol, Bran. "'The Memoir as Self-Destruction': A Heartbreaking Work of Staggering Genius." In Modern Confessional Writing: New Critical Essays, edited by Jo Gill, 100–114. New York: Routledge, 2009.

Nichol, Eleanor. Personal communication to Mike Borkent. 28 November 2012. Email.

North, Anna. "The Rise of the 'Girly' Narrative." BuzzFeed. 5 July 2012. http://www.buzzfeed.com/annanorth/the-rise-of-the-girly-narrative.

Nowell, Iris. P11, Painters Eleven: The Wild Ones of Canadian Art. Toronto: Douglas & McIntyre, 2010.

Obrist, Hans Ulrich. "Walter Hops." In A Brief History of Curating, 10–31. Zurich/Dijon: JRP Ringier/ Les Presses du Réel, 2013.

"Of the North." Dokufest, Edition XV (2015). http://dokufest.com/2015/movie/of-the-north/.

Ohlsen, Becky. "'How Should a Person Be? Review: Young Woman's Navelgazing Frustrates but Makes You Think." The Oregonian. 13 June 2012. http://

www.oregonlive.com/books/index.ssf/2012/06/how_should_a_person_be
_review.html.

Orr, Catherine. "Charting the Currents of the Third Wave." *Hypatia* 3.12 (Summer, 1997): 29–45.

Page, Benedicte. "Headline to Publish Texts from Dog." *The Bookseller*. 23 July 2012. http://www.thebookseller.com/news/headline-publish-texts-dog.

Parker, Trey, dir. "HUMANCENTiPAD." *South Park*. 27 April 2011. http://www.imdb.com/title/tt1884035/.

Penny, Laurie, "Laurie Penny on Lena Dunham's Girls: It Can't Represent Every Woman, but Shouldn't Have To" *NewStatesman*. 4 February 2014. http://www.newstatesman.com/culture/2014/02/why-lena-dunhams-girls-cant-represent-every-woman-and-why-it-shouldnt-have.

———. "Laurie Penny on the Feminist Writer's Dilemma: How to Write about the Personal, Without Becoming the Story." *NewStatesman*. 4 February 2014. http://www.newstatesman.com/politics/2014/07/feminist-writers-dilemma-how-write-about-personal-without-becoming-story.

Perloff, Marjorie. "After Language Poetry: Innovation and Its Theoretical Discontents." In *Contemporary Poetics*, edited by Louis Armand, 15–38. Evanston: Northwestern University Press, 2007.

———. "A Conversation with Kenneth Goldsmith." *Jacket* 21 (February 2003). http://jacketmagazine.com/21/perl-gold-iv.html.

———. *Unoriginal Genius: Poetry by Other Means in the New Century*. Chicago: University of Chicago Press, 2010.

———. "Unoriginal Genius: Walter Benjamin's Arcades as Paradigm for the New Poetics." *Études Anglaises* 2.61 (2008): 229–252.

Peters, Carl, ed. *bpNichol Comics*. Vancouver: Talonbooks, 2002.

Philip, M. NourbeSe. *Zong!* Middletown: Wesleyan University Press, 2008.

Place, Vanessa. "Artist's Statement: Gone with the Wind @Vanessa Place." Genius.com. 19 May 2015. http://genius.com/Vanessa-place-artists-statement-gone-with-the-wind-vanessaplace-annotated.

———. "The Case for Conceptualism." Electronic Poetry Center. http://epc.buffalo.edu/authors/place/Place_Conceptualcase1A.pdf.

"Poetic Visuality and Experimentation." Canlitguides.ca. 23 March 2015. http://canlitguides.ca/canlit-guides-editorial-team/poetic-visuality-and-experimentation/.

Poggioli, Renato. *The Theory of the Avant-Garde*. Cambridge: Harvard University Press, 1968.

Pound, Ezra. "Paris Letter: December 1921." *Dial* 72.1 (1922): 73.

Povinelli, Elizabeth. *Economies of Abandonment: Social Belonging and Endurance in Late Liberalism*. Durham: Duke University Press, 2011.

Puchner, Martin. *Poetry of the Revolution: Marx, Manifestos, and the Avant-Gardes*. Princeton: Princeton University Press, 2006.

Queyras, Sina. "How to Do Silence: A Conversation with Vanessa Place." *Lemon Hound*. 29 July 2010. http://lemonhound.blogspot.ca/2010/07/how-to-do-silence-conversation-with.html.

———. "Lyric Conceptualism, A Manifesto in Progress." *Harriet*. 9 April 2012. https://www.poetryfoundation.org/harriet/2012/04/lyric-conceptualism-a-manifesto-in-progress.

———. *M x T*. Toronto: Coach House Books, 2014.

Rankine, Claudia. *Citizen: An American Lyric*. Minneapolis: Gray Wolf Press, 2014.

Reid, James. "Editorial." In *TISH: No. 1-19*, edited by Frank Davey, 71. Vancouver: Talonbooks, 1975.

Rhodes, Shane. "Reuse and Recycle: Finding Poetry in Canada." *Arc Poetry Magazine*. 1 May 2013. http://arcpoetry.ca/?p=6644.

———. *X : Poems and Anti-Poems*. Gibsons: Nightwood, 2013.

Robertson, Lisa. *Cinema of the Present*. Toronto: Coach House Books, 2014.

———. *Nilling: Prose*. Toronto: BookThug, 2012.

Robinson, Adam. *"How Should a Person Be?" BOMB Magazine*. 11 June 2012. http://bombmagazine.org/article/6654/.

Robinson, Joanna. "Watch Jennifer Garner Read an Expletive-Laden Bedtime Story." *Vanity Fair*. 1 March 2016. http://www.vanityfair.com/hollywood/2016/02/jennifer-garner-go-the-fuck-to-sleep.

Roeder, Katherine. *Wide Awake in Slumberland: Fantasy, Mass Culture, and Modernism in the Art of Winsor McCay*. Jackson: University Press of Mississippi, 2014.

Roiphe, Katie. "Her Struggle." *Slate*. 7 July 2014. http://www.slate.com/articles/double_x/roiphe/2014/07/what_if_karl_ove_knausgaard_s_my_struggle_were_written_by_a_woman.html?wpisrc=burger_bar.

———. "Not Quite How a Person Should Be: Grow Up, Sheila Heti!" *Slate*. 6 July 2012. http://www.slate.com/articles/double_x/roiphe/2012/07/sheila_heti_s_how_should_a_person_be_compelling_and_irritating.single.html.

Rosenberg, Alyssa. "Sheila Heti, Lena Dunham, and the Challenges of Telling 'Girly' Stories in Film and Television." *Slate*. 9 July 2012. http://www.slate .com/blogs/xx_factor/2012/07/09/sheila_heti_lena_dunham_and_the_ challenges_of_telling_girly_stories_in_film_and_television.html.

Rosenkranz, Patrick. *Rebel Visions: The Underground Comix Revolution, 1963–1975*. Seattle: Fantagraphics, 2008.

Sabin, Roger. *Comics, Comix and Graphic Novels: A History of Comic Art*. New York: Phaidon, 1996.

Sales, Leila. *The Leila Texts*. 13 August 2007. http://theleilatexts.blogspot.ca/.

Sartwell, Crispin. *Act Like You Know: African-American Autobiography and White Identity*. Chicago: University of Chicago Press, 1998.

Scanlon, Jennifer. "Sexy from the Start: Anticipatory Elements of Second Wave Feminism." *Women's Studies* 38 (2009): 127–150.

"Schlemiel." Oxforddictionaries.com. http://www.oxforddictionaries.com/ definition/english/schlemiel.

Schulte-Sasse, Jochen. "Forward: Theory and Modernism versus Theory of the Avant-Garde." In *Theory of the Avant-Garde* by Peter Bürger, vii–xlvii. Translated by Michael Shaw. Minneapolis: University of Minnesota Press, 1984.

Scobie, Stephen. *Signature Event Cantext*. Edmonton: NeWest, 1989.

"Shane Rhodes—X: Poems and Anti-Poems (An Interview)." *The Toronto Quarterly*. 19 September 2013. http://thetorontoquarterly.blogspot.com.au/2013/09/ shane-rhodes-x-poems-anti-poems.html.

Shattuck, Roger. *The Banquet Years: The Arts in France, 1885–1918*. London: Jonathan Cape, 1969.

Shaw, Nancy. "Expanded Consciousness and Company Types: Collaboration since Intermedia and the N. E. Thing Company." In *Vancouver Anthology: The Institutional Politics of Art*, edited by Stan Douglas, 85–103. Vancouver: Talonbooks, 1991.

Shearer, Lynda M. *Painters-Eleven*. http://www.painters-eleven.com/.

Shepherd, Reginald. "Who You Callin' 'Post-Avant'?" *Harriet*. 6 February 2008. https: //www.poetryfoundation.org/harriet/2008/02/who-you-callin-post-avant/.

Sheringham, Michael. *Everyday Life: Theories and Practices from Surrealism to the Present*. Oxford: Oxford University Press, 2006.

Shklovsky, Viktor. "Art as Technique." In *Russian Formalist Criticism: Four Essays*, edited and translated by Lee T. Lemon and Marion J. Reiss, 3–24. Lincoln: University of Nebraska Press, 1965.

Silliman, Ron. "Disappearance of the Word, Appearance of the World." In *The L=A=N=G=U=A=G=E Book*, edited by Bruce Andrews and Charles Bernstein, 121–132. Carbondale: Southern Illinois University Press, 1984.

Simpson, Leanne Betasamosake. *Dancing on Our Turtle's Back: Stories of Nishnaabeg Re-creation, Resurgence and a New Emergence*. Winnipeg: ARP Books, 2011.

Smith, Russell, "So You've Never Heard of This Important Movement in Poetry? Don't Worry—the Poets Don't Care." *The Globe and Mail*, 11 March 2000, R5.

Solt, Mary Ellen, ed. *Concrete Poetry: A World View*. Indiana: Indiana University Press, 1968.

Spahr, Juliana, Mark Wallace, Kristin Prevallet, and Pam Rehm, eds. *A Poetics of Criticism*. Buffalo: Leave, 1994.

———, and Stephanie Young. "Foulipo (Talk for CalArts Noulipo Conference, Fall 2005)." *Drunken Boat* 8 (2006). http://www.drunkenboat.com/db8/.

Spear, Monroe K. "The Poetics of the New Formalism." *The Hudson Review* 43.4 (1991): 549–562.

Spenst, Kevin. "Garry Thomas Morse." Kevinspenst.com. 24 June 2011. http://kevinspenst.com/?p=600.

Stacey, Robert David. "Mad Translation in Leonard Cohen's *Beautiful Losers* and Douglas Glover's *Elle*." *English Studies in Canada* 40.2–3 (June/September 2014): 173–197.

Stein, Gertrude. *The Autobiography of Alice B. Toklas*. Edited by Carl Van Vechten. New York: Vintage Books, 1962.

———. *Tender Buttons*. Mineola: Dover Editions, 1997.

Stoeffel, Karl. "The Problem Child: Why Won't America Publish Sheila Heti's Second Novel?" *The New York Observer*. 16 December 2010. http://observer.com/2010/12/the-problem-child-why-wont-america-publish-sheila-hetis-second-novel/#ixzz3ItSjmJFi.

Suleiman, Susan. *Subversive Intent: Gender, Politics, and the Avant-Garde*. Cambridge: Harvard University Press, 1990.

Tallman, Warren. "'When a New Music Is Heard the Walls of the City Tremble': A Note on Voice Poetry." *TISH: No. 1-19*, edited by Frank Davey, 67–68. Vancouver: Talonbooks, 1975.

Toronto Research Group, ed. "Introduction." *Canadian "Pataphysics: Open Letter* 4.6–7 (1980–81): 7–8.

Town, Harold. "Confessions of a Literary Nibbler." *The Globe and Mail*, 25 December 1965, A14.

———. *Harold Town Enigmas*. Toronto: McClelland & Stewart, 1964.

Tranter, John, ed. "Jacket Flarf Feature." *Jacket2* 30 (July 2006). http://jacket magazine.com/30/index.shtml.

Trasov, Vincent. "An Early History of Image Bank." http://vincenttrasov.ca/index .cfm?pg=cv-pressdetail&pressID=3.

Turner, Michael. "An Interview with Michael Turner on Letters: Michael Morris and Concrete Poetry." *Here and Elsewhere*. 31 January 2012. http://hereelsewhere .com/see/letters-michael-morris-and-concrete-poetry/.

Vickery, Ann. *Leaving Lines of Gender: A Feminist Genealogy of Language Writing*. Hanover: University Press of New England, 2000.

Vizenor, Gerald Robert. *Manifest Manners: Narratives on Postindian Survivance*. Lincoln: University of Nebraska Press, 1999.

Voyce, Stephen. *Poetic Community: Avant-Garde Activism and Cold War Culture*. Toronto: University of Toronto Press, 2013.

Wah, Fred. *Faking It: Poetics and Hybridity*. Edmonton: NeWest, 2001.

Wain, John. "Making It New." In *Leonard Cohen: The Artist and His Critics*, edited by Michael Gnarowski, 23–26. Toronto: McGraw-Hill Ryerson, 1976.

Walker, Kara. "Manuscript for a Proposition." In *Rethinking Contemporary Art and Multicultural Education*, edited by Eungie Joo and Joseph Keehn II, 36–53. New York: Routledge, 2011.

Wall, Jeff. "Vancouver: Concrete Poetry." *Artforum* 7 (1969): 70–71.

Wallace, Ian. "Literature—Transparent and Opaque." In *Concrete Poetry: An Exhibition in Four Parts,* edited by Ray Johnson and Michael Morris, n.p. Vancouver: University of British Columbia Fine Arts Gallery, 1969.

Wallace, Keith. "A Particular History: Artist-run Centres in Vancouver." In *Vancouver Anthology: The Institutional Politics of Art*, edited by Stan Douglas, 23–45. Vancouver: Talonbooks, 1991.

Wark, McKenzie. "The Game of War: Debord as Strategist." *Cabinet* 29 (2008): 73–75.

Waters, John, dir. *Pink Flamingos*. Baltimore: Dreamland/Saliva Films, 1972.

Weir, Lorraine. "Discovery Passages." *Canadian Literature* 214 (Autumn 2012): 178–181. https://canlit.ca/article/discovery-passages/.

Wershler, Darren. "Conceptual Writing." In *The Johns Hopkins Guide to Digital Media*, edited by Marie-Laure Ryan, Lori Emerson, and Benjamin J. Robertson, 89. Baltimore: Johns Hopkins University Press, 2014.

———. "Conceptual Writing as Fanfiction." In *Fic: Why Fanfiction Is Taking Over the World*, edited by Anne Jamison, 363–371. Dallas: Smartpop, 2013.

———. *The Tapeworm Foundry: Andor the Dangerous Prevalence of Imagination*. Toronto: House of Anansi, 2000.

Wiens, Jason. "Avison and the Postmodern 1960s." *Canadian Poetry* 59 (2006): 27–39.

———. "Kootenay School of Writing: History, Community, Poetics." Ph.D. diss., University of Calgary, 2001.

Wilkins, Peter. "'Nightmares of Identity': Nationalism and Loss in *Beautiful Losers*." *Essays on Canadian Writing* 69 (1999): 24–50.

Will, Barbara. *Gertrude Stein, Modernism, and the Problem of "Genius."* Edinburgh: Edinburgh University Press, 2000.

Witek, Joseph. "The Arrow and the Grid." In *A Comics Studies Reader,* edited by Jeet Heer and Kent Worcester, 149–156. Jackson: University Press of Mississippi, 2009.

Wood, James. "True Lives: Sheila Heti's 'How Should a Person Be?'" *The New Yorker.* 25 June 2012. http://www.newyorker.com/magazine/2012/06/25/true-lives-2.

Wood, James M., M. Teresa Nezworski, and William J. Stejskal. "The Comprehensive System for the Rorschach: A Critical Examination." *Psychological Science* 7.1 (1996): 3–10.

Wood, William. "The Insufficiency of the World." In *Intertidal: Vancouver Art and Artists*, edited by Dieter Roelstraete and Scott Watson, 63–78. Vancouver: Morris and Helen Belkin Gallery, 2005.

———. "Some Are Weather-Wise; Some Are Otherwise: Criticism and Vancouver." In *Vancouver Anthology*, edited by Stan Douglas, 137–171. Vancouver: Talonbooks, 1991.

Woolf, Virginia. "A Room of One's Own." In *The Norton Anthology of English Literature*, 7th ed., vol. B, edited by M. H. Abrams and Stephen Greenblatt, 2414–2475. New York: Norton, 2001.

———. "Professions for Women." In *The Norton Anthology of English Literature*, 7th ed., vol. B, edited by M. H. Abrams and Stephen Greenblatt, 2475–2479. New York: Norton, 2001.

Yancy, George. *Look, A White! Philosophical Essays on Whiteness*. Philadelphia: Temple University Press, 2012.

Zolf, Rachel. *Janey's Arcadia*. Toronto: Coach House Books, 2014.

Index